Terror and the
Cinematic Sublime

Terror and the Cinematic Sublime

Essays on Violence and the Unpresentable in Post–9/11 Films

Edited by TODD A. COMER and LLOYD ISAAC VAYO

Afterword by Patrick Fuery

McFarland & Company, Inc., Publishers
Jefferson, North Carolina, and London

ALSO OF INTEREST: *Sexual Ideology in the Works of Alan Moore: Critical Essays on the Graphic Novels.* Edited by Todd A. Comer and Joseph Michael Sommers (McFarland, 2012)

LIBRARY OF CONGRESS CATALOGUING-IN-PUBLICATION DATA

Terror and the cinematic sublime : essays on violence and the unpresentable in post–9/11 films / edited by Todd A. Comer and Lloyd Isaac Vayo ; afterword by Patrick Fuery.
　　p.　　cm.
Includes bibliographical references and index.

ISBN 978-0-7864-7207-9
softcover : acid free paper ∞

1. Violence in motion pictures.　2. Motion pictures.
I. Comer, Todd A., 1972–　　II. Vayo, Lloyd Isaac, 1981–
PN1995.9.V5T47　2013
791.43'655—dc23　　　　　　　　　　　　　2012049760

BRITISH LIBRARY CATALOGUING DATA ARE AVAILABLE

© 2013 Todd A. Comer and Lloyd Isaac Vayo. All rights reserved

No part of this book may be reproduced or transmitted in any form or by any means, electronic or mechanical, including photocopying or recording, or by any information storage and retrieval system, without permission in writing from the publisher.

On the cover: Poster art for the 2008 film *Cloverfield* (Paramount Pictures/Photofest)

Manufactured in the United States of America

McFarland & Company, Inc., Publishers
Box 611, Jefferson, North Carolina 28640
www.mcfarlandpub.com

Table of Contents

Preface and Acknowledgments 1
Introduction: Terror and the (Post)Cinematic Sublime
   TODD A. COMER and LLOYD ISAAC VAYO 5

Hits and Missives: Excluding/Embracing 9/11

Plummeting to the Pavement: The Fall of the Body in
Spider-Man
   KARTIK NAIR 15
When Does the Hurting Stop? *Cloverfield* and the
(Re)Enabling of Fantasy in the Post-9/11 City
   SCOTT WILSON 29
Keeping Terror Alive: The Political Economy of Visibility
in *Inside Man*
   SVEN CVEK 42

Pushing the Enveloped: Exposing the Limits of Freedom

Aronofsky's Cinematic Vision and the Ethical Meaning of
Freedom as the Sublime Horizon of *Amor Fati*
   DONALD CALLEN 57
The Apocalyptic Sublime: Hollywood Disaster Films and
Donnie Darko
   SEUNG-HOON JEONG 72
History Is Always Virgin: Quentin Tarantino's *Inglourious
Basterds* and the Lyotardian Sublime
   MARCO GROSOLI 88

Tarrying with Sublimity: The Limits of Cinematic Form in
Duncan Jones' *Source Code*
    MICHAEL J. BLOUIN 103

Communiqué-tion Breakdown:
(Post)Cinematic Interruptions

Pleasure and Pain: Post-Cinematic Remakes
    HOLLY WILLIS 119
Watching the World Burn: Intensity, Absurdity and Echoes
of the Sublime in Contemporary Science Fiction Destruction
    JOHN P. WARTON 134
The AIllusion: Intelligent Machines, Jacques Derrida's "Ethical
Turn" and Oren Peli's *Paranormal Activity*
    LARRIE DUDENHOEFFER 150
The Indigestibility of the World: Birthing the Posthuman in
Spielberg's *A.I.*
    TODD A. COMER 165

Afterword: Afterwards
    PATRICK FUERY 181
Selected Bibliography 187
About the Contributors 199
Index 201

Preface and Acknowledgments

It was unexpected, the birth of this book. In April of 2010 we circulated a call for papers dealing with "terror and the cinematic sublime" for the conference of the Midwest Modern Language Association, and were deluged with proposals. Proposals on "splatter films," on the "aesthetics of the disgusting" in *Antichrist*, on the "bifurcated gaze of terror in Tarantino's *Death Proof*," on "authorial choice" in *No Country for Old Men*, and on ethics and representation in *Hiroshima mon amour*, among many others, clotted our email boxes. Shocked at such an unexpected profusion, we formed several panels — tiny, well-rationalized boxes whose sole purpose was to contain such a delightful, if messy birth. And, unlike so many dry and arid conferences, we were thrilled, intellectually and relationally, with our eventual experience. After such an experience, it became impossible not to continue grappling with the complexities of "terror and the cinematic sublime." We took it, or, rather, it took *us* to the next level — yes, to a new beginning and to a new birth.

But the above is merely the formal reason for this material object you now hold, opened and exposed, in your hands. The sublime, however defined and named, is an experience that touches, and by touching, defines humans, and for this reason remains of perennial interest. For some, it is an emotional, awe-ridden link, verging on the mystical, to an amorphous "being" (the Universe, God, Nature); or a reminder of limits, a sort of structural humility, built into the human psyche as its totalizing representations founder; and, for others, it designates the originary stuff of freedom. Todd's interest in the sublime began with his study of Jean-Luc Nancy's *The Inoperative Community*, in particular the manner in which death (and birth) interrupts human subjectivity, leading to a relation *with* the other. Nancy, as with Lyotard and Derrida, also simultaneously critiques the violence of the rationalizing subject, and the community that lives, and moves, and has its being in the Western Subject. Added to his interest in the medium of film, these two motifs — communal violence, and an exposure, via the sublime — motivate his interest in "terror and the (post)cinematic sublime," our earliest title for this collection.

Isaac's interest follows a different trajectory, one grounded in the experience that we now too colloquially, and too immediately, refer to as "9/11," that event, at least for the population of the U.S., that best defines the contemporary sublime. In particular, he has been preoccupied (and continues to be so) by what seems to be missing in visual representations of 9/11, of the inherent lack in such imagery and the manner in which the paradoxical overabundance of iconic photos and videos comes to nullify their representative capacity. Rather, he finds that the aural artifacts of 9/11, especially the voice recordings of the hijackers, both address that representative lack while also demonstrating that such failed representation is inevitable in the face of the sublimity of 9/11.

The goal was never univocal. We wanted to examine post–9/11 and post-cinematic (as opposed to analog, or non-digital) film in light of theories of the sublime. And we wanted to do this from many, many different points of view simultaneously, demonstrating the theoretical heft and ambidextrous conceptual nature of the sublime, while attending to the essential problem of our historical moment: violence (hermeneutic, ontological, physical). Much has been written over the centuries and even in the last decade on the sublime, including at least three edited collections, Simon Morley's *The Sublime* (2010), Luke White and Claire Pajaczkowska's *The Sublime Now* (2009), and Bill Beckley's *Sticky Sublime* (2001). Other books include Christine Battersby's *The Sublime, Terror, and Human Difference* (2007), Philip Shaw's *The Sublime* (2006), Amy Elias' *Sublime Desire: History and Post 1960s Fiction* (2001), and Gene Ray's *Terror and the Sublime in Art and Critical Theory: From Auschwitz to Hiroshima to September 11* (2005). Despite the demonstrable quality of all of the above (and we recommend them all without reservation), there is no thoroughgoing collection of essays focused on (post)cinema and the sublime, situated at this historical moment, and deeply attuned to the problem of violence.

* * *

A collection such as this, despite being an ostentatious act of *collection*, involves, in fact, dozens of people, its influences, direct and indirect, spidering out in countless directions. We extend particular appreciation to our contributors — including Patrick Fuery who graciously agreed to pen our afterword — whose work is fascinating, and whose patience (with us

Preface and Acknowledgments

and our challenging work schedules), has exceeded all limits. We loved working with you and hope to reconnect in future projects. To Patrick Fuery, Ellen Berry, Lance Norman, David Cecchetto, Joseph Sommers, Mary Catherine Harper, David Sheridan, and Amy Drees, thank you! All of you have encouraged us, and/or provided much needed feedback at important moments in the slow labor which birthed this collection (the faults of this collection of essays, and there are sure to be a few, are ours, and ours alone). Our appreciation also extends to Bernadette Steele and David Posner, organizers of the annual meeting of the M/MLA, and to our 2010 panelists. Such conferences, and such people, continue to spark crucial reflection and discovery. And, lastly, we thank Stephany Blackston, our editorial assistant, for her energy, her critical eye, and her precision.

Individual thanks are also in order:

Todd thanks Dawn, Elliot, and Lucy. Only you know the intangible benefits and, all too often, *tangible* liabilities to my work. It is because of you that such "work"—all of those 5:30 A.M. mornings of editing and late-night e-mails—can be so easily transformed into play (*I promise, I will take next summer off*). Much more than my previous McFarland collection (*Sexual Ideology in the Works of Alan Moore*, 2012), this book reflects my history at Michigan State University, where I picked up my theoretical proclivities (some say "obsessions") from such teachers and scholars as Scott Michaelsen, A.C. Goodson, Patrick O'Donnell, and Eyal Amiran (thank you, all!). And, finally, my appreciation goes out to Collette Knight of the Pilgrim Library, for aiding me in my search for various and sundry dusty volumes.

Isaac thanks Lauren, my constant companion through the entire collection process, sounding board for my many enthusiasms and bearer of good humor despite obsessive e-mail checking and an inability to pull myself away from late-night editing binges; Ellen Berry, for helping me to refine my own interest in the sublime through countless dissertation drafts; and my parents, Sue and West Vayo, for encouraging my love of scholarship, research, and the desire to understand the world that manifests itself in this collection.

* * *

As with any birth, this collection is not tidy. While there are many conversations and engagements throughout, our hope is that this collection does not merely *collect* or *gather*, slowing or—worse—stalling the spiral of learning. Our hope is that this collection births other such projects.

Introduction: Terror and the (Post)Cinematic Sublime

Todd A. Comer and *Lloyd Isaac Vayo*

> "We have paid a high enough price for the nostalgia of the whole ... let us be witnesses to the unpresentable; let us activate the differences and save the honor of the name" — Jean-François Lyotard, *The Postmodern Condition*, 81–82

First comes terror, swaddled in its carriage, ferried in Buda's wagon.[1] This terror is itself a product of the marriage of the latter, a post- which not so much (or not only) antedates, but rather anti-dates, is timeless, enacts a courtship premised less on the rendezvous than the rude arrival, the shining violence of the act. Which is to say, our tripartite concern, our labor of love, wedding terror, the (post)cinematic, and the sublime, will not be an easy one. Its lineage is long, littered with cul-de-sacs, larded with fractures, layered, sedimented with interpretations; in passing, presenting futures. This trinity, this test, slouches, toward what, it is difficult to say, the destination remaining obscure, being obscured, curdles reflexively, spoils and is spoilt, its labyrinthine treble-backs dizzying, vertiginous. Once more to say, to call a thing by its name: terror, yes, and more terror still; the cinematic, and its post- child, surely; and the sublime, rapturous rupture. So here we begin.

* * *

A decade on from a signal terror, to some avenged just now by a singular demise, 9/11's shocking, awe-inducing becoming, a deliberate, symbolic, and unending production of fear, the hijackers' and victims' "I am become death" yields less a destruction of worlds than a destruction of a certain idea of "world." It is a destruction of a certain conceptualization of being, of a relationality to that which is in some senses larger than our-

Introduction

selves, yet in others reducible to a solitary moment in a dusty room half a world away, to a muzzle blast and an ignominious splash. Here, then, is not fear *per se*, but rather a rending, a tear or, perhaps, a separation or perforation, a line already scored and awaiting parting, a world in which terror is rule, not exception, a state of acceptance reigning in which terror, unless paradoxically exceptional, is more a bore than boring. How this terror comes to us, how the act is enacted within individual and collective reception, is by rote, though not in writing. Rather, it is visuality, the locus of the spectacle, where this nebulous terror sets up its housekeeping, establishing an uncanny abode, an unsettled settlement for an equally spooked citizenry, though the visual is too general: anyone can see, but it is something altogether different to create the seen, the scene, in the realm of the cinematic.

Yet, this cinematic, this framing of the moving image on screen in accordance with, or at least in dialogue with, certain aesthetic conventions standardized in mainstream film, is itself unstable, undermined, scored and cored, subject to a sequentiality, a periodization, followed by the post-cinematic, described only as that which comes after, the next, the once and future screen. All, the above and otherwise, is undergirded, at once given foundation and foundered, by sublimity, by the sublime variously configured. Such a sublime is at once the enormity before which one is speechless (an aural aporia common to cinematic discourse), the natural grandeur, yet also an alternate configuration, the post- of the cinematic meeting with the post- of the modern sublime. This meeting results in a fragmentation, a rupture, a negativity, an inability to present or represent, a discontinuity that continues on from its forbears while bearing a substantial difference in its insubstantial gossamer.

Our concern, then, is with terror and the (post)cinematic sublime, with the representation of terror in contemporary film and visual media, including *avant garde* film, such recent media "revolutions" as CGI, and 3D, and, of course, dramatic film. Our questions, though many and varied, coalesce around a number of central ideas: How are "nostalgia" and the "whole" linked to terror and the (post)cinematic form? Is terror synonymous with the unpresentable? Or is the unpresentable that which exposes terror to its finitude? How do cinematic and post-cinematic media — or do they — communicate that which is unpresentable? How do films mediate the sublime trauma of the events of September 11? How do (post)cinematic media confront the unpresentable in an age in which capitalism and the military are intimate bedfellows, exerting incredible pressure on our rep-

Introduction

resentational practices? How do contemporary films represent our imaginative limits? How does recent cinema frame human freedom in terms of the sublime? What sort of sublime arises from and/or elicits the (post)cinematic representation of horror? Can the sublime be used to understand the movement from cinema to post-cinematic media, from human to posthuman? Though sundry, these are certainly not all or even a significant fraction of the inquiries that may be posed in this area, and to these we may, might, will add others.

Taking the sublime, the last but, lest we forget, far from the least of our considerations, that sublime taking on an immensity both at the contemplative and conceptual levels, as our initial focus, two crude periodizations may be established as a means of grounding our discourse from the start: the original, foundational, classical sublime of Edmund Burke, Immanuel Kant and the like-minded, and the somewhat rogue, relational, postmodern sublime of the epigrammatic Lyotard. This is, of course, a substantial reduction, an *uber*-simplification, a twinning that trims, but the inertia of being stopped in one's tracks by the considerable largesse of the matter at hand calls for measures disparate, if not desperate. The Burkean/Kantian iteration itself draws on Longinus' rhetorical formation, where the sublime is a lofty, persuasive language enacted in the discursive field, moving beyond it to complicate simplistic notions of beauty within the natural world (beauty in that understanding being a uniformly positive and pleasurable experience) with a differential aesthetics. Within this alternate aesthetics, that which is less than beautiful, other than beautiful, perhaps even ugly, may instill intense emotion such that an equivalent, if not greater, pleasure is produced in the viewer. In accordance with its positioning in relation to nature, this sublime deals often in immensities, the sheer scale of natural features, such as towering mountains, sweeping plains, and tumbling cataracts evoking a terror-charged awe in their witnesses. The Lyotardian iteration, on the other hand, is preoccupied with the politics of representation in a manner at which the classical form only hints, spending less time on the act of oversaturation, on the confrontation with the sublime object or experience, than on the confrontation that such a meeting demands from the viewer, where the inability to adequately represent that which is, at base, unpresentable, forces the viewer to address deficiencies within the rational mind. Where the Burkean/Kantian sublime focuses primarily on the spiritual and moral transcendence endowed by encounters with the sublime (though Burke also makes preliminary note of the implication of limitation at this early date), Lyotard's sublime stands

Introduction

as a manifestation of the postmodernity that he elsewhere conceptualizes, a world marked less by stability or singularity than by variability and multiplicity, a sublime for all giving way to a sublime for each (and every). Complexity occupies the interstices between these titans, but let two stand as giants, to give way to the many in what follows.

Heretofore, perhaps as a reflection of either the conceptual enormity of the sublime, the literal heft of that which embodies it (in the case of natural forms or unnatural events), or the theoretical complexity that it unfurls, treatments of the sublime within the extant body of literature have been partial, incremental, willfully incomplete or, in some cases, haltingly general, so distanced as to allow for a superficial appraisal and little more. The former approach in some ways mimics the conclusions drawn by Lyotard, resembles the perception of the postmodern sublime as a site of fragmentation, as a locus of conceded imperfection and inability, as the spot where humanity confronts its incapacity for representation or even presentation. The sublime object eludes description with any degree of accuracy, instead sliding by, sliding through, remaining largely untouched save for a fumbling graze of the fingertips. It is easier, in a sense less daunting, to tackle the part rather than the parcel, to look at a specific aspect of or area in which the sublime manifests, be it horror films (a frequent focus of the more specific sort) or, in the absence of a specific toehold within the imposing face of the sublime, a more general, at times generic look at the concept as a whole, either through a historiographic survey (the more prevalent) or a purportedly original theoretical venture (less prevalent). This is not to say that these approaches are unworthy, unsustainable, inappropriate; rather, there is a usefulness in parsing the sheer bulk of the sublime into more manageable serving sizes, in selecting certain foci with demarcated parameters, in identifying a particularly fascinating aspect. Too, there is value in the grander sweep, the all encompassed in a broader cartography of the sublime, though in this there is a danger of encountering the very limit which is the sublime, the inability to represent the totality. In any case, one should keep trying.

What is offered here is another such effort, though to call it more of the same would be a disservice, both an inaccurate claim for the homogeneity of previous texts (which, though often possessing much in the way of theoretical or topical overlap, are yet distinct works) and, more importantly, a preemptive writing off of a collection less novelty than novel, an accusation of paths twice trod where new footprints are laid. On the one hand, what follows is not a singular specificity, but a multiple one, each

Introduction

area, be it 9/11, freedom, or (post)cinematic interruptions, capable of standing on its own as a unique area study akin to the narrower texts within the existing literature. Yet, in many cases, these multiple singularities are still singular, not in their freestanding nature, but in their first address of some aspects of the sublime, their original attention to topics previously left unattended, abandoned for others more familiar. To the second hand, an inverse movement from the larger to the smaller, the multiple specificities coalesce into a comprehensive overview, one which does not make claims for exhaustive coverage, but one which comes very near to achieving such expansiveness due to its incorporation of new ground constructed on and making mention of older turf. Overview suggests oversight, both a limiting guidance to a certain end and a paradoxical shortsightedness, an over- which results in an under-examination. This collection avoids either pratfall, thematizing perhaps, but letting the invisible hand of the free market of inquiry guide the analyses that follow, while yet taking the long view, identifying new frontiers for the sublime while avoiding the colonial excesses that such a language implies. What we have, then, is a failure to conflate, to elide various sublimes into a single one, and to merge our singularity with previous such monovocalities; a new voice for the hearing, a new sight for the seeing, a new understanding for the age of terror, for its (post)cinema, and for their union in the sublime.

* * *

We demarcate three areas of concerns, concerns whose limits exclude, but also embrace (at moments) the others: *Hits and Missives: Excluding/Embracing 9/11*; *Pushing the Enveloped: Exposing the Limits of Freedom*; and *Communiqué-tion Breakdown: (Post)Cinematic Interruptions*. The first section opens with Kartik Nair's "Plummeting to the Pavement: The Fall of the Body in *Spider-Man*." Nair discusses the "premediation" (Richard Grusin) of traumatic events, how, in other words, films attempt to assimilate the possibility of trauma ahead of time before said trauma can take hold. He asks, "how might one begin to think of images of terror that belong neither to the memory of the past nor to a vision of the future?" Nair focuses his attention on images of the "falling man" (of 9/11 fame) which have not been visually pre- or remediated, he argues, but, instead, "blacklisted." Specifically, Nair focuses on the innumerable falls in the *Spider-Man* movies which he sees as a sublime "encounter, however provisional, with [this] unacknowledged past."

Scott Wilson's "When Does the Hurting Stop? *Cloverfield* and the (Re)Enabling of Fantasy in the Post-9/11 City" focuses on the traumatic

Introduction

sublime, the question of how healing from the traumatic events of September 11 can occur in the midst of complex representational and ideological forces. To heal requires a *direct* confrontation with trauma; however, as Wilson argues, representations of the New York skyline (i.e., the Twin Towers) became "locked in a socially enforced structure of performance trauma" so that the skyline was not (re)presented, or, at best, representations became mere memorializations of the traumatic event. *Cloverfield*, however, with its more direct representation of the cityscape, marks an end and a new beginning of sorts for the representation of NYC. Wilson sees the film as a "recuperation of the uncanny geography of the ruined landscape and the commodification of the specific tropes of 9/11."

Hits and Missives: Excluding/Embracing 9/11 ends with Sven Cvek's "Keeping Terror Alive: The Political Economy of Visibility in *Inside Man*." Cvek analyzes the "political (invisibility of the dead) and technological (hypervisibility of the living)" in the post 9/11 context. Politically, of course, the (Iraqi or U.S.) dead need to be erased or risk becoming a ground for political activity; the living (Iraqi or U.S.) need to be visible in order to be tracked, just in case, by power. Spike Lee's *Inside Man*, a case in point, plays with visibility to an extraordinary degree — it is *not* about 9/11 and yet it *is*, in light of all of the references to terror(ism). Using Lee's film, Cvek argues that today the sublime event, which is 9/11 and terror, more generally, is visible, yet immediately, as it is assimilated by a military-economic structure, made invisible.

Donald Callen's "Aronofsky's Cinematic Vision and the Ethical Meaning of Freedom as the Sublime Horizon of *Amor Fati*" opens the second section, *Pushing the Enveloped: Exposing the Limits of Freedom*. Callen uses Aronofky's *oeuvre* to work through issues of ontology, aesthetics, and freedom. Specifically, he opens with a reading of *Black Swan*, teasing out the tension between the Apollonian and the Dionysian in that film, before arguing for the importance of that which escapes an Apollonian rationality. Against a simplistic notion of the individual (tied to Apollo), Callen argues that "an adequate consciousness would reflect back to us the abyssal, sublime mystery of our existence." Living in view of this sublimity allows a person to be aware of fate, aware of the forces that would pin him or her down, and, thereby, able to self-reflexively contemplate a "free" — as long as freedom is not defined by the subject — existence.

With its emphasis on freedom and the apocalyptic, Seung-hoon Jeong's "The Apocalyptic Sublime: Hollywood Disaster Films and *Donnie Darko*" complements Callen's essay. Against the backdrop of the assimilation or kitschification of the Holocaust and other disasters by Hollywood film, Jeong uses *Donnie Darko* to argue for an ethical sublime, for a "sublime effect that leads us beyond the screen toward unthought dimensions of the world and our mind." The lesson of *Donnie Darko* is that a catastrophe, seen/represented correctly, "explode[s] repressed social desires and traumas," leading to a profound rethinking of society.

Marco Grosoli's "History Is Always Virgin: Quentin Tarantino's *Inglourious Basterds* and the Lyotardian Sublime" focuses on the conservative formal tendencies of cinema — how an audience is "tease[d]" by a narrative's "delightful, aberrant, irregular movements" which are then erased at the moment of "synthesis." Tarantino's filmography, however, is atypical in that it teases audiences with excessive moments that are scarcely able to be reintegrated into the assimilative movement that Grosoli identifies with the basic *modus operandi* of Western rationality. Connecting Nazism to U.S. capitalism, Grosoli argues that *Inglourious Basterds* is neither "pro" nor "con" terrorism; rather, what the film demonstrates is that it is both, foregrounding the viewer's own desires for totality, while, simultaneously, critiquing totalitarianism: "being a democratic citizen means, today, being *also* a terrorist."

Michael J. Blouin's "Tarrying with Sublimity: The Limits of Cinematic Form in Duncan Jones' *Source Code*" follows Grosoli with a close analysis of the representational limits of cinema. Against Adorno's critique of mass culture conservatism, Blouin sees *Source Code* as engaged in an attempt to pass beyond the formal limits of film. *Source Code*, for example, allegorizes the entrapment of the cinematic audience, only to then place us in a position to "feel the terrifying — and liberating — edges of an enclosed social space in transition ... as a (post)cinematic sublime." Sensing this transition, the viewer recognizes the limits and desires containing him or her; the viewer, staggered, confronts the limits of representational thought.

Holly Willis' "Pleasure and Pain: Post-Cinematic Remakes" opens our final section, *Communiqué-tion Breakdown: (Post)Cinematic Interruptions*. Her essay takes as its object a series of recent *avant-garde* media projects, Peter Tscherkassky's *Outer Space* (1999) and Douglas Gordon's *24 Hour Psycho* (1993), among others. Such media art pieces signal a move to a "post-cinema," undermining "spatial" and "temporal codes" of traditional cinema which assist in creating an "illusion of coherence," and giving expression to a new sense of subjectivity in our heavily mediated world.

John P. Warton's "Watching the World Burn: Intensity, Absurdity and Echoes of the Sublime in Contemporary Science Fiction Destruction"

Introduction

focuses on Roland Emmerich's *2012*; Warton demonstrates how, while retaining an intra-diegetic sublime, advances in digital technology have undermined the extra-diagetic possibility of the sublime as disaster scenes become more and more "cartoonish" and "absurdist" due to an *excessive* distance between the viewer and the viewed. Warton argues, however, that "some mass destruction sequences still reveal a capacity to produce echoes of the sublime through the images' associations with recent historical traumas."

In "The AIllusion: Intelligent Machines, Jacques Derrida's 'Ethical Turn' and Oren Peli's *Paranormal Activity*," Larrie Dudenhoeffer discusses how a camera normally allows for the illusion of the self-presence of its object *and* alludes to objective reality's distance. However, in Peli's film, the camera is digital, allowing for the "instantaneous creation of a camera-subject that does not exist at the moment the image is taken." The camera, as an incipient artificial intelligence, *is* the demon antagonist, he argues, as it "re-elaborat[es] the supersensible enormity of the sublime as the data-transfer of the organismic into an altogether different format."

Todd A. Comer's "The Indigestibility of the World: Birthing the Posthuman in Spielberg's *A.I.*" focuses on how the work of representation grounds Humanism, and on that which fragments the representations upon which the Human is built. Holding that the work of representation is really a work of assimilation, a *digestion* of alterity, he argues that this digestive cycle, fueling an engineering of the world into more and more human dimensions, is the essence of Humanism. Framed by an apocalyptic world in which digestion has faltered, Comer argues for a posthumanism prompted by a sublime confrontation with birth. Patrick Fuery, dean and professor of English at Chapman University, author of numerous books on film and critical theory, and scholar of the cinematic sublime, provides us with our afterword.

* * *

As we conclude, it is useful to return briefly to our tangential example, our opening salvo, the dual salvational acts of 9/11 and the assassination of its purported mastermind. To the aforementioned literal and figurative fragmentings engendered by the event itself and their consequences for preexisting conceptualizations of "world," one may add a more Burkean/Kantian sublime, the sheer scale of the event itself, not only in terms of the notable height and symbolic import of its targets, but also in terms of the intended and realized death toll, realizing that sublime and complicating the more Lyotardian fragment. In both cases, the confrontational

Introduction

act requires a second confrontation, that of the witness with representation and the associated failures thereof, be they the failings of the visual, aural, either or both, the unfamiliar feeling of vulnerability, such representation being at once impossible to perform and equally impossible to bypass.

However, it is the fresher wound, that issued to the man behind the curtain, that perhaps best illustrates the elusive nature of the (post)cinematic sublime as its exists within the realm of terror. Bin Laden's demise is freighted with a wealth of related details that significantly alter perceptions of the man and his deeds, of the large, multitudinous enemy lurking in primitive climes. Where it was assumed that the sheik was ensconced in a network of caves in the lawless hinterlands, cut off from his compatriots amid a spartan, romanticized rebel lifestyle, giving him the legendary carriage of a folk hero, the realities of the intervening years since 9/11 are something altogether different. The caved but uncaving hero gives way to the shut-in, the hermit, less rebel than rabble, tucked away with relative safety in the borders of an uneasy ally, trading the cave for the cloister, in touch with those touched by his message yet, for whatever reason (be it a matter of simple logistics, of will, or of difficulty in the face of increasing scrutiny and counterterror measures), unable to act in any significant way, less the man of action than of traction, satisfied with the toehold and nothing more. Representation fails, has failed; what was once a giant is now a broken man, lesser and yet perhaps more, greater in his flaws and failings, a (once) living, breathing embodiment of the new sublime, an agent of terror, a practitioner of the (post)cinematic (in video/audio dispatches and attacks-as-spectacles), what was, is, and may be.

NOTES

1. The reference here is to Mike Davis' 2007 book *Buda's Wagon: A Brief History of the Car Bomb*, more specifically to the 16 September 1920 Wall Street bombing, allegedly perpetrated by Sacco and Vanzetti associate Mario Buda.

HITS AND MISSIVES:
EXCLUDING/EMBRACING 9/11

Plummeting to the Pavement: The Fall of the Body in *Spider-Man*

Kartik Nair

Almost immediately after the attacks on the World Trade Center in New York City, it was evident that the terrorist event had been rehearsed countless times in Hollywood blockbusters. Particular reference was made to disaster films, and their deployment of cinematic spectacle as an anticipation of the burning, collapsing Twin Towers. Consider, for example, Roland Emmerich's films of the late 1990s, in which an alien spacecraft obliterates New York (*Independence Day*, 1996) or a giant lizard whips its tail through the city's skyscrapers (*Godzilla*, 1998). "The question we should have asked ourselves as we stared at the TV screens on September 11," proposed Slavoj Žižek, "is simply: Where have we already seen the same thing over and over again?" (17).

Of disaster films, Susan Sontag wrote: "In such films, it is by means of images and sounds that one can participate in the fantasy of living through one's death and more, the death of cities, the destruction of humanity itself" (213). Yet, even as it evoked (and invoked) the generic markers of a disaster film, 9/11 exceeded the banality with which catastrophe is distributed to Hollywood's global audiences. The fall of the towers, argued Jean Baudrillard, provoked an "excess of reality," "a resurgence of the real, and of the violence of the real, in a supposedly virtual universe" (28). The truly paralyzing effect of 9/11 came not from its audacious execution, its spectacular scale, or the cost to human life, but from the ferreting of these elements together out of the image and into the "real." The terrorist thus improves on Hollywood:

> In this case the real is superadded to the image like a bonus of terror, like an additional *frisson*: not only is it terrifying, but, what is more, it

is real. Rather than the violence of the real being there first, and the *frisson* of the image being added to it, the image is there first, and the *frisson* of the real is added [Baudrillard 29; original's emphasis].

To prevent another such awesome excess of the real would require expanding the kingdom of images — to capture and convert every possible real into an image, to imagine it now so it cannot be realized later. According to Richard Grusin, 9/11 — the first "live" global media event — influences the production of images that can insulate us from the threat of a terrible "liveness": he terms this aggressive media reaction "premediation." Whereas "remediation" involves the re-presentation of traumatic images from the past, premediation "imagines multiple futures which are alive in the present" (Grusin 8), making available these futures as consumable images in an attempt to prevent the trauma of their ever *really* happening. Premediation as cultural policy attempts to check the "immediacy of the catastrophe, the immediacy of disaster," working to ensure that "when the future comes it will already have been remediated, prepar[ing] the public to be ready for the future not as it emerges immediately into the present but before it ever happens" (Grusin 12).

Indeed, the ten years since 9/11 has seen Hollywood insistently return to New York as its destination of choice for disaster. Every year, it seems, another apocalypse descends on the city and the box office. In *The Day After Tomorrow* (2004, Roland Emmerich), tidal waves come crashing down Madison Avenue. In *War of the Worlds* (2005, Steven Spielberg), alien tripods burst through the asphalt and blast humans to nothingness. In *I Am Legend* (2007, Francis Lawrence), the protagonist races through a derelict Manhattan now overgrown with vegetation and overrun by animals. In *Cloverfield* (2008, Matt Reeves), a monster hits the city by night, sending the head of the Statue of Liberty rolling past terrified hundreds. Understood in terms of Grusin's theory of premediation, these are films in which the future of global terrorism is itself remediated, the dread of the real contained within an intelligible image; cinematic spectacles neutralize the unknowability and contingency of the unpredicted attack, making the terror of the future part of our past, our communal memory. "After 9/11," writes Grusin, "mediality has followed a trajectory of premediation as a means of mobilizing collective affect in order to protect us from the impending threat of global terrorism" (9). For even as these films remediate 9/11 — ash-covered New Yorkers fleeing for their lives, hand-held cameras capturing an unfolding disaster — they also premediate its possible, imminent variations — bio-terror lacing the streets, monuments flaming against the horizon. Within this complex double logic of mediation and premediation, how might one begin to think of images of terror that belong neither to the memory of the past nor to a vision of the future?

I refer to images that belong historically to the event designated as "9/11" but became invisible soon after, never mourned or canonized in the media memory of the event. Arguably, the most controversial story of that day was not the death of the thousands who burned inside the buildings or the destruction of the buildings themselves, but the 200 people who jumped to their deaths from the towers. At 9:41 A.M., AP photographer Richard Drew took a photograph of a man falling down the side of the North Tower. When the picture was printed in newspapers the next day, editors received angry letters and complaints. The picture ran no longer, but it inspired a story in *Esquire* by Tom Junod titled "The Falling Man." The story begins, "Do you remember this photograph? In the United States, people have taken pains to banish it from the record of September 11, 2001. The story behind it, though, and the search for the man pictured in it, are our most intimate connection to the horror of that day." More unbelievable it seems than the fall of the towers was the fall of these men and women. Junod describes the falling figures seen in rare photographs and videos as "struggling against horrific discrepancies of scale," overwhelmed by the towers, "which loom like colossi" and by the magnitude of "the event itself." Unlike images of the planes crashing into the Twin Towers or smoke billowing in the city's streets, these *other* images blasted onto our screens without a sense of remediation or reassuring cinematic precedent.

To commemorate the first anniversary of September 11, the Rockefeller Center displayed *Tumbling Woman*, a large-scale bronze nude by celebrated New York sculptor Eric Fischl. A week later, a screen was placed over it. When the *New York Post*'s Andrea Peyser published her review, authorities scrambled to have Fischl's homage removed from the Center altogether. "Is this Art? Or is this Assault?" Peyser asked, shocked that such a "violently disturbing sculpture" had "popped up ... right in front of the ice-skating rink," and outraged at the sculpture for depicting a woman "at the exact moment her head smacks the pavement following her leap from the flaming World Trade Center." In fact, Peyser was mistaken, for the bronze commemorates not the instant of death, but the hauntingly unknowable delirium of a fatal leap: the *tumbling* woman.

Falling man or tumbling woman, an unholiness scorches such images of 9/11. "From the beginning," recalls Junod, "the spectacle of doomed people jumping from the upper floors of the World Trade Center resisted redemption." Why? What places this spectacle beyond redemption? Given the seemingly unchecked proliferation of televisual material immediately following the attacks, what is it about this specific set of images that prevents them being assimilated and distributed as part of the memory of the event? Among all the instances of pain, trauma, and bodily suffering captured on film that morning, why is the image of the falling blacklisted?

Perhaps the answer lies in the way we received the events of September 11, 2001. As billions of viewers convened around television screens, we all gaped at Ground Zero, the locus of the terrorist strike, along with our surrogate viewers within the image pointing, gasping, screaming, running. In many ways, 9/11 was rendered as traditionally 2-D: as a closed frame from the edges of which planes swam into view; at the center of which occurred the pyrotechnics of explosion, fire, and smoke; and to the base of which one saw the wreckage piling. The event persists in media memory as one that is objectified before the viewer, unspooling as on a flat-screen. Further, this flat-screen encloses other flat-screens — the facades of the Twin Towers — which in turn screen off the deaths of thousands.

One must ask therefore if there is room for a different perspective on 9/11, perhaps one that looks upon the event not from the outside but from its *inside*? Is it possible to re-visualize the event not from New York's pavements, but from a window on the 110th floor of the World Trade Center? This would entail not just elevating our point of view by a thousand feet, but following that point of view as it changes over time. It would entail accompanying the jumper on his journey to the pavement; it would mean inhabiting the present continuous of Richard Drew's photograph, and its terrible futurity. There is an obscenity in attempting identification with any one of those 200 people who jumped or fell; it means taking a voyeuristic interest in an experience both lethal and oddly beautiful; it means inhabiting, however briefly, a sublime, mobile sensorium characterized by its velocity, its fatalism, its radical disorientation, its embrace of death. It means immersion in an ambience of noise and speed, falling through smoke and flames, racing past flying debris and floating sheets of paper, and being hit by the wind and drawn by gravity toward one's destiny.

Following our discussion of the complex double logic of premediation, I will now focus on a constellation of cinematic moments that work less as disaster-film style images of vast cataclysm and suffering, and more as visceral contraventions of taboos surrounding 9/11. Sam Raimi's *Spider-Man* films (2002, 2004, 2007) are taken not with the metaphysics of a fallen world "after the event," but with the physics of a falling New York City. When the *Spider-Man* films attempt to apprehend images of falling—and the affective experiences entombed inside them—are they "remediating" 9/11 or "pre-mediating" it? In this case, as I shall argue, pre-mediation works not to describe an unknowable future but an unknown past; this is a past, like a future, that has not yet been lived through. By bringing them into our present, *Spider-Man* engages with the sublime terror of their "liveness," creatively reworking the intolerable immediacy of experience that made these images taboo in the first place.

Fantasy Island, Falling City

In *Delirious New York* (1978), Dutch architect Rem Koolhaas writes the history of Manhattan as a heady exercise in make-believe that comes true. In Koolhaas's account, the island fades *into* existence as tentative, a half-whisper that survives the ages. The purchase of Manhattan is the first delusion: Twenty-four dollars are exchanged with the Indians, but these Indians never owned the place. Then follows the city's grid of streets and avenues, the "most courageous act of prediction in Western civilization" based, as it is, *on a guess*: "the land it divides, unoccupied; the population it describes, conjectural; the buildings it locates, phantoms; the activities it frames, nonexistent" (18). A dream from which there has been no awakening, Manhattan for Koolhaas is a speculative image that has materialized "without manifesto"—something akin to "living inside a fantasy" (10).

Within this world of make-believe, it is Coney Island that most interests Koolhaas. A "fetal" Manhattan, Coney Island is the "incubator" for the island's "incipient themes and infant mythology.... The strategies and mechanisms that later shape Manhattan are tested in the laboratory of Coney Island before they finally leap toward the larger island" (30). In a curious turn, the appurtenances of amusement—electricity, air-conditioning, tubes, telegraphs, tracks and elevators, the "incipient tradition of Fantastic Technology" (87)—are laundered into Manhattan. It was among the "paraphernalia" of Coney Island's "artificial paradise" that the skyscraper was truly born (87).

The American skyscraper developed in Chicago, but assumed dominance only in New York City. From the 1880s onward, prominent experiments began erupting off the ground in Manhattan. These eruptions were initially framed within the context of a *fin-de-siècle* contest for possession of the city between *civic horizontalism* and *corporate verticality*. Civic horizontalism, coming out of the 19th century's "City Beautiful" movement, called for a topography of parks, pavements, playgrounds: a city for its children, in other words. By contrast, and standing at the end of a complicated history of access, corporate verticality charted a city of high-rises, in which the recently-invented passenger elevator had flipped the fortunes of the upper floors (Wigoder 152–169). Inventor Elisha Otis first presents the elevator as a theatrical spectacle. At the 1854 New York World's Fair, he orders an axe-man to cut the rope supporting his raised cart. The eager crowd is prepared for a booming crash. Nothing happens (the safety catches), leading Koolhaas to observe that Otis has sounded a note that will be "a leitmotiv of the island's future development: Manhattan is an accumulation of possible disasters that never happened" (27).

More than anything else, the skyscraper is iconic of Manhattan, embodying its arrogant, ambitious defiance of gravity. One morning in 1988, Michel de Certeau stands at a window on the 110th floor of the World Trade Center. Staring out over Manhattan, "no longer clasped by the streets," Certeau's elevation makes him a "solar Eye, looking down like a god" (91). Equally, consider Corbusier on the viewer-on-high: "he becomes radiant. He sees the ocean and boats; he is above the other lice" (133). Certeau or Corbusier, euphoric or hostile, the view from on high assumes a solidity of perspective arising from the solidity of the monumental high-rise. Over the course of the twentieth century, the skyscraper would assume its place as one of the central definers of perspective in urban modernity. But in the 21st century, on a morning in 2001, a new choreography of perspectives was set in motion. The spell is broken: The stability of perspective surrenders to a hurtling, immeasurable mobility; skyward ambition surrenders to earthbound gravity. Hapless eyes and cameras witness what they cannot believe, the collapse of the Twin Towers, more than a hundred stories in just over a hundred minutes. An "accumulation of disasters that never happened," Koolhaas's Manhattan is, in the space of one morning, one giant calamity: the falling city.

Spider-Man *in New York: The Real Time of Falling Bodies*

The first big action sequence in *Superman Returns* (Bryan Singer, 2006) involves a NASA mission gone awry. An airplane catches fire and begins its rapid descent through the skies; a fiery spectacle that first loses one wing then another, it spirals earthward from the stratosphere. Navigating the trail of the disintegrating plane, Superman whizzes in to rescue its load of hysterical passengers. Bracing himself against the head of this massive projectile, he uses all his superhuman strength to arrest its fall. He succeeds, laying the plane down safely in a baseball stadium. The crowd erupts in enthusiastic applause. This airborne fireball, with the additional shock of a suicidal airplane and helpless Americans is perhaps a bold image, coming merely five years after 9/11. However, the vocabulary of the image (NASA, "U.S. Air Force" emblazoned on the side of the plane, baseball, red-and-blue Superman and Stars-and-Stripes fanfare on the soundtrack) belongs to the language of the *national. Superman Returns* has taken the urban out of 9/11.

By contrast, Sam Raimi's popular *Spider-Man* situates itself within the dynamics of the city, featuring on-location shoots in the city's meat-packing districts and on its piers, in addition to filming its cabs, its cops, and its fire-fighters. The film's visual effects designer John Dykstra says: "It's *real* New York City, right down to the rust stains underneath the drain pipes and pigeon droppings ... the dirt and the dust and debris of this city." Of course, the "real" New York is always somewhere in a shuffling deck. For an elaborate showdown in *Spider-Man*, producers contemplated shutting Times Square down for the weekend, but the city administration refused them permission. Hence, Times Square emerges on the screen via a stream of matte paintings, pre-visualization work, green screens, pipelines, CGI, animation, motion control, and 60,000 textures. According to J.P. Telotte, this is how "speculative images come alive" in sci-fi film (8), that is, through the painstaking process of *world-building*. Further, location shooting is dicey, subject to the vagaries of availability, money, and time. A recently restored theatre in downtown LA provided the interiors for a Broadway performance in *Spider-Man 3*, and these were then welded to exterior shots of the "real thing." At various points, Sony-Columbia studio sets simulated New York City, and location scouts recreated the city in such improbable places as Cleveland, Ohio, (*Spider-Man 3*) and Chicago, Illinois (*Spider-Man 2*).

We see Spider-Man perch atop such sites as the Art-Deco Chrysler Building on Lexington Avenue, and when he swoops down into New York's streets his body is reflected furtively in the glass-and-steel facades of a later international modernist style. Predictably, the *Spider-Man* films indulge a touristic fascination with the Manhattan skyline. "Sam [Raimi] always wanted to use the verticality of the city," says producer Laura Ziskin, as part of the DVD commentary. "When Spider-Man flies to the top of a building," notes Art Director Andrea Dopaso, "he is supposed to appear very small in comparison with the enormous architectural pieces that adorn the building." Raimi and his production team choose repeatedly to throw their superhero against a Manhattan skyline that is, in production designer Neil Spisak's words, "slightly over-scaled." The distortion of proportion manifests as a kind of architectural sublime. Halfway through *Spider-Man 2*, Spider-Man (Tobey Maguire) chases Doctor Octopus (Alfred Molina) up a skyscraper. The tentacled villain lures him toward the giant, gothic clock at the summit. As Spider-Man approaches, Doc Oc rips out the hands of the clock, each a few dozen feet in diameter, and flings them down at his foe. Hit by one, barely missing the other, Spider-Man loses his grip and takes a dive down the north face of the building. He is dwarfed by the wrought-iron clock hands as they whiz past him, cutting through the air in magnified, contemplative silence.

Likewise, the following sequence from *Spider-Man*: The setting is the World-Unity Science Fair on Times Square. Green Goblin, having hijacked a military glider, makes a surprise visit to the Fair. His contrail is first glimpsed; the glider comes into view as it dips into the Square. Watching from a balcony, Mary Jane (Kirsten Dunst) is stunned to see the glider hovering so dangerously close. Goblin approaches the balcony. He dispatches a bomb; the force of the blast rips the balcony out of the firmament and sends Mary Jane dangling over the edge. When the balcony gives, she begins her headlong nosedive to the earth. As she screams for help and dear life, we switch from a frontal shot to a shot in free-fall, escorting her body to the pavement. A reverse zoom seems to bring the pavement closer as she falls farther. Spider-Man to the rescue — he catches her at the last instant. Or consider the climax, in which Mary Jane is dropped by the Green Goblin over the George Washington Bridge: As she plummets, dead-track blankets the sound; in the silence, all we hear is the sound of the wind as she cuts through it. The action is rendered in slow-motion, with comic-book like close-ups of her hands and her face; on the soundtrack, we get a kind of auditory close-up of her scream. Then, Spider-Man swings in and breaks her fall.

I count above a dozen such falling bodies in the three *Spider-Man* films. Just by herself, Mary Jane falls thrice; Peter Parker once, and, as Spider-Man, countless times; ancillary characters, regularly. Of course, these scenarios can be explained within the logic of the arachnid athleticism of a figure like Spider-Man, as well as the logic of spectacle that summer blockbusters work hard to render with cutting-edge visual effects, inviting comparisons to roller-coaster rides or bungee jumps. As such, they represent the latter-day, transversal return of the "cinema of attractions," espousing the abruptness of affect over the development of narrative: trading in visual thrill, shock, and astonishment over story, character, or meaning. However, the aesthetic strategies employed in the cited sequences — dead-track, slow motion, visual and aural close-ups, unstable and accelerated points-of-view that move with the falling subject — destabilize perspective and abandon frontality, immersing us in a sense of heightened terror and eerie calm at odds with the outsized tendencies of contemporary blockbusters. Imbuing the screen with a quieter sense of time and space, the journeys of falling men and women in the *Spider-Man* films fill out the present with immediacy. Time dilates, space contracts: The few seconds of the fall last longer, the thousands of feet come closer together. The poetics of falling brings to life the unknowable, near-post-mortem and essentially sublime experience of falling to one's death.

The sublime, as Istvan Csicsery-Ronay writes, "is a response to an imaginative shock, the complex recoil and recuperation of consciousness coping with objects too great to be encompassed" (72). The sublime provokes a break in cognition, "a sudden estrangement from habitual perception," abolishing narrative for a momentary plunge into uncertainty, "suspend[ing] one's confidence in knowledge about the world" (71). In courting an aesthetics of the sublime, *Spider-Man* forces an affective encounter, however provisional, with the unacknowledged past. In his story for *Esquire*, Junod writes that the men and women who jumped from the twin towers on September 11

> were called "jumpers" or "the jumpers," as though they represented a new lemminglike class. The trial that hundreds endured in the building and then in the air became its own kind of trial for the thousands watching them from the ground. No one ever got used to it; no one who saw it wished to see it again....

The *Spider-Man* films not only stare into this world beyond redemption, they boldly inhabit it. In fact, one might argue, had the story of the jumpers been pursued after the event, had the alterity of their experience been acknowledged in public discourse, the poetics of falling would not have figured so prominently in the *Spider-Man* trilogy, or would have been re-mediated differently. As they appear now, images of falling in *Spider-Man* premediate 9/11, giving cinematic shape and volume to images that were banished from the record, helping us confront a past we never lived through.

Since they draw out the past rather than pre-empt or predict a future, these images prompt us to rethink Grusin's theory of premediation. Insofar as premediation is a cultural reaction against the threat of "liveness," Grusin notes that it militates against the 1990s discourse of technological optimism. Specifically, Grusin identifies Paul Virilio's concepts of "time freeze" and "real time" with the 1990s' techie euphoria about instantaneity. Virilio, according to Grusin, predicted the general movement of telecommunications and digital technology to "collapse space and time into a moment of instantaneity and thus to produce a preoccupation not with the past or future, but with the present" (12). In *Open Sky* (1997), Virilio begins by claiming that while Renaissance perspective has controlled space for nearly four centuries, a new conquest is underway today. "The urbanization of real space," Virilio proposes, is "giving way to a preliminary urbanization of real time" (9). The old depth of field vanishes, "the optical density of the landscape is rapidly evaporating" (22). In the era of the transmission revolution, the couch-bound viewer inhabits "tele-existence," a form of perception that privileges the *now* over the here. Forget classical space, forget historical time—*speed* will from now be the measure of experience.

Let us turn to an example from *Spider-Man 3*. On the roof of a skyscraper, a crane is moving massive iron ledges during repair-work over New York City. In the office high-rise across the road, blonde bombshell Gwen Stacy (Bryce Dallas Howard) is modeling for a photo-shoot. Suddenly, the crane blows a fuse and goes out of control. The ledge it is carrying sways violently, and shoulders in to the building across, three floors below Gwen. Tearing out windows and columns, it creates a hailstorm over 6th Avenue, sending whole floors of office stationery—boxes, tables, lamps, paper—down with glass and steel. Horrified onlookers jump out of the way to escape the falling debris. The convulsing crane then guts into the building, pulling floors out like so many shelves, and Gwen with them. She is in rapid descent. Spider-Man approaches the scene. His "spider-sense" attunes him to the sights and sounds of the unfolding catastrophe: As everything else fades, Gwen's body, and the many chunks of concrete she is plummeting with, come into sharp focus; the only sounds we hear are of these bodies slicing the wind with speed, along with a thudding heartbeat.

As such, spider-sense imitates the "headlong rush of perception" Virilio ascribes to falling bodies, taking the example of a parachutist:

In this experience, at a certain moment, the ground no longer approaches, but parts and splits open, going suddenly from a "whole" dimension *with no receding lines*, to a "fractional" dimension in which the visible spectacle gapes open.... The *headlong* perspective is no longer so much that of the real — vertical or horizontal — space of the Italian geometers; it is first and foremost that of the real time of falling bodies. The horizon of visibility of the "faller" prior to being smashed to smithereens depends essentially on the speed at which his eyes adapt, focusing and an imperceptible time freeze depending on the mass of his body itself.... The falling body suddenly becomes *the body of the fall*... [29; original's emphasis].

What Virilio calls the "real time of falling bodies," of time instantly perceived, of an over-extended present-ness, finds its comic-book equivalent in spider-sense, the temporary augmentation of sensory faculties in moments of mortal danger. The films often cue us into these moments via a visual and sonic amplification of things moving through time and space. Spider-Man thus carves out an architecture of the journey, a dynamic *mise-en-scène* of disaster. These are not apocalyptic spectacles glimpsed from the outside, but urban calamities experienced from the inside, the underside to living inside the Koolhaasian fantasy of Manhattan. In his *Esquire* piece, Junod notes that those who jumped or fell were probably "accelerating at a rate of thirty-two feet per second squared ... [then] traveling at upwards of 150 miles per hour, upside down." *Spider-Man*'s own Falling Men and Tumbling Women are, like the subject of Richard Drew's controversial 9/11 photograph, "in the clutches of pure physics" (Junod), contraband images of what it must feel like to plummet to the pavement.

We are in the zone of the post-modern accident, where time and space converge with speed. "The accident," writes Virilio, "is solely *what occurs*, and not, like substance, *what is*..." (123; original's emphasis). Thus it is that the thinness of a dematerializing city defines *Spider-Man*. Indeed, when it proceeds beyond the obligatory pleasures of world-building, it finds itself replete with an unequal and opposite emphasis on *world-(un)building*. A creature of the city accident, Spider-Man can be seen coasting on and clambering over flying debris (*Spider-Man 2*), escaping two bits of debris colliding in mid-air (*Spider-Man 3*), pulling helpless citizens out from under falling debris (*Spider-Man*), rammed into debris by villains (*Spider-Man 3*), and burying villains under it (*Spider-Man*). Producer Laura Ziskin, on the DVD commentary, affectionately calls Raimi "Debris King." Mass cedes to surface; earthbound detritus is replaced by airborne debris. More than anything else, urban forms can be seen in these movies participating in their own destruction. Here we have a popular-cultural intuition of the accident not as contingent event, but as structural necessity; what Virilio describes in "The Primal Accident" as a "failure" that is "programmed into the product from the moment of its production" (212). Whether as the Roosevelt Island Tram falling into the Hudson (*Spider-Man*), cabs flung at unsuspecting crowds (*Spider-Man 2*), or office stationery hailing down on 6th Avenue (*Spider-Man 3*), the city regularly and readily dismantles itself into the units of its fantastic technologies. Distinct from the by-now hoary means of wreckage — tidal waves/aliens/giant lizards — this cinema delights in the intimacy of a city breaking down. It might be tempting to see this as a city of destruction. Not quite. The New York of *Spider-Man* is a kinetic space of geometric forms and accelerating production, albeit the auto-production of auto-destruction. Luxuriating in the *élan vital* of bodies falling apart — man and mass — Raimi's Manhattan uncannily echoes Baudrillard on 9/11: "When the two towers collapsed, you had the impression they were responding to the suicide of the suicide planes with their own suicide" (18). Is it a surprise that the climactic action sequence for *Spider-Man 3*, the biggest set-piece in all three films, with seven different crews and months upon months in pre-production, is staged at a massive construction site? Here we see the dynamic interaction of tons of sand, concrete blocks, floors on stilts, iron rods, and load-carrying trucks, the very Lego-blocks of a skyscraper under construction!

This is also the scene that confronts visitors to Ground Zero today. Of course, unlike that space, heavy with the sense of death and mourning, *Spider-Man*'s sites of urban disaster are blessed with comic-book levity. Manhattan is compelled into virtual weightlessness, the zone of the postmodern accident. Lacking the world-weary heaviness of *The Dark Knight* (Christopher Nolan, 2008) or the visionary gravity of *Blade Runner* (Ridley Scott, 1982), the cinematic city comes into view as approximating *postmaterial* territory, like some speculative image of New York once again dematerializing.

Postscript: "We are all falling men"

Images of falling have a long cinematic history, and cannot be understood solely in terms of the double logic of (p)re-mediating 9/11. After all, Alfred Hitchcock's *Vertigo* (1958) famously evokes a sense of fatal falling into the twilight zone between dream and consciousness, past and present, life and death, truth and appearance. The "reverse zoom" perfected for the film is now often remembered as the "Vertigo zoom," and images of falling in the *Spider-Man* films benefit immeasurably from the disorientation it produces. Further, images of falling in the *Spider-Man* films must also be appreciated within the context of the sensational summer blockbuster and Hollywood's constant drive to discover new attractions. In *Inception* (2010), for instance, director Christopher Nolan fuses *Spider-Man*'s high-tech realization of bodies in freefall with the ambiguities set forth in *Vertigo*: Through layers of the dream-world, through different temporalities and spaces, through different genres and *topoi*, our guide is the falling body, whose very literal plummet, we are to believe, provides a metaphysical exit into the real beyond the image.

Likewise, in early 2012 as part of the run-up to the fifth season of *Mad Men*, television network AMC took out a promotional image that was soon visible in New York City's subway stations, at bus stops and elsewhere. In the image, against a clear white-grey background, we see the minuscule but instantly recognizable figure of the ad-man, placed upside-down at the top of the frame, while the words "March 25" are printed across the bottom. With his body presumably in mid-tumble, his arms and legs flailing, his suit and tie in disarray, the *Mad Men* mascot elicited flak; was AMC exploiting a traumatic national memory to peddle a TV show? Indeed, the entire advertising strategy seemed to be premised on the anticipation of a fall — of the closing of the gap between the top of the frame and the bottom, between the man who has lost his perch and the deadline on the pavement — which climaxes not in an ending but a beginning, a season premiere. In a brief online essay for *Esquire* defending AMC against charges of exploitation, Tom Junod revisits the debate around 9/11, noting that the poster, by dispensing with the "corporate context specific to *Mad Men*, indeed with context altogether, and by concentrating on one falling man ... remind[s] viewers that the show is really about the Falling Man." One can see what Junod means; the fall projected in the poster only prefigures other falls on to which the new season of *Mad Men* will presumably open out: The fall of the show's famous title sequence, which itself prefigures the figurative fall of heroic masculinity that the show has thus far chronicled. The "legacy of 9/11" that the show taps into, writes Junod, is an atmosphere of "moral unease — an almost vertiginous sensation of the ground giving way beneath our feet, along with just about everything else." In thus defending the show's deliberate invocation of 9/11, Junod also shifts the goalposts, re-aligning the disturbingly literal and affective power of a photograph taken more than ten years ago with an abstract sense of descent and disorientation a decade later; Junod converts a very physical fall into a symbol of the zeitgeist, the perpetual plunge of a nation: "for all its American-Century trappings," he writes, *Mad Men* is "set squarely in the age of American decline." Perhaps he concedes that such abstraction is the only way that a memory as terrifying as that of the falling men and women could ever be made intelligible.

Laura Frost has recently argued that most mainstream representations of 9/11 prefer figurative narratives of heroism to "bodily and antiheroic responses" to the event (34). In such films as Paul Greengrass's *United 93* and Michael Moore's *Fahrenheit 9/11*, the traumatic event itself, 9/11, is draped over with a black screen which "implies that the bodily, human destruction ... at the center of the events must not be shown" (23). The *Spider-Man* trilogy's fascination with the skyline articulates an anti-gravitational soar typical of the superhero genre, but it also paves the way for the franchise's death images, its visions of falling bodies and falling debris that perforate the skyline. Death images are regularly retailed by action movies, but their febrile, repetitive, insistently embodied quality in *Spider-Man* calls for attention. Isolated, encased, and over-extended, these moments constitute a generic strobe peculiar to the trilogy. In these moments, the films step outside the warm sunlight of a daydream and into the contingency of nightmare, carving out spaces in which the most taboo memories of 9/11 resurface.

When Does the Hurting Stop? *Cloverfield* and the (Re)Enabling of Fantasy in the Post-9/11 City

Scott Wilson

The horrifying events of September 11, 2001, served to illustrate, in the most terrible fashion, the kinds of cognitive, ideological, and representational strategies that surround the possibilities of the sublime, both as experience and as fabrication. In the aftermath of September 11th, it quickly became clear that "the most photographed 'event' in human history" (Melnick 65) would be problematically aligned both to public discourses of representation and memorialization, and also to the manner with which cinema and other media might deal with (or be permitted to deal with) this situation. The events of that day, which eluded the means of those witnesses to describe directly without resorting to other clichés of representation, quickly became locked in a socially enforced structure of performative trauma, whereby any direct references to the attacks were removed from broadcast media and a collective representational silence became the mark of a seemingly respectful longer-term memorialization. Yet, as explorations into trauma have manifestly demonstrated, for as long as the traumatic event is unspoken, no recovery from trauma can occur. Therefore, by exploring the problematic relationship of trauma and representation to the sublime (and to this event in particular), it is possible to comprehend the ways in which representational discourses regarding 9/11, aided by a cinema that does not represent the sublime so much as find a way to cope with it, have worked through a process that moves the event from unspoken trauma, through to shock and, therefore, into mourning and grief.

For Freud, mourning—when correctly negotiated—has both an object and an end point, a moment at which the mourning is completed, the object is understood as lost, dead or gone, and the ego, to quote Freud (1991), "becomes free and uninhibited again" (253). Mourning that is incorrectly negotiated and uncompleted shifts into the perpetual twilight of melancholia, a psychic complex Freud likens to "an open wound" (262) and which functions as a form of mourning that is not, and can never be, completed. Judith Butler, writing in response to the events of 9/11, utilizes Freud's work and, especially, Jacques Derrida's own development of notions of continuous mourning, to explore the relationship of mourning to individual and communal loss as a mechanism that results in a more cohesive sense of social and political community. Both Derrida and Butler consider mourning to be an ongoing and subjectively vital process, essential to the development of self-knowledge and an understanding of the relationship of self to other. As Butler writes in *Precarious Life*:

> ... each of us is constituted politically in part by virtue of the social vulnerability of our bodies.... Loss and vulnerability seem to follow from our being socially constituted bodies, attached to others, at risk of losing those attachments, exposed to others, at risk of violence by virtue of that exposure [20].

Becoming a social subject, in Butler's terms, occurs as a result of, and depends on, exactly these kinds of relationships whereby the collective experience of mourning becomes one of the ways in which social groups can coalesce and create common ground between ordinarily disparate individuals. The point of departure for later writers on mourning appears, therefore, to be related to the possibility of mourning as never entirely completed, counter to Freud's original suggestion. Nevertheless, it is possible to draw a distinction between the experience of mourning as an intersubjective phenomenon—one that is continuous and provides a developmental trajectory—and the function of mourning as an ideological construction, generated by, sustained and then terminated by a series of broader hegemonically-aligned mechanisms. What links these later explorations of Freud's work to Freud's own discussions is the way in which all writers recognize that for mourning to be possible at all, the object of mourning needs to be comprehensively available to the speaking subjects; as remembered experience and also, crucially for Freud, as the subject of fantasy (as in dreams and parapraxes, for example). This is exactly what he means, as Freud notes in "The Psychotherapy of Hysteria," when he comments, "We must not expect to meet with a single traumatic memory and a single pathogenic idea as its nucleus: we must be prepared for successions of partial traumas and concatenations of pathogenic trains of thought" (373). As Gene Ray makes clear:

> Trauma is a category of damage. It marks the limit of conventionalized, assimilable experience and the vulnerability of the psychic organization to disrupting penetrations from outside. As such, it is a threat to the imaginary integrity of subjectivity [*Terror and the Sublime in Art and Critical Theory* 1].

Thus whilst the traumatic event may have a singular origin, the work of moving from trauma through to mourning (and thence to healing) involves repeated attention to the manner with which the original event will be played out across a variety of experiences and, one might be tempted to add, media forms. Thus, as Susan J. Brison notes, when discussing the ways in which trauma might be alleviated by representation, "saying something about the [traumatic] memory does something to it" (xi) and that for as long as the traumatic event and its aftermath remain unspoken, or off-limits to all kinds of representation, then no healing (in the form of mourning) can occur.

What role, therefore, could cinema play in this process? After all, my contention above is that there is a relationship between the events of 9/11 and the manner with which those events, marked as traumatic, are therefore unable to be represented, which the proliferation of post–9/11 documentaries and tributes would seem to belie. Here we find a further link between the notions of the sublime and the work of both Freud and the post–Freudian users of his work on trauma. That the events of 9/11 might constitute a sublime experience of the "wildest and most irregular disorder and desolation" (Kant, *The Critique of Judgment* 76) seems to be clear. As Sean Cubitt explains, "the sublime stands above and beyond time," meaning that the "the nonnegotiable evil — sublime binarism enacted in the television images of the September 11 events" (324), for as long as they are experienced *as* a kind of trauma (which is also, remember, located "above and beyond time"), will always evade the contextualizing activity of representation.

Yet, as Kant notes, sublimity "does not reside in any of the things of nature, but only in our own mind" (94) which means that, as Richard Kearney explains, "It is in this specific sense that we might say that the feeling of awe and shock experienced by many who witnessed (largely on TV) the event of 11 September, might be called 'sublime'..." (38), even as we might also seek to recognize these events as traumatic without doing an injustice to prior uses of the term. Indeed, as Julia Kristeva (*Black Sun*) makes clear, the "shock and awe" associated with such a large-scale public event, even for those whose only connection to the attacks was via mass media, is enough to lead to a "shattering of psychic identity" (222), itself increasingly dependent on the ebb and flow of media discourse. As she continues elsewhere:

> ... these monstrous and painful spectacles disturb our mechanisms of perception and representation. Our symbolic modes are emptied, petrified, nearly annihilated, as if they were overwhelmed or destroyed by an all too powerful force ["Pain of Sorrow" 139].

Yet the fact that these potentially sublime events, recognized as such by the ways in which they generated an "astonishment amounting almost to terror" (Kant, *Critique of Judgement* 99) are also communally coded as trauma is demonstrated by the ways in which the representations of the event were thoroughly policed and, in some instances repressed. As Žižek comments:

> The fact that, after September 11, the openings of many "block-buster" movies with scenes which bear a resemblance to the WTC collapse (tall buildings on fire or under attack, terrorist acts ...) were postponed (or the films were even shelved) should thus be read as the "repression" of the fantasmatic background responsible for the impact of the WTC collapse [*Welcome to the Desert of the Real* 16–17].[1]

Consequently it is important to consider both the manner with which mourning, especially communal and public mourning, might ever be said to be completed, as well as the possible rationale driving the delivery of a visible and viable movement from a politically-mandated representational repression through to a fictionalization, not just of the events themselves, but of the tropes of those events. It is therefore my primary assertion that the Matt Reeves' and J. J. Abrams' 2008 monster movie *Cloverfield* marks, however unwittingly, the end of a particularly political legislation regarding the possibilities for dealing with, and therefore representing, the events of 9/11. Further, it is my contention that the film *Cloverfield* stands as a nexus point between four very different, but necessarily interrelated, mechanisms that work to demonstrate the state of the industries that have produced this multi-media object and the populations that consume it. With this in mind, *Cloverfield* will be discussed in relation to the psychic mechanisms of trauma and shock before I explore the manner with which this film marks the recuperation of the uncanny geography of the ruined cityscape and the commodification of the specific tropes of 9/11, demonstrating an attempt to articulate a conclusion to the specifically legislated and ideologically circumspect public face of mourning the 9/11 event.

Cloverfield: *Shock and Trauma*

For those that missed the film — and it turns out that many did — *Cloverfield* concerns the attempts of a series of twenty-somethings — variously described as "scruffily-handsome" careerists (Douthat 55) and "hateful yuppies" (Travers 88) — to survive the mayhem and destruction wrought when a monster attacks New York. The film, whose central narrative device is that it is shot and presented in the first-person during the events that it records (lending a shaky real-time aesthetic to the unfolding disaster), spends its time unconcerned with the larger questions at play: What is this monster? Where did it come from, and, more importantly, how do "we" stop it? Instead, the film portrays the actions and reactions of a group of "normal Americans" whose lives are suddenly, and monstrously, inverted. That is pretty much the entirety of the narrative although, to be fair, the object of the film's content — the narrative of the monster and its arrival in New York — spans a number of alternative media platforms, including a highly innovative and successful Internet viral marketing campaign that, in the way of such marketing, layered clues, hints, and fragments of meta-narrative information across a variety of blogs and websites. This included a broader framing device that "solved" the monster's origin and located the film's narrative causality in a conspiracy involving mysterious Japanese food consortia, crashed spy satellites and slowly-revealed coded messages across YouTube videos, "leaked" documents, and a "Missing Persons" website.[2] I am less concerned with these, especially as such attempts to place the events of the film in some kind of larger, conspiracy-focused context limits and reduces the ambiguity that was, at least in my opinion, the film's strongest suit. Indeed, one is tempted to suggest that these para-cinematic texts, in their work to both embellish and solve the film's ambiguity, work in much the same way as the various cognitive strategies I explore below, insofar as they take the overwhelming and irreducible material of the primary text and give it meaning, locating it within a schema by which it can be contained and understood.

Clearly the first, and most obvious way of exploring — or explaining—*Cloverfield* is to see the film's overt content as evidence of the traumatic events of 9/11. This is the kind of exegesis that has circulated around the film's reception, and it is exactly this kind of critical exploration at work in Susan Sontag's seminal essay "The Imagination of Disaster," and in other writings about disaster films and that glorious subset, the monster / disaster film. With *Godzilla* (Ishirô Honda, 1954) as our most obvious exemplar, the monster is understood retrospectively as a discursive mechanism that provides the means for a population to confront and cope with some traumatic event, or the fear of trauma, that otherwise cannot be consciously articulated.[3] With this reading, the authors' repressed "anxieties about contemporary existence" (Sontag 45) are cathected through the narrative that, utilizing the cinematic equivalents of displacement and condensation, provide enough experiential or cognitive distance between the site of trauma and its representation to permit some kind of critical, or, at the very least, conscious, consideration of that which might not otherwise be said. With this is mind *Cloverfield* is obviously "about" 9/11 in a very banal way. The monster is either, then, a condensation of the terrorists who perpetrated the attacks, or a conflation of the various Western doxa surrounding the perception of al Qaeda, or a way to represent all those who would attack America, seemingly without reason.

That this film's narrative directly confronts the events of 9/11 and displaces the terrorists onto, or into, a monstrously foreign body can be read as part psychic mechanism and part wish-fulfillment (insofar as the allegorical destruction is played out as a spectacular fiction designed to provide spectatorial pleasure). In this fashion *Cloverfield* is "more advanced" in its discursive landscape than, say, Spielberg's *War of the Worlds* (2005) insofar as it can confront the events of 9/11 within the same geographic location as the events themselves, while Spielberg's film worked to displace the events away from New York and generalize the aftermath globally, rather than retain the specificity that *Cloverfield* utilizes. Nevertheless, *Cloverfield*, to continue this exegetical reading, must still displace and condense the unsayable into the figure of the monster. This is where such an exegetical exercise leads us; if the monster is the "displaced" representation of the terrorists, or of those that support, fund, or provide for terrorists and terrorism, then the film evidences a deeply felt sense of America's other *as* monster. In this fashion we might conclude that the trauma *Cloverfield* works through is still not completely resolved; certainly the film is closer to a direct confrontation of this repressed material than *War of the Worlds* but not so entirely as to permit the kinds of direct reference that would mark the movement of the traumatic material toward direct representation.

Here we might usefully compare the repressing and repressive mechanisms of trauma with what is, in many ways, its opposing psychic mechanism: shock. Freud, in *Beyond the Pleasure Principle*, explores the ways in which consciousness works to limit, prevent or, at the very least, negotiate those experiences that might otherwise generate trauma. Because "consciousness arises instead of a memory trace" (Freud 25), those memory fragments that risk generating trauma are "often most powerful and most enduring when the incident which left them behind was one that never entered consciousness" (25). For Freud, consciousness does not remember — indeed, as Mary Ann Doane explains, "Its most important function is rather to protect the organism against excessive stimuli, to act as a stimulus shield in operation against external energies" (13).

Usefully, Doane brings the work of Walter Benjamin to bear and it is here with Benjamin that we see a comprehensive exploration of shock, both as an experience that emerges in response to the demands of modernity and as a mechanism to prevent excessive experiences bypassing consciousness and settling as unresolved trauma. For Benjamin, as for Doane who utilizes his thought, shock involves the opposite of trauma: Shock keeps the event in the forefront of consciousness. As Benjamin makes clear:

> The greater the share of the shock factor in particular impressions, the more constantly consciousness has to be alert as a screen against stimuli; the more efficiently it does so, the less do these impressions enter experience..., tending to remain in the sphere of a certain hour in one's life ... [163].

Thus, one of the most important acts associated with the experiencing of shock — particularly in line with the effort to prevent experience from bypassing consciousness and generating trauma — is the way in which the experience of shock is memorialized by consciousness. As Benjamin explains, "Perhaps the special achievement of shock defense may be seen in its function of assigning to an incident a precise point in time in consciousness at the cost of the integrity of its contents" (163). With this in mind, we see how *Cloverfield* works to occupy both positions: The superficial exegesis demonstrates how the film's narrative provides a way to cathect the repressed energies of the event experienced as trauma ("at the cost of the integrity of its contents"), even as the film — which is publicly and commercially recognized exactly *as* a discussion of 9/11 — permits a memorializing of the event in order to provide support for the mechanisms of shock which would operate should the events of 9/11 be repeated in any form.

Memorialization, the Uncanny, and the Cinematic Reclamation of New York City

It is the method of *Cloverfield*'s memorializing 9/11 that has drawn the most critical attention. While the film has, largely, sunk without a trace (despite some discussion of a sequel), what slight controversy that did erupt around the film's content occurred over the perception of the film's trivializing of 9/11, primarily through the film's use of what have become some of the most recognizable representative tropes of the event. As Ross Douthat laments:

> There's no problem with a monster movie drawing on real-life fears and horrors and imagery; the best ones always have. But if you're going to rip off the worst day in recent American memory for a film in which a scaly creature the size of the Chrysler Building makes a snack out of screaming adultescents, you have a moral obligation to make a better, deeper, richer monster movie than this [55].

This comment is typical of a number of similarly oriented reviews of the film, which all held that the events of 9/11 deserved a more fitting memorial than *Cloverfield* was prepared, or able, to provide. Thus what emerges is a claim that whilst the events of 9/11 may typically be memorialized in a more respectful fashion, they may not be trivialized, which is to say, utilized as fiction.[4] Here we can consider the manner with which *Cloverfield* utilizes one of the most recognizable tropes of 9/11: the collapsing and collapsed skyscraper. Early in the film, before the magnitude of the unfolding disaster is made clear, our protagonists are forced to flee the clouds of smoke and debris generated when, as a result of the monster's rampage, buildings collapse. Roger Friedman, writing for *Fox News*, responds to these images thus: "Does no one recall what was said following the World Trade Center disasters? There was such sensitivity about the huge human losses that images of the Twin Towers were erased from movie posters and excised from films."

This dichotomy illustrates exactly the kinds of work the film is undertaking; its narrative permits a conscious articulation of material that, as trauma generated by the experience of a sublime event, cannot be approached directly, whilst the affront experienced by those who respond to the film negatively demonstrates the manner with which the trauma is being worked through by the memorializing activities of the film as a site of shock. The memorializing activities of the film — as with those of the more "respectful" or "appropriate" representations of the event — work to keep the experience fixed within a conscious articulation, and yet that activity, which for some means confronting traumatic material, necessarily generates resistance to the text that forces such confrontations.

As Friedman's comments make clear, one of the more striking consequences of 9/11 was the manner with which the New York skyline was rendered immediately problematic — so much so that, as he notes (and Žižek explains), representations of the pre–9/11 skyline were immediately removed from post–9/11 media objects. Of course, the actual skyline and especially the marked absence of the towers stood as testament to the events themselves, but the representation of the skyline became problematic insofar as the only representational tropes available were those that had already been long aligned to the various fictions of large-scale destruction. This is reflected in the large number of contemporaneous reports that made direct reference to 9/11's many cinematic prefigurations. For example, two of the most obvious and immediate reports comment:

> Over and over Tuesday, after the planes tore through the World Trade Center towers and then the Pentagon, benumbed spectators said the same words: "It was like a movie." Which was to say they had seen it before in countless disaster movies. The explosion and fireball, the crumpling buildings, the dazed and panicked victims, even the grim presidential address assuring action would be taken — all were familiar, as if they had been lifted from some Hollywood blockbuster [Gabler].
>
> "It was like something out of a movie." Not everyone said that, but enough people did, watching on television or from the streets of Lower Manhattan.... The "money shots" were eerily reminiscent, the towers falling to earth with the same instant, awesome symbolism as the atomisation of the White House in *Independence Day* [Steyn 56].

Thus, as alluded to above, to represent the post–9/11 events seemed to require a greater publically-performed moral responsibility than the very tropes of that representation would permit, meaning that the 9/11 event could only be discussed directly in such a way that retained a constant focus on the processes of repressing alternative forms or possibilities of representation without necessarily indicating some kind of end-point for that interdiction. As represented by the reports above, in an effort to overcome the "nothing" of trauma that Kristeva explores in *Black Sun* — and to therefore deal with the excess of affect produced by the experience of a (negatively) sublime event — the witnesses reached for the only representational language equipped to provide some context for their experience: that of disaster cinema. What then occurred, exactly as Žižek explains (in *Welcome to the Desert of the Real!*), was both a pro-active censoring of post-event representations that might echo or too-closely resemble the events of that day, as well as a retrospective fetishization of the towers and the New York skyline itself.

In this fashion, the events of 9/11 rendered the New York skyline uncanny insofar as each representation, be it pre- or post-event, was both familiar and unfamiliar, homely and unhomely — uncanny. This link between the sublime and uncanny should not surprise us: Like the sublime, the uncanny is a product of the subject in relation to an experience or an object and, like the sublime, the uncanny stands in a problematic relationship to the possibilities of representation, not least of which because the uncanny object (much like cinema itself) is always-already a representation (of the vanished, or remembered original [homely] object or situation). Yet, the uncanny can also be distinguished from the sublime in the manner with which it is mobilized in the act of representation: As Kerstin Mey explains in her *Art and Obscenity*, "[t]he uncanny leans towards the 'negative' pole of the aesthetic force field, towards the fright, repulsion and distress," meaning that while "[t]he uncanny and the sublime are linked to different levels of emotional intensity ... the uncanny temporarily shakes and corrodes the psychically regulated equilibrium of the experiencing subject" (66).

Thus each moment of post–9/11 representation — each sequence that worked to negotiate the relationship between trauma and shock — worked also to render the affected cityscape uncanny by providing a constant comparison between the before and after; the temporal nature of the memorial constantly drawing attention away from the mechanisms of coping or resolution and back, in a conservative action, to the way things were. This is where the struggle between the demands of opposing psychic mechanisms comes into conflict with the demands of a series of industries which, as a consequence of the uncanny aspect of the New York skyline, were unable to represent it at all, for fear of alerting their audience to the trauma they sought to avoid. Needless to say, the New York skyline is a lucrative piece of real estate; as a thoroughly overdetermined landscape, its hermeneutic function is too valuable to be isolated as a result of these events. For as long as the landscape was linked inexorably to the specific events of 9/11, it could not function as anything other than a specific memorial to those events. In essence, the previously overdetermined nature of this skyline was overwhelmed, such that this skyline was unable to connote anything but these events. This explains the ways in which the majority of films made in New York since 9/11—and there have been, at time of writing, over two hundred—worked to find ways to avoid representing the skyline at all, while those that did were required by the overdetermined demands of this uncanny landscape to find ways to confront the events directly and appropriately, by which I mean, respectfully. *Cloverfield*, therefore, engages with the uncanny cityscape directly (and, according to the criticisms noted above, disrespectfully), which is why I claim it can be considered as more advanced in its discursive actions than *War of the Worlds*, itself also a function of the intervening three years between the two films. The outcome of this direct encounter is, through the utilization of both the landscape and tropes of the 9/11 event, a defusing, even if only partially, of the uncanny pall that had rendered the New York skyline off-limits.

As a result of the manner with which *Cloverfield* deliberately utilizes the representational tropes of the 9/11 event, we can see that it both forces a confrontation between a publicly-mandated desire to maintain a respectful non-fiction distance from the events of that day (evidenced in the slight controversy over, and resistance, to the film's content) and a broader industrial desire to reclaim the actual and cognitive geography of New York as a site for continued cinematic fantasy. The repressive activities of trauma work to prolong the ways in which the traumatic event, be it communal or singular, can be worked through and resolved, and for as long as the means of representing that trauma remain off-limits, no such resolution can occur. The narrative of *Cloverfield* therefore permits a working through of the events of 9/11 in such a way that they occur as superimposed upon the actual geography whilst remaining an obvious, if thinly disguised fiction. At the same time, the very fact that the film's narrative is so thinly disguised permits it to function as a shock mechanism, to utilize Benjamin's term, ensuring that the consciousness of the film's spectators are suitably prepared for, and cushioned against, similar events.[5]

The ways in which 9/11 was represented and reported during and immediately after the collapse of the towers rendered the New York skyline problematic and, as a result, uncanny; any representation of the skyline forced the spectator to be both aware of the events that had so recently occurred as well as of the ways in which the skyline had previously functioned as a site of overdetermined interpretation. As above, this conflict between the desire to avoid representation in order to preserve the memory of some time prior to the events, and the demand to continue utilizing the skyline as a routine commercial landscape, could only be resolved by adapting the tropes of 9/11 to fiction which, as explored above, forced the conflict between trauma and shock once again. Having forced the issue, the skyline and its attendant geography is, in effect, freed from the burden of dual-representative service and can begin, once more, to provide a site for cinematic fantasy that need not respond or attend to 9/11 so closely. Regardless of whether mourning is a singular activity that has a discreet end-point, or a life-long activity that generates inter-subjective affect, the actions of *Cloverfield* demonstrate that, with regards to the events of 9/11, the repressive actions of trauma are completed and a new phase of mourning, and thus remembering, speaking and fictionalizing, can begin.

NOTES

1. This decision to restrict the kinds of representations of 9/11 extends beyond cinema and television. In her article "Teaching 9/11 and Why I'm Not Doing it Anymore," Louise Spence comments on the ways in which the events of that day, perhaps because they were treated with such deference by the mainstream media, remained essentially meaningless for her students. In the absence of, and concomitant search for any narrative resolution that might answer the question of "why," Spence notes that her students run the risk of "sentimentalizing 9/11 and contributing to the fetishistic attempt to adorn the attacks with an aura of sacred piety" (104).

2. Interested readers are directed toward www.tagruato.jp/ (the homepage of a fictional Japanese deep-sea drilling company linked to the monster) and www.slusho.jp/ (a softdrink subsidiary of Tagruato). All of these are further explored in the associated prequel Manga *Cloverfield/Kishin* (Yoshiki Togawa. Kadokawa Shoten, 2008).

3. Gene Ray explores the relationship between Hiroshima and New York through both the public and official mobilization of the term "Ground Zero," convincingly suggesting that the re-emergence of this term points, in effect, to a kind of "return of the repressed." As he comments:

Certainly a collective wound is being marked here, but which wound, exactly? The wound of losing 2,830 innocent citizens (and noncitizens) in a spectacular, Hollywood-style attack, or that of seeing the symbols of U.S. postwar and post–Cold War power punctured so effectively? Or is it in fact a more complex narcissistic wound that tracks back from the shock of realizing that "America" is not loved by all to the haunting suspicion that perhaps the use of U.S. power in the world has not matched the moral exceptionalism proclaimed by its rhetoric? [52].

With this in mind, it is significant then that a comparison be made between the exegetical readings of *Godzilla* and *Cloverfield* in exactly these terms.

4. In a fascinating postscript, the British newspaper *The Guardian* faced public censure for its ten-year anniversary Twitter stream (@911tenyearsago), devoted to recounting the events of 9/11 as a real-time series of Tweets. Unlike other, similar uses of Twitter (*The Associated Press* and *The Daily* ran similar Twitter streams), *The Guardian*'s stream relayed the bare facts of the original events, without contextualizing them as a memorial activity. As one on-line correspondent noted:

The Daily (with 955,000 Twitter followers) and *the AP* (with 509,500 followers) continued their tweets of the events from ten years ago right up to the collapse of the second tower of the World Trade Center. Meanwhile, *The Guardian*'s dedicated feed, with just 3,800 followers, was forced to abandon its retelling early [Bryant].

Another blogger commented:
Had they [*The Guardian*] been providing context to the events — linking to the stories of loved ones, survivors and families of the victims — there may even, just, have been a narrow justification to it. But *The Guardian* failed to do that. There was no humanising of the event, just a stark publishing of facts ... [Hepburn].

So it would seem that, despite my argument regarding the fictionalizing of the various representational tropes associated with the attacks, the events themselves must still be approached cautiously, which is to say, with due deference to the existing, and still powerful, discourses surrounding the manner with which 9/11 can be represented.

5. In 2008, writing in the online *Huffington Post*, Jessica Wakeman succinctly summarized this way of receiving *Cloverfield* as an audience member who had also undergone the events of September 11:

The first 45 minutes of *Cloverfield* is the closest I think I can get to showing sometime [sic] else what 9/11 was like for me on an emotional level. *Cloverfield* nails what that morning felt like: the confusion at first, and then fear overwhelms and all you can think about is the possibility of dying and needing to escape by getting *out-out-out* but where can you go because the subways and trains aren't running? It gets what it *looks* like and *feels* like to believe there's 8 planes in the air, that the president ordered any non-grounded aircraft to be shot down, they could be shot down above your city and kill you, and what if there's a ground attack? It depicts what it's like to be convinced that that day is the day you are going to die. You are 17 years old and you are going to die on a sunny Tuesday morning in the middle of New York City [original's emphasis].

Keeping Terror Alive: The Political Economy of Visibility in *Inside Man*

Sven Cvek

It is generally agreed that *Inside Man*, Spike Lee's commercially "most successful film" (Guthrie), represents somewhat of a departure from the director's usual thematic concerns and formal interests. Lori Harrison-Kahan critically summed up the bulk of the film's reception by stating that "many reviewers reductively described the film as simply good old-fashioned entertainment. While a few critics expressed disappointment that Lee had left his moral concerns behind, most appeared to find the film's lack of a political agenda refreshing" (39). Situating the movie in the context of "post–9/11 entertainment," Harrison-Kahan argues that Lee remains political even in this "ostensibly escapist genre picture" (46). In her view, the central targets of his critique are the related post–9/11 issues of "American imperialism abroad" and "racial profiling" at home (54). The many references to the contemporary moment support her contention that Lee's 2006 movie should indeed be understood as a post–9/11 allegory.

Harrison-Kahan's argument rests on the important insight that the film constantly blurs the lines between some of the central categories dominating the U.S. public sphere after the September 11 attacks: the distinction between reality and fiction, victim and perpetrator, us and them, guilt and innocence. The persistent motive of "costuming" and "disguising," she argues, serves precisely this destabilizing purpose (53–54). This is a compelling remark that, in my view, opens the possibility for an analysis that would address the problem of visibility in the movie. Variously articulated, the issue of visibility has often taken a prominent place in U.S.

debates surrounding the 9/11 attacks as well as the wars in Afghanistan and Iraq that followed. While agreeing in many respects with Harrison-Kahan's analysis of Lee's "critique of the shifts in racial politics" after 9/11 (39), I will put forward some thoughts on the problem of visibility in *Inside Man* that are critical for the contemporary historical conjuncture.

9/11 and the Sublime Visibility of Terror

The hyper-mediation surrounding the September 11 attacks put the visual aspects of the event to the forefront of many of the responses that ensued, be they critical or artistic. Ranging from politicized eye-witness accounts such as Art Spiegelman's *In the Shadow of No Towers*, to studies of "the reconstruction of safe spectatorship in the photographic record of 9/11" (Lurie), this development is now as evident as it is well documented. Visibility has also, and in different ways, been raised as a problem by the critics of the U.S.-led wars in the Middle East. The work of the Iraqi American artist Wafaa Bilal is particularly illustrative in this respect. In one of his performances ("... and Counting"), Bilal had his back tattooed with dots representing the Americans and Iraqis killed in the war: "The 5,000 dead American soldiers are represented by red dots (permanent visible ink), and the 100,000 Iraqi casualties are represented by dots of green UV ink, seemingly invisible unless under black light" (Bilal). The commentary on the artist's website suggests that the point of this play with visibility was to draw the public's attention to the fact that "the deaths of Iraqis like [Bilal's] brother are largely invisible to the American public." Another of Bilal's projects focused on hyper-visibility. In "Shoot an Iraqi," the artist spent a month living in a room, constantly in the line of fire of a paintball gun. The gun was remotely controlled by Internet users who could log on to the artist's website and shoot at him (Bilal).

Bilal's work makes palpable two closely related aspects of visibility that, provisionally and for the sake of analysis, we could term political (invisibility of the dead) and technological (hyper-visibility of the living). The first problem concerns the victims of U.S. military actions. Invisibility removes their deaths from the U.S. public, and effects what Judith Butler termed "violence through omission" (34): Because they are invisible, these deaths cannot be mourned and potentially made into a basis for political mobilization.[1] The other problem has to do with the permanent and near-total visibility of humans as military targets, and leads to questions about the far-reaching implications of the strategic connection between visual technologies and U.S. military power. What these examples suggest is that the alternation between invisibility and visibility does not offer a conclusive choice, although in any given situation, as the examples also show, choices do have important political or tactical value. What emerges in the background of this alternation is the recognition that, in the context of the global war on terror, these two positions are equally anchored in the reality of military operations and the economy of the military industry.

I would like to argue that *Inside Man* can be approached in that context and in the manner sketched above. In my view, the film's obsession with practices of veiling and revealing, as well as the functions they perform — the interpretive ambivalence and indefinite delay of the final resolution they dramatize (the justice that the movie announces is never executed) — are also structurally central to the operation of Lee's allegorical discourse. The game of hide and seek that is at the center of the plot foregrounds visibility as a problem, while, as I will try to argue below, certain formal aspects of the movie dramatize the specific historical conditions in which visibility as a problem is implicated. The ambivalent business of displaying and hiding from view that takes place in *Inside Man* constantly points to an underlying substratum not only of this film, but of the 9/11 archive as a whole, namely, the interdependence of U.S. world-wide military presence and the role of military industry in national economy.

Although admittedly inconsistent, this foregrounding of the contemporary involvement of visuality, terror, and capital accumulation in *Inside Man* represents somewhat of a departure from the more direct fictional engagements with the events of 9/11, many of which tend to remain trapped in the traumatic moment around which they revolve. I have argued elsewhere how this proclivity becomes evident in those 9/11 narratives in which the traumatic event represents a turning point in teleological development, or the moment of emergence of a new subject.[2] Such narratives are in line with what LaCapra described as "an important tendency in modern culture and thought to convert trauma into the occasion for sublimity, to transvalue it into a test of the self or the group and an entry into the extraordinary." "In the sublime," LaCapra writes, "the excess of trauma becomes an uncanny source of elation or ecstasy" (23). In the political aftermath of 9/11, a certain sacralization of the event has been made into the basis for different extraordinary measures, both at home and abroad. The fictional accounts of 9/11 as a sublime founding event have thus often been consonant with the hegemonic employments of a similar rhetoric. It is possible to look at the ways in which *Inside Man*, as a post-traumatic narrative, deals with this political potential of the sublime.

LaCapra's coupling of trauma and sublimity makes the proposition about an affinity between the aesthetics of Lee's film and the notion of the sublime somewhat less unlikely, however. Moreover, many of the analytical categories introduced here — visibility, obscurity, power, terror — do recall Edmund Burke's classical study of the sublime. It seems to me that Burke's classical definition, which locates the source of the sublime in "whatever is in any sort terrible, or is conversant about terrible objects, or operates in a manner analogous to terror," provides us with a possible description of the representational mechanisms at work in *Inside Man* (36). But, as I will argue in more detail below, the movie de-sublimates the apparent sublimity of contemporary terror, as it articulates "the manner" in which terror operates to the historical conditions of its occurrence. As the film shows the binary of visibility and invisibility taking a central place in the contemporary practices of terror, it also stages the sublimity of terror as a visual, media spectacle, a kind of veil that both hides and is implicated in a more fundamental, and perhaps more obvious truth. Furthermore, if *Inside Man* represents a possible political allegory of the state of the nation after 9/11, it also offers a testimony to the limits of the post–9/11 discourse on terror.

Terror Placement

That Spike Lee patches up his heist thriller out of scraps from the cultural archive of 9/11 is clear from the start. *Inside Man* stages a scene obliquely reminiscent of 9/11: A bank in New York City downtown area is under siege, as anonymous attackers (whose leader seems to have a foreign accent) interrupt the regular flow of finance and everyday life. The bank robbers take hostages, and in that way deepen the sense of crisis. However, the virtual state of emergency they establish by making impossible demands turns out to be only a tactic for buying the time needed to execute the criminal plan. Their bank robbery — apart from the obvious financial motive — has a pronounced political justification. We learn that the founder of the bank accumulated his wealth by acquiring the valuable possessions of the Jews deported to concentration camps during World War II. This fact makes him a fundamentally and unquestionably evil character, while the robbers' actions are now ethically justified and can be seen as part of a noble struggle.

It is difficult not to read an allegorical quality into this story of a politically motivated attack on a financial institution in downtown New York City. The heist drama functions as a microcosm of the post–9/11 United States. *Inside Man*'s connections to its contemporary moment are many, encompassing problems of racial profiling (of a Sikh bank clerk, recognized by the police as an "Arab"), interrogations and detentions of suspects (which recall real-life treatment of terrorist suspects), intensified policing and surveillance after 9/11, as well as the role of visual technologies in the so-called "global war on terror." Moreover, the central question of the movie echoes the one often asked during and immediately after the 9/11 attacks: What really happened? *Inside Man* is a story about an event that appears opaque and incomprehensible, at least to the official authorities. This moment, however, does represent one significant departure from the hegemonic narrative patterns of the 9/11 archive, since in the film the viewers do get a privileged insight into the unfolding of the critical event as well as its prehistory.

In addition to all this, the genre story of bank robbery is supported by a continuous flow of iconic post–9/11 images, which provide a spectral background for the main line of action. These images appear as flashes in a linear sequence, thus both constituting a flow and a series of interruptions. First, we see the two main characters, the policeman in charge of the case (Denzel Washington) and the "fixer" (Jodie Foster), talking in front of a billboard modeled on the American flag. The repeated phrase "We will never forget" forms the stripes, whereas the stars corner is taken by an image of the Statue of Liberty with the Twin Towers in the background. A couple of minutes later, while the policeman is being searched by a masked and uniformed bank robber (Clive Owen), the camera suddenly switches angle, giving the viewers a bird's eye view of the scene. The outlines of the two bodies now reproduce the silhouette of the infamous "hooded man" photograph of the Abu Ghraib torture scandal. A few minutes after that, the bank robbers show the police a video of an (ultimately fake) execution of a hostage. The video, with the grainy image of a hooded victim being shot in the back of the head, directly references the videos of Afghan and Iraqi insurgents killing enemy soldiers or civilians, which were disseminated through the Internet as a part of their war effort.

It is possible to regard these sequences as traumatic returns that, more or less obliquely, all point back to the event of 9/11 and its global impact. This post-traumatic proclivity for retrospective repetition is a common feature of many post–9/11 fictions, but it should not prevent us from considering these returns in the contexts in which they emerge, and where they are re-articulated in other, non-original situations. It is these discursive re-articulations of staple elements from the U.S. cultural archive of 9/11 that interest me here.

The three iconic moments also emphasize Lee's interest in the connection between visual technologies and technologies of terror. All of them refer to events that are both unimaginable without intensive processes of visual mediation surrounding them, and whose affective and political repercussions thoroughly depended on the dissemination of the images of these events through global communication networks. Moreover, as familiar scenarios from the ongoing wars, these three moments also point to the role of visual technologies in military contexts.

The centrality of the connection between visual technology and terror is further emphasized when a boy hostage is shown playing a graphically violent video game, in which a gang shootout is resolved by way of a hand grenade. Curiously, the visual technology used in the scene, and with it the diegetic reality of *Inside Man,* shifts from film to computer animation, if only for a few short moments. The blurring of the distinction between the virtual and the real in this scene could be seen as corresponding to the contemporary "interpenetration" of entertainment and war. In Nick Turse's words, "Through toys, especially video games, the military and its partners in academia and the entertainment industry have not only blurred the line between entertainment and war, but created a media culture[3] thoroughly capable of preparing America's children for armed conflict" ("Bringing"). This interpenetration, to which Bilal's "Shoot an Iraqi" also points, finds one of its lethal realizations in the unmanned aerial vehicles (U.A.V.s), whose controllers are modeled precisely on the Playstation (cf. Caryl).

Considering the pronounced presence of military weaponry in the video game, as well as the historical connection between this form of entertainment and military technology, the scene seems to suggest that everyday life — including the images of violence that pervade it — cannot be easily disarticulated from the ongoing practice of war and the military industry that supports it and plays a significant role in the U.S. economy as a whole. As a report from the Institute for Policy Studies argues, "military spending has risen at an average rate of 10 percent per year from 2000–2006," or "from 3.0 to 4.4 percent of GDP during the Bush Presidency." The authors of the report further show that "the $600 billion military budget creates approximately five million jobs, both within the military itself and in all the civilian industries connected to the military" (Pollin and Garrett-Peltier 1–2). Indeed, the extent of the defense industry's involvement with the U.S. economy as a whole has recently led Robert Reich to conclude that "national security is a cover for job security." These cursory statistics help outline the political-economic background against which *Inside Man*'s imagery of terror emerges.

Let me add here, for now only as an aside, that the video game scene is also one of the numerous instances of product placement in *Inside Man*, the product in question being a Sony Playstation portable gaming device. This, I think, should not be viewed as a mere externality, or an irrelevant additional element in the otherwise tightly-knit plot of the movie, but as yet another connecting point that attaches *Inside Man* firmly to its contemporary moment and that, in a sense, speaks of the conditions of its own existence. This intrusive, non-diegetic element speaks of and comes from the material, economic infrastructure within which *Inside Man* is produced. The many instances of embedded advertising obviously point to the embedded nature of *Inside Man*, both as a Hollywood product and a post–9/11 narrative, in the flow of capital, thus putting on display the mechanisms of the underlying system that provides the actual infrastructure for the flow of images of terror. What becomes visible in these instances is in the first place the capitalist economy itself. Here, we get a glimpse of what I suggest is the central articulation of *Inside Man*, between visuality, capital accumulation, and terror.

The Abu Ghraib scene and the execution video are a particularly strong testimony to the involvement of visual technologies with terrorism and war on terror. They do, however, differ. While the execution video has a clear role in the structure of the narrative, the spectral appearance of the Abu Ghraib icon appears completely unmotivated and cannot be easily explained by appealing to the compositional or thematic logic of the film. It remains a disruption, an excess, an uncanny, and apparently sublime moment. I would like to suggest that this excessive quality makes this scene of terror structurally similar to the practice of product placement. Both represent moments of "cinematic excess,"[4] and both suture the narrative of *Inside Man* to the wider systems of political economy (in the Playstation scene) and of U.S. military power (in the Abu Ghraib scene).

Shocking & Awesome

In order to understand the presence of this intrusive specter of terror in *Inside Man*, it is useful to briefly recapitulate its public history. First of all, the reappearance of Abu Ghraib in *Inside Man* is not without a real-life equivalent. The debate about torture, initiated two years earlier thanks to the publishing of images of torture at the U.S.-controlled Iraqi prison, was revived in 2006 due to the proposition (and eventual passing) of the controversial Military Commissions Act. The "Torture Bill," as it was nicknamed by its numerous critics, was widely criticized as anti-constitutional and anti-democratic. A *New York Times* editorial summed up the virtual explosion of critique that at one point flooded the blogosphere, stating that the bill gives "[President] Bush the power to jail pretty much anyone he wants for as long as he wants without charging them, to unilaterally reinterpret the Geneva Conventions, to authorize what normal people consider torture, and to deny justice to hundreds of men captured in error" (Editorial).

By 2006, the Abu Ghraib images had already become stock inventory of the 9/11 archive, and were often used by the opponents of the Bush administration as a terrifying warning against the unseen consequences of war. The passing of the Military Commissions Act was understood by many as a failure of the democratic public sphere: How could the "Torture Bill" be passed after such graphic and unambiguous evidence of torture? The question seemed even more pressing in light of the fact that it was precisely the images, not the news of torture, that prompted the Abu Ghraib scandal in the United States. A massive public response ensued only after the photographs of U.S. soldiers abusing prisoners in Abu Ghraib were published. This happened in late April of 2004, three months after the information about the existence of torture in Abu Ghraib was first made public by CNN. Apparently, the brief CNN coverage, which only alluded to the existence of incriminating photographs but did not include any, failed to spark any significant public reaction. The bland journalistic language, in which "U.S. soldiers reportedly posed for photographs with partially unclothed Iraqi prisoners," could not possibly match the vivid evidence of the actual photographs (CNN).

The debate that followed focused on the publicized images of torture, revolving mostly around questions of representation: Are the abusers representative of the U.S. military's actions in Iraq, and, by extension, the U.S. nation? What are the consequences of these representations for the abused Iraqis depicted in them? Other critics moved away from the shocking imagery and focused instead on the institutional context in which these actions were carried out: the place of torture in U.S. history, the structural conditions for the emergence of abuse (state of U.S. prisons, economic deprivation at home), and so on.[5]

Very soon, American visual artists joined in the debate and began reworking the controversial images. From the 2004 *Inconvenient Evidence* exhibition at the International Center of Photography in New York to the activist portrait art of Daniel Heyman, this work most broadly focused on the close involvement between techniques of representation and technologies of power.[6] The Abu Ghraib images, although at first subjected to government suppression and censorship, were soon disseminated globally, both in their original form and through various reproductions (cf. Mitchell 2005, 2011). These reproductions insistently focused on one notorious photograph in which a hooded prisoner stands on a box while holding wires in his hands, an image which was eventually turned into a visual cypher for the events at Abu Ghraib and their fallout. The public life of these images was then characterized by a trajectory of increasing visibility as well as abstraction, as the event of which they testify became more visible and, at the same time, was sublimated in one suggestive and terrifying icon.

Critics have tried to explain the choice of the hooded man image as the iconic reference to Abu Ghraib and torture variously. Stephen F. Eisenman summarizes some of those arguments in *The Abu Ghraib Effect*, saying that "[the hood] recalls dunces' caps once used to punish schoolchildren, the hoods worn by members of the Ku Klux Klan and subsequent American racist organizations, and the hoods worn by the executioners and their victims" (13). Eisenman's actual concern is the ineffectiveness of these images to produce any significant political effects. This, he argues, is due to the fact that they comply with the formula of "beautiful suffering" — "the motif of tortured people and tormented animals who appear to sanction their own abuse" — which "constitutes an unacknowledged basis of the unity of the classical tradition in European and Western art" (16). Eisenman's formula of "beautiful suffering" certainly resonates with Burke's definition of the sublime, in which "danger or pain" become sources of pleasure "at certain distances," such as, for example, the distance between the viewer and the image (Burke 36). Eisenman's argument implies that the social work of representations which turn terror into mere opportunity for awe is basically assimilatory.[7]

This implication gains in relevance if we take a brief look at some institutional practices of the U.S. military. These show that the shocking familiarity of the hooded man cannot be simply reduced to an aesthetic issue. In his embedded-journalistic account of the 2003 invasion of Iraq, Evan Wright writes:

> Survival Evasion Resistance Escape school (SERE), a secretive training course where Marines, fighter pilots, Navy SEALs and other military

personnel in high-risk jobs are held "captive" in a simulated prisoner-of-war camp in which the student inmates are locked in cages, beaten and subjected to psychological torture overseen by military psychiatrists — all with the intent of training them to stand up to enemy captivity. When Gunny Wynn [one of Wright's main characters] went through SERE, his "captors," playing on his Texas accent, forced him to wear a Ku Klux Klan hood for several days and pull one of his fellow "inmate" Marines, an African American, around on a leash, treating him as a slave [22–23].

This transgressive episode suggests that the cultural resonance of the images of Abu Ghraib is neither a matter of accident, nor a purely formal matter, but rather a symptom of existing, quite non-exceptional processes in which the military, as a powerful social actor, is unavoidably implicated. A persistent and exclusive focus on the shocking effect of the images that created the "Abu Ghraib scandal" also works to cover its systemic background. Almost immediately after the publishing of the original photographs, the L.A.-based political design group Forkscrew authored an Abu Ghraib-inspired series of posters parodying Apple's iPod advertising campaign. On one of these, the hooded man of the Abu Ghraib series reappears under the label "iRaq," now taking the place of a silhouette of a relaxed young man listening to his iPod. Instead of the Apple slogan, "10,000 songs in your pocket. Mac or PC," the poster reads, "10,000 volts in your pocket, guilty or innocent." By blending the image of terror with the form of the commercial, the iRaq posters pointed to the mutual dependence of a normally functioning domestic economy and the distant war. However, in the context in which it is found — pasted on walls and surrounded by actual Apple ads — the subversive iRaq poster can also go unnoticed, and simply blend in the flow of commercial images. This interpretive ambiguity is certainly always there where parody is concerned, since this mode is by definition divided, as Linda Hutcheon put it, "between complicity and distance" (32). Still, it could be argued that, all ambiguities aside, the image of terror nevertheless remains in place, and thus might enter and remain within the field of vision subliminally or unconsciously.

Beyond the Sublime

A similar situation — defined not merely by ambiguity, but by an indecisiveness between ambiguity and certainty that appears to make any interpretive act irrelevant — characterizes the glimpse of Abu Ghraib in *Inside*

Man. It seems safe to say that the flashing image of torture is in this case not at all supposed to raise questions about representation (as it did in the wake of the Abu Ghraib scandal). Neither is this a scene that would encourage viewers to rationally consider their role, as consumers, in the workings of the military-entertainment complex; it is way too fleeting to do that, and the momentary shock of recognition that it produces, if registered at all, is soon suppressed by the teleological push of the suspenseful plot. Devoid of representational value and defined primarily by its affective power — by its proximity to the sublime — the image of terror here figures neither as a document of a tragic historical episode, nor an iconic anti-war message. Instead, it seems to appear simply as itself, a terrifying visual thing plugged in the flow of other exchangeable things, namely, of commodities.

I propose to read this scene in two, mutually non-exclusive ways. First, we can understand it as an instance of defamiliarization followed by assimilation, since the recognition of the image of terror produces a shock that will last only as long as the unfolding of the ongoing thriller will allow. In this, the brief scene could be said to re-enact the social process that followed the appearance of the scandalous Abu Ghraib images in the U.S. public sphere, where the initial shock was soon followed by cultural assimilation abetted by the work of the mass media. Instead of producing political action, massive public exposure and hyper-visibility of the photographs drowns the event in the flow of commodity-images.[8]

The other way to make sense of this enigmatic display of terror in *Inside Man* is to see it as a structural analogue of that other filmic gesture which appears similarly redundant (if considered strictly as an element in the plot), but which is actually essential (if considered in its economic function). In short, the unmotivated hint to Abu Ghraib in Lee's film can only be compared to the practice of product placement that the movie also engages in, showing us casually iPods, Dell computers, and cans of Pepsi. What can be said about this uncanny gesture, in which display of terror literally falls in line with the display of commodities? Two apparently contradictory things: First, that terror — with all the implications pertaining to the post–9/11 historical situation — is easily assimilated in the channels of commercial transaction; and, second, that terror can, momentarily, disrupt the steady flow of commodities. I do not think the film allows for the possibility of making a conclusive choice here. The logic of terror does not prevail over the logic of advertising, and the processes of commodification do not totally eliminate or assimilate terror. They coexist in a state of mutual embeddedness, not exclusive opposition. The manifestation of Abu Ghraib in *Inside Man*, in a sublime, excessive, compositionally unmotivated and disintegrative element of the plot, therefore simultaneously connects the pervasive post–9/11 imagery of terror to the economic practice of product placement and U.S. world-wide military presence. If we approach the scene this way, dialectically, instead of the impasse of irresolvable contradiction, we get a glimpse of the co-involvement of capital accumulation and terror in its contemporary historical form.

Just War

Another, quite central element of *Inside Man*'s plot makes such a reading possible. The Abu Ghraib scene is not the only moment in the film in which capital accumulation and terror are articulated. However, while through the video game and Abu Ghraib scenes the film outlines the connection between the wider political-economic system and contemporary practices of terror, this other moment is there to contain the film's excesses within the limits of the hegemonic post–9/11 discourse. As mentioned earlier, the actions of the bank robbers are ethically grounded in the fact that the financial empire under attack was built on human suffering: The diamonds that are the main target of the robbery come from the European Jews from whose deportation and death the banker profited directly. An official Nazi document bearing the bank owner's name also suggests that his empire was founded on war profiteering. Evidently, at the origin of capital accumulation in *Inside Man* lies terror. Moreover, this connection to the Holocaust allows for the staging of a fundamental inversion that, if considered in the context of the post–9/11 moment, might potentially carry certain subversive implications, considering that those who initially appear to be the bad guys are actually good (the robbers, or "terrorists"), whereas the system they are attacking, since it was built on violent expropriation, appears fundamentally corrupt after the secret of its origin is revealed.

The way in which the Holocaust motive here makes the robbers basically likable is somewhat reminiscent of a similar procedure in the classic heist-with-a-twist, Sidney Lumet's *Dog Day Afternoon* (1975), which Lee's film explicitly pays tribute to at several occasions. In *Dog Day Afternoon*, in which a young man robs a bank in order to pay for a sex change operation for his boyfriend, the justification for the bank robbery is also not (primarily) personal financial gain, but again a nobler cause, although clearly more controversial, and arguably a political one. In *Inside Man* this is not the case. The Holocaust here figures not only as an exceptional traumatic historical event, but also as a necessary, safe, and uncontroversial point of reference that will assure that the robbers' actions remain politically and ethically beyond doubt.

The fact that Lee resorts to what in *Inside Man* figures as a mere cliché—a variation on the "Nazi gold" motive—is significant. One wonders whether in a politically charged moment and in a movie with so many references to some of the burning problems of the contemporary United States the dark secret of the arch-capitalist of the story could not have been a more distinctly post–9/11 one. Every other post–9/11 issue that appears in the movie is foregrounded, questioned, made problematic—from racial profiling and government secrecy to terrorism and victimhood. It is certainly difficult to think of a more recent war that was initially, although falsely, justified through an appeal to nobler causes. If we insist on the allegorical immediacy of *Inside Man*, the U.S.-proclaimed "liberation" of Iraq in the name of democracy and human rights could quite as well serve as the model for the actions of the bank robbers in the movie. Still, the contemporary problems of a political economy of terror remain left out of the narrative structure, appearing only as moments of sublime excess, and are hidden by a generic explanation that both reveals capital's connection with systemic practices of terror and displaces it to a safe temporal and ideological distance. The presence of the Holocaust motive works to exclude the problem of capital accumulation from the post–9/11 allegory, and render its place in the contemporary moment unquestioned and unproblematic.

Paradoxically, then, the only reference to the historical past in the movie seems to contribute more to a de-historicizing and de-politicizing of the contemporary conjuncture than to its possible genealogical or systemic grounding. This is so, I would argue, because the Holocaust motive in this post–9/11 allegory is filtered through the hegemonic discourse of the 9/11 archive. In that sense, it is not a reference to the actual historical occurrence at all. In the context of 9/11, allusions to World War II have often served as rhetorical props supporting revived narratives of American exceptionalism, with Ground Zero and Pearl Harbor as the most obvious examples. Reflecting on this problem, Gene Ray observed that,

> in official and popular American memory, World War II has become the "last good war," fought and won by the "best generation." As this generation dies out, a desire to honor its surviving members has found

cultural expression in a string of mythifying Hollywood blockbusters from *Saving Private Ryan* to, indeed, *Pearl Harbor*— to say nothing of post–September 11 Hollywood fare. In this light, the revival of the categorical rhetoric of World War II can be read as a collective reach back for the morally unambiguous position of the United States in that conflict. And the folding of this rhetoric into the response to September 11 has been politically effective, if ultimately naive [52].

Viewed from this perspective, the just bank robbery of *Inside Man* becomes a post–9/11 re-enactment of the "good war," and the criminal act itself takes the place of the U.S. military intervention in Europe. That way, the more recent military invasion can completely and safely disappear from the narrative, while its terrifying consequences and implications — racism, torture, murder — are put on display as peculiar ads for the global war on terror.

Although both the Abu Ghraib scene and the Holocaust sub-plot are there for the articulation of capital accumulation and terror to come to the fore, they might be considered complementary elements in this story, mirroring and canceling each other out. By recurring to the stock imagery of the 9/11 archive, and relating its apparently sublime intrusion in the plot to the logics of advertising and war, the film gestures towards uncovering the systemic, material substratum of contemporary terror — but only in order to remove it from the present moment on another level (by reducing the Holocaust to a narrative cliché). The fragmented terrifying imagery of *Inside Man* evokes the sublime as if to point out the unspeakable complexity of the political-economic structures within which particular traumatic events emerge. But the unspeakable, the traumatic, and the sublime are here openings into and products of larger networks of power and signification. The allegories of *Inside Man* put the systemic involvement of the production of terror and a normally functioning everyday life at the heart of the contemporary United States. In this sense, even when staging terror as excessive or sublime, *Inside Man* ultimately shows that it is neither too terrible nor that exceptional, but part of the substance of the post–9/11 reality.

Notes

1. Susan Lurie's article on the fate of the infamous photograph of people falling from the WTC towers shows how the politics of visibility functioned in the domestic, U.S. context in the wake of the 9/11 attacks.

2. See Cvek, especially chapter 3, "Common Ground: Melodramas of 9/11."

3. Turse goes on to substantiate this claim by referring to collaborative projects between the U.S. military, University of Southern California, and Hollywood. The extent of the militarization of everyday American life is also the subject of Turse's informative book *The Complex: How the Military Invades Our Everyday Lives* (2008).

4. In "The Concept of Cinematic Excess," Kristin Thompson argues that excess is "counternarrative" and "counter-unity," and explains its function by relying on Russian Formalists' notion of motivation: "Strong realistic or compositional motivation will tend to make excessive elements less noticeable; the perception of the narratively and stylistically significant will dominate. But at other times, a lack of these kinds of motivation may direct our attention to excess" (57). The moments of cinematic excess discussed here direct our attention to the political-economic systems within which terror emerges.

5. For more on these topics see Brown, Klein, Sontag, Strange. The iconic images from Abu Ghraib are also the subject of W.J.T. Mitchell's book *Cloning Terror*, which offers a more in-depth analysis of the role of images in the "war on terror." To date, two American documentaries have been made about the torture scandal and its implications: Rory Kennedy's *Ghosts of Abu Ghraib* (2007) and Errol Morris' *Standard Operating Procedure* (2008).

6. Daniel Heyman's work would certainly deserve a separate study. In 2006, Heyman traveled to Jordan with a group of U.S. human rights lawyers who were conducting interviews with former prisoners of Abu Ghraib in order to collect evidence for a lawsuit on their behalf (see Gladstone). According to Heyman, "these particular people's human identities had already been removed twice: first as wrongly accused and brutally tortured prisoners, second in the photos their captors took of them, hooded and faceless, where they became global icons but lost their individuality. I wanted the Iraqis to regain their humanity, to regain their faces and their voices." Heyman's work — clearly positioned against the mass-media representations of torture — poses numerous questions about art, humanitarianism and imperialism, and the role of visual culture in times of war (Gladstone).

7. Eisenman's argument also implies a causal relationship between public images and political action. This common, often unspoken assumption has been convincingly criticized by Thomas Keenan in his "Publicity and Indifference."

8. Lila Rajiva has argued that the political failure of the Abu Ghraib scandal can be related to the ways in which the event was represented in the U.S. media. These, according to her, took two basic forms, "forensic drama" and "pulp drama": "On one hand we have reports, so numerous, detailed, and specialized that public attention has been lost among them; on the other, singular acts of hostage-taking and beheading [the Nick Berg case], which portrayed violence inundating the country whose victims most of all are Iraqis themselves, create the illusion of symmetry in suffering and turn the victimizer into the victim. Abu Ghraib is seen in split screens — one limited and lurid, finding its way to well-publicized court-martials, and the other so encumbered with legal documentation that it seems arcane and politically motivated " (158). Her book seriously questions any easy notion of a direct connection between publicity and political action. As she writes, "at one point, the Pentagon turned over 21,600 pages of documents in two months, after having already made 16,600 pages available on the Internet" (154). This clearly shows how the Abu Ghraib case might give support to Fredric Jameson's claim about the repressive "ideological function of overexposure in commercial culture" (39).

PUSHING THE ENVELOPED:
EXPOSING THE LIMITS OF FREEDOM

Aronofsky's Cinematic Vision and the Ethical Meaning of Freedom as the Sublime Horizon of *Amor Fati*

Donald Callen

"... it is only as an aesthetic phenomenon that existence and the world are eternally justified"—Nietzsche, *The Birth of Tragedy*, 32

At the climactic moment of the narrative arc of Darren Aronofsky's *Black Swan* (2010) Nina recognizes that she has not killed her nemesis, Lily, but has instead struck herself in what will turn out to be a death blow. Interpreted as a psychological thriller, the moment is Nina's awakening from the paranoid delusion that Lily is out to violently replace her as principal dancer in Thomas Leroy's new production of *Swan Lake*. Her ensuing death is the tragic cost of a psychological illness caused by the combined stresses of being infantilized by a jealous, domineering mother and the perfectionist demands of an art she can comprehend only in terms of achieving absolute technical mastery.

Undoubtedly, the film can be interpreted along these lines. However, such an interpretation distances us from the narrative's existential drama that casts Nina's story as embodying universal themes that establish a more intimate connection between the spectator and Nina, one in which her abnormality is much more a matter of dramatically stressing what is archetypically human rather than a character portrait of illness.

So let's begin by recovering paranoia from the psychoanalytic lexicon and sketching briefly its fundamental location in a horizon of existential anxiety. Following the main lines of a phenomenological analysis of anxiety by Heidegger (132), we can do so by making it one pole in a relation whose opposite is occupied by a feeling of the sublime. The sublime is our main focus but for now let us simply speak of the feeling of the sublime as a detached or distanced sense of an incapacity to find sense and meaning in existence, of confronting existence as an awesome and infinite abyss of "sound and fury signifying nothing." (In Heidegger, death is the nothingness that absolutely seals off every possibility of being [232].) What makes paranoia a polar opposite to the sublime is the need to identify something as causally responsible for what is felt — no longer as an uncanny and distant threat, but as approaching, coming ever nearer, and as overwhelming. At its heart, paranoid anxiety is the perhaps altogether reasonable sense that *something* is responsible for one feeling threatened with abyssal nothingness. However, typically assuming a background metanarrative of redemption or healing, paranoid anxiety's projected object is a stand-in for a cause that one is unprepared to recognize, paradigmatically oneself, a self dominated by an imaginary ideal that one is unwilling to give up but that must be surrendered if the creation of meaning is to be possible. In a familiar net of existentialist concepts, sublime nothingness must in the end be welcomed as the ground of the possibility of being. In the problematic of the film, Thomas Leroy, the choreographer, says that there is nothing seductive or creative in Nina so long as she is under the spell of a vision of artistic beauty dominated by technical perfection, that is, under the spell of academic ideals and rules already given and familiar. To see her excel under such rules is nonetheless to see nothing new in her, nothing that can seduce us into loving *her*. This is the explanation offered for why she is unable to give a convincing rendition of the black swan in the company's new performance of *Swan Lake*. This existentialist reading of Nina's story is loaded, however, with a presumptuous if yet fascinating confidence that meaning is a kind of free mastery of existence, albeit accomplished through the *creation* of ideals rather than the mastery of a *given* essence or ideal. Recognizable here is Sartre's familiar formula for human being, "existence precedes essence" (15). It seems to me, for reasons to be adduced, that we need a much more modest conception of the scope and significance of freedom and the feeling of the sublime. However, we need to begin by giving a richer exposition of the existentialist concept in its roots in the philosophy of Immanuel Kant.

Kant's Concept of the Sublime

Existentially, for Kant, throughout his *Critique of the Power of Judgment*, the sublime emotion is an episode in a drama of freedom, centered in the imagination's effort to unify the manifold of experience as a purposive or meaningful whole. It is a most notable symptom of an inability to either unify the manifold under a concept or to find beauty in things — a matter of a free play of imagination in which a semblance of a purposive or meaningful whole is constructed. In a different way, semblance is at work in the feeling of the sublime since, as a triumph, upon self-reflection freedom wakens to its supreme power, a will that is able to act under the moral law, whatever the abyssal, unhappy, or initially fanciful representation of one's situation. In brief, one could say that for Kant, *the aesthetic is a realm of illusion where in freedom we play between enjoying the construction of a beautiful semblance of purpose or meaning in things and a reflected terror of powerlessness in the face of apparent irremediable contingency and chaos.* This polar conception of beauty and the sublime will become Nietzsche's conception of art in *The Birth of Tragedy*—that is, art conceived as the weighing of an Apollonian impulse to the construction of illusions of form and securely delineated, equipoised individuals *against* a Dionysian surrender to intoxication and ecstatic embrace of formless impulses destructive to individuals.

In this realm of aesthetic semblance we are squarely in the cinematic vision of Darren Aronofsky — minus the Kantian card in the hole, namely, the power of freedom to determine action and character in virtue of a moral vision of one's humanity, one's belonging to a Kingdom of Ends, a community of mutually respectful similar free powers. For Kant, ultimately, existence is justifiable, able to be made sense of, *morally* in a rational recognition and appropriation of the force of the moral will. We could say that for Kant the truth of the matter of existence lies *outside* the aesthetic illusion in waking to the power of the moral will. In Aronofsky and Nietzsche there is no representation of such a power and such wakening (though, with Aronofsky, perhaps an occasional nostalgia in its absence). The truth of existence is to be found in the aesthetic illusion itself. The "free" play of imagination has no transcendental or transcendent meaning. Yet, it is only as we grapple within the virtual realm of seeming free, that we blithely mask the nothingness that is the banality or hopelessness of everyday reality. In Aronofsky's *The Wrestler*, finally, Randy gives up hope of finding meaning outside the wrestling stage in real relationships of love and caring.

He chooses the aesthetic illusion, within which he is loved, at the cost of death. He judges the "world out there" to be a morally unredeemable reality. Allying Aronofsky to Nietzsche in *The Birth of Tragedy*, the only justification of existence is aesthetic (Nietzsche 32). It is in the aesthetic play between the Apollonian and the Dionysian that early Nietzsche philosophically reflects Aronofsky's cinematic vision. Dionysian art reveals suffering and death to be the truth of existence — albeit a truth dramatically masked by a "hero" whose theatrical face is molded by Apollonian illusion (29).[1]

The pivotal issue between Kant and Aronofsky/Nietzsche is the latter's judgment concerning the fate of morality as understood by Kant, the moral as a positive power of freedom to determine action as meaningful and ideal. With Kant the moral ideal is expressed as a principled regard for the freedom of others. Negatively, this means a hands-off respect for their capacity for self-determination. Positively, it means an active nourishing of this capacity and, then, holding persons morally responsible for their actions, blaming, and, perhaps, punishing immorality, as well as praise for and pride in moral uprightness.[2] Take away this possibility of a moral escape from aesthetic illusion and we are left with something very close to Aronofsky's cinematic vision and Nietzsche's Dionysian mask. But within the aesthetic illusion, minus any chastening recognition of or interest in the moral, others are either obstacles to or servants of one's *narcissistic* imaginary construction of free mastery. The aesthetic illusion as such, purely within the parameters of both the Kantian and Nietzschean conceptions, appears to be (non-erotically) loveless, and love is therefore inimical to the illusion inasmuch as a truly loving relation to the other disrupts egoism. (Love is present in Aronofsky's cinematic vision, but it emerges authentically only within the throes of broken dreams, as above, in Randy's ultimate rejection of the world "out there" for the dramatic world of the wrestler's stage but also in Harry Goldfarb's nostalgic love for Marion in *Requiem for a Dream*, reflected in the romantic idealization of the first year of their shared addictive bliss.)

In *Black Swan*, almost all of Nina's story seems to unfold within this narcissistic imaginary. Clearly her paranoid anxiety is entirely self-occupied. When she lets herself go, breaking with her mother and embracing the Dionysian intoxication of sexual desire, the object of her leap is a perfection that will make her seductive and make her able to dance the black swan. Her wakening from paranoid anxiety seems to take place entirely within a narcissistic frame. She becomes aware of the self-destructiveness of her paranoid anxiety, but accepts it, embraces it as the condition of her artistic-and-self-transcendence. No longer does she worry over the breaks in the Apollonian perfection of her skin. She accepts damage, even death, as an essential condition of aesthetic transcendence. These themes cinematically reflect postulates in Nietzsche's conception of art in *Thus Spoke Zarathustra* and *The Will to Power* as well as his conception of idealization as a trans-valuation of value and the possibility of becoming overman.

All of this sets the conceptual stage for our philosophical problem and our reflection concerning the truth and limits of Aronofsky's cinematic vision. Suppose that, for good reasons, we should indeed reject Kant's confidence in morality as a power of freedom to determine action in a break with aesthetic illusion but also be able to break with the irremediable narcissistic cast of aesthetic illusion which we find in Nietzsche and, apparently, in Aronofsky. Nietzsche himself is skeptical about the Kantian conception of a legislative autonomous moral will, deeming it to be the product of reactive and uncreative resentment. He regards "moral" feelings of remorse and guilt or pride and desert[3] as reactive constructions of weakness, displacements from potentially creative appropriations of suffering and the moment (*Genealogy*, Part Two, 40–93). Moreover, arguably, Nietzsche's determinism required him to judge such feelings to involve irrational assumptions concerning one's capacity to be self-determining.

However, such feelings are not reactive merely because they foreclose on creative self-determination. That argument only works if we accept Kant's and Nietzsche's shared existentialist conception of the meaning of freedom as autonomous action. *They are reactive because they conceptually irrationally cage in the potentially open and "free" contemplation of the indeterminate meaning of one's being.* Perhaps, we should rethink the "moral" not in terms of a *power of action* but as a *reflective feeling* about the violent or non-violent quality of one's character and deed. Within an aesthetic reflective construction, there remains room for "moral" feeling and a kind of "moral" judgment, issuing from a reflection on the affective quality or *élan* of the person and deeds one narratively images in the contemplation of the sort of motivations one observes oneself to have. We may well still value mutual respecting and loving beings even if we are utterly without the power to make ourselves such beings in the same way that we value and ponder the indeterminacy of the meaning of an artwork without supposing that the work of art might have been other than it is. Replacing the polar concepts of guilt and pride, shame or gratitude, in contemplating one's fortune are perhaps better affective markers of the "moral" quality of the person one *aesthetically* observes oneself to be.

A reflective dialectic of the sublime temporality of one's being and the meaning of the moment will be necessary in order to properly gauge the work of art that is the aesthetically reflected person. There one recovers the question of the meaning of the sublime feeling as central to an episode not of free self-determination but of "morally" affected "free" contemplation.

Why, though, should we abandon the Kantian conception of the moral meaning of the sublime feeling? And why does doing so leave us at best with an aesthetic justification of existence, that is, with a justification found only within an aesthetic contemplation of self and world?

Finding the Sublime in the Machine

> "Restate my assumptions: One, mathematics is the language of nature. Two, everything around us can be represented and understood through numbers. Three, if you graph the numbers of any system, patterns emerge. Therefore, there are patterns everywhere in nature. Evidence: The cycling of disease epidemics; the wax and wane of caribou populations; sun spot cycles; the rise and fall of the Nile. So, what about the stock market? The universe of numbers that represents the global economy. Millions of hands at work, billions of minds. A vast network, screaming with life. An organism. A natural organism. My hypothesis: Within the stock market, there is a pattern as well ... Right in front of me ... hiding behind the numbers. Always has been" — Maximillian Cohen, *Pi*

In broad terms, the reason we should abandon the Kantian conception of the moral meaning of the experiences of beauty and the sublime is that they imply his conception of the human person as self-determining, as autonomous, a sort of supernatural being. Kant, himself, was double-minded about this matter since he held that as phenomena all actions, as with all other events, are subject to a transcendental law of deterministic causation. In order to make room for freedom, he had to posit, in his *Critique of Pure Reason*, an ontological realm of things-in-themselves, strictly unknowable, though, since knowledge is limited to what we can experience. This is a long story. Suffice it to say that philosophers have had great difficulty in seeing how we can be both determined and free in Kant's sense. For freedom as he conceives it means being self-determining and responsible for the choices we make — it being understood that we must be able to choose from multiple real options in order for feelings of responsibility, merit, guilt and desert to make sense. Yet, as Kant understood, the natural sciences are able to operate only on the assumption that the world of events in time is a deterministic or near-deterministic matrix. If the world is that way, the future is not open. Among the possibilities that we imagine for ourselves at any given time, one at most is already laid out for us as real, conditioned by forces and events that, ultimately, lie outside ourselves even if our thoughts and desires channel our fate. Our sense that the future is open is only a product of our ignorance of the causes and consequences of our actions. If determinism is true, our feelings of beauty and the sublime are functions of a necessarily limited perception of ourselves and our situation, a perception that is itself unable to know or determine the true and basic pattern of the complex phenomenal beings that we are. *In short, the meaning of the sublime is not concerned with freedom. It is not existential in the ordinary sense. It has to do with perception only.*

So if we are not autonomous beings, we are heteronomous. Our choices and acts issue from mechanistic procedures having conditions that lie outside ourselves. If we *could* grasp the deterministic pattern in things, we would be able to do (in fact, sometimes *see* ourselves doing) marvelous things, as Max in *Pi* insists. Talking with his former teacher and mentor, Sol Robeson, he rejects the claim that the sequence of decimal-place elaborations of pi may just be irrational. Kidnapped by a group of Kabalistic Hasids, he shouts that only he is fit to be given the number-name of God, since, unlike them, he grasps the principle in the sequence. They want the number only to intone it so as to receive God's blessing. A gang of corporate stock manipulators wants the number so it can profit from truly insider knowledge about how the market will move. Max repeats, "Restate my assumptions ... The basic language of the world is mathematics." If so, it seems, we should be able to predict what will happen, for example, how the stock market will turn, if we can discover the numerical principle that governs the sequence of events in question. Hence, we get the puzzle governing the basic problematic of the film. "Pi" denotes a number that seems in its sequence of decimal elaborations to admit of no rational principle. To discover the principle for pi is the film's metaphor for uncovering the number of "God," the number governing the deterministic unfolding of the natural creation or world in time.

Actually, it turns out that even if determinism is true, it is very likely false that macro-events of the sort that Max is interested in, such as stock market cycles can be predicted (Hoefer). The language in which we describe everyday actions and events is not able to be mathematically mapped. The material micro-level at which determinism works requires the language of the physical sciences to express the mathematical pattern in the deterministic or near-deterministic matrix of events.[4] The ordinary language in which we "scan" or reflect our situation, actions, and "possibilities" leaves us with a merely apparently open future and an "existential" indeterminacy that issues from an essential ignorance. If determinism is true, we shouldn't expect to find its workings at the level of complex social and historical macro-phenomena. But by the same token, conversely, we have little reason to suppose that consciousness, which self-evidently operates in the everyday language within which we reflect action and experience, has any determining role to play in the unfolding of the physical universe in time. As conscious beings we are odd creatures, able to variously reflect necessarily indeterminate shapes and patterns in ourselves and in our deeds but we are beings in which consciousness as such, in the terms with which we are ordinarily aware of self and world, has no determining role to play in the world. Consciousness has an essentially passive and reflective rather than active function. Pursuing a thought experiment along these lines, some philosophers have speculated on the logical possibility of another Earth where, physically speaking, everything unfolds in a way that is strictly identical to the way in which events unfold on our planet but where consciousness is missing. There, zombie-like creatures looking just like us, with identical brains and brain-processing, and acting just like us wander about without any reflective awareness of what they are doing. For consciousness *as such* can't be admitted as being physically causal. A physical causal system must be closed, admitting only physical causes. This is a fundamental axiom of the physical sciences (Chalmers).

Given this reconstruction of existence as radically heteronomous, terror, paranoid anxiety, and the feelings of beauty and the sublime, which also feature importantly in *Pi,* have an altogether different meaning than what we take them to have when we suppose ourselves to be free or self-determining. As emergent from complex and big-brained organisms in which language has evolved, arguably, reflective perception or consciousness is *always* aesthetic, always tracking at a distance, or more or less closely, the textured and quasi-holistic patterns and semblance of meaning in what happens to us in our doings. In the aesthetically sophisticated but scientifically crude language of consciousness we are constantly outputting descriptions and interpretations of our behavior. Given the ignorance that is essentially involved in using such language, there is an inherent indeterminacy of meaning in our actions and interactions. The indeterminacy in the meaning of a work of art is merely an instance of the indeterminacy of the meaning of being in human existence. At the end of *Pi,* having effectively lobotomized himself with a drill, Max contentedly sits on a park bench, gazing up at the beautiful canopy of rustling leaves over his head. Unlike a day earlier, he is unable to play and win the complex calculation game with the little girl who, calculator in hand, asks him questions of complex arithmetical sums. But he is now able to feel beauty in things. Gone is the paranoia that was a constant companion when he insisted on perfecting his understanding of the phenomenal world as a whole by laying hold of the principle of pi. Gone is his obsession with conquering the sublimely unknowable and apparently irrational world by discovering the mathematical principle of its temporal unfolding. For, aesthetically speaking, perfection is not gained that way. In *Black Swan,* Nina's last words before dying are "I was perfect." But as the choreographer of her dance makes clear from the beginning, perfection in art is gained only in letting go of the demand to conquer the work through a technical tracking of action. Aesthetically, freedom means a release into an illusion of imaginative play within the multiply determinable forms and meanings of the manifold of perception, and the satisfaction or frustration one feels is a registering of achievement in perception and interpretation, not in free action and self-creation.

Excluded from Thomas Leroy's morally insensible conception of the aesthetic realm is any conception of love beyond the seduction of beauty. The world of aesthetic reflection appears to be a semblance without any kind of "moral" feeling. But if we cannot escape the aesthetic illusion by having recourse to autonomy and morally governed self-determination, must we give up on an affective semblance thereof altogether? Is there a place for it within a purely aesthetic and reflective hold on human existence?

The Sublime Moment

Writing about Spinoza's *Ethics* and Nietzsche's critique of morality, Gilles Deleuze reconstructs a conception of an ethics without morality, that is, without concepts of duty, blame, guilt, pride, moral responsibility and desert (Boundas 69–77). The problem with morality as it is commonly conceived is that it is rooted in inadequate ideas of consciousness. Self-consciousness is a witness to effects rather than to causes. Even our acts are effects the causes of which are unknown to us. Rather than reflect our existence within the terms of our ignorance we construct illusions in which we take effects for causes. We take purposes or intentions, will or desire, or, more grandly, the self, to be originating causes of deeds when they themselves are affections or types of effects whose causes we do not fathom. In short, an adequate consciousness would reflect back to us the abyssal, sublime mystery of our existence. Priests and tyrants take existence to be something whose form we can command. They suppose that we come to desire a thing because we judge it to be good where in truth we only judge things to be good when we already desire them. Priests, tyrants, and those under their sway are dangerous because they conjure up laws the knowledge of which they suppose to be sufficient to determine action in accordance with them. Feelings of guilt, blame, desert, and praise are affections that involve inadequate and presumptuous illusions concerning the nature and power of awareness or knowledge. When we understand them, we understand that these feelings reflect bodies as disposed by fundamentally violent motions toward others and toward ourselves. An ethical, as opposed to moral, life would be one in which, under the awareness of the sublime mystery of one's existence, one lives *within* an understanding and constant contemplation of existence as a matter of fate. Affections thus reflected would constitute us as suited to or in harmony with a more adequate idea of what happens to us. Our lives would unfold within an *amor fati*, a love of fate. Such "moral," or, better, ethical feelings are, arguably aesthetic. They involve what amounts to freedom from the violent emotions and bodied impulses that are reflected in illusions of autonomy, responsibility, and desert. They allow "existential" contemplation to interpret and envision our lives and relationships differently.

Such a feeling of the sublime mystery of existence knits up the position for paranoia that occupies the polar opposite to the feeling of the sublime within a dramatics of freedom and autonomy. Paranoia is egocentric. It is the imagination-infused sense that someone or something is set upon injuring or punishing you and often, if not always, that this assault is undeserved. It imputes violent motives (broadly speaking) to someone who, if one could only escape the fear and muster a defense, deserves violence in response. Nina yells, "It's *my* turn," as she drives the blade of broken glass into the hallucinated Lily (my emphasis). But an ethical (as opposed to a moral) response to uncanny danger recognizes the inadequate ideas involved in anxiety. That is, paranoid anxiety typically involves ideas of undeserved assault and deserved punishment, or, more broadly, the egocentric sense that the world is set against *me*. I may certainly wrestle with fate, but my fate does not finally befall me as having chosen *me*, much less as an undeserved or punishing assault that in freedom might really have been different or avoided. Ethically, one may accept a feeling that condemns violence but only in an aesthetically contemplative sorrow in the senseless suffering that human beings endure and delusively and cruelly inflict upon one another. Such a reflection is testimony to the way in which within an ethically shaped aesthetic contemplation of life the affections and horizons of awareness involve a break with the motives and perspective of narcissism. In the final shots of *Pi*, Max's wonder-filled gaze at the rustling leaves above his head shows us how fortune has enabled him to become free (not to free himself) from the tightly circumscribed boundaries of his paranoid self. His freedom is not the freedom of autonomy but the freedom of having a vision of open horizons, grounded in his sublime ignorance of the future. In an attitude of pacific joy and amusement, he tells the little girl that he doesn't know the number that correctly answers her desire for a marvelous feat of calculation. But, then, she is a child. Only intellectual children seek such answers.

Broaching another dimension of the sense of the sublime in one's fate, Deleuze extends his account of an ethics without morality in a discussion of what is involved in an adequate judgment of fate, of what has happened to one (Boundas 78–82). One could say (although Deleuze does not himself put it this way) that *amor fati* does not imply fatalism. The reason for this is that an adequate idea of the moment is one that is suffused with a sense of the sublime. Interpreting what happens to one is a matter of seeking out an event in what happens. The essential ignorance of consciousness entails that an adequate awareness of the meaning of the moment is indeterminate. There is a philosophical tradition that stresses the temporal complexity of the sense of the moment (Kierkegaard, Nietzsche, Husserl, Bergson, Heidegger, Derrida, and Deleuze, among others). The moment is not a clearly defined instant, distinct from all those that have gone before and those yet to come. It is a complex present, the awareness of which involves both memory and anticipation. Hence, the present, or what has happened (on the scale and in terms of common experience), is essentially a construction, an interpretation. Typically, we elide the sublime indeterminacy of the moment, glossing it over with the sameness of settled and familiar concepts. We fail to see the "possibility" of the event in what has happened, an original insight into a "possible" arc of meaning that fate may hold in store. Consciousness is an activity and can have a creative dynamics in its unfolding purview. As an effect, it is a dynamics the causes of which are unknown. Yet, given the essential inherent indeterminacy of consciousness, we can still speak of the originality in the activity and in the result, in the work of art we are left to contemplate. Hence, there is no need to regard one's fate fatalistically, as if what happens to us *as we reflect it in consciousness* is determinately fixed within the terms of a given and closed framework of concepts. There is a dramatic instance of an awareness of an event in what has happened in *Black Swan*. Nina has come to Thomas to plead to be given the role of the swan queen. Thomas sneers at her "seductive" get-up and violently kisses her. But he is taken aback when Nina bites his lip. We soon discover that he has seen something unexpected in Nina's action, an arc of meaning in which her being able to dance both the white swan and the black swan can be envisioned. To be sure, seeing the event here does not seem to have an ethical significance. Yet, his own narcissistic prospect is temporarily broken by the perception of the event and he is able to see another person as having dispositions and motives he had not thought possible.

However, the ethical implications of the indeterminacy of the moment are yet to be drawn out more fully. If there is sublimity in the moment, what can be said about the dimensions of the infinity that lies before us? Here we need to consider Nietzsche's "most burdensome of thoughts," the thought of the possibility of an eternal return (*Gay Science*, 273–4).

In an interview (included as an extra on the DVD) Ellen Burstyn asks Hubert Selby, Jr., co-screenwriter and author of the novel, *Requiem for a Dream*, about the darkness of his story in which the dreams and lives of the protagonists are destroyed by addiction. The presumption in the question is that the culprit here is addiction. But Selby answers the question in a way that suggests a broader existential perspective. He remarks that coming to the end of their lives, most people feel regret, a sense that they got it all wrong. Is it that their dreams come to nothing? Or is it that they have had the wrong dreams? The film, as far as I can see, does not condemn the protagonists' dreams. Rather, it presents them as worthy of respect, as worthy of a requiem. Selby's claim involves an inversion of Nietzsche's idea of the eternal return in which the quality of the dream is clearly being addressed. Imagine, Nietzsche says in *The Gay Science,* that one day a demon whispers to you, "You must live this life, in every detail just as you have lived it, infinitely many times." Is this, asks the demon, a thought you are able to bear, to welcome joyfully (273–4)? Nietzsche's thought experiment is notoriously ambiguous, but one thing fairly clearly can be drawn from it. The implication is that the stakes of life, the standard by which its quality is to be judged, applies to a final moment, from which one has the perspective to make a judgment of life as a whole. The demon asks us to imagine the way we live our lives in detail and as belonging to a whole. The quality of the judgment we make is a matter of whether the picture we thus paint is viewed with joy or with sorrow. It is an aesthetic judgment of our story that the demon calls us to make.

However, Nietzsche countenances no possibility of an ethical quality in the aesthetic judgment he envisages. In his book, *Shame and Necessity*, Bernard Williams claims that we should give up the concept of moral responsibility given what science teaches us about the causal necessity in our actions (75–102). He looks to the narratives composed by the ancient Greeks for inspiration in reconstructing our moral concepts and our ethics. He argues that a concept closely akin to shame would be a more fitting way of registering ethical disapproval. Crucially, however, we need to conceive of shame not as a feeling that appeals to a community standard or custom of behavior as its ground (historically the norm when it comes to the concept of shame). Rather, we should reconstruct the concept of shame such that it is grounded in an ethical concept or standard that, on best reflection and reasoning, one formulates for oneself. If guilt, a form of feeling morally responsible, implies the judgment that I should have acted differently and that I could have done so, the feeling of shame concerns simply the matter of whether my character and acts are humanly fitting. Nothing is imputed as to some original power to determine my action and, ultimately, character in virtue of being free in a sense that would contradict the necessity in my deeds (Williams, *passim*). Still, there is in the concept of shame so understood nothing specifically ethical. I may simply feel, as Selby says, that I got it all wrong. And a joyful positive answer to Nietzsche's demon may still be entirely self-occupied. Finally, says Nina, "I was perfect!" Nina and Randy "get it right" but only within a "corrected" aesthetic illusion in which death is necessary yet made meaningful as the cost of the perfection of the dream. However, this is as far as Aronofsky takes us.

In *Thus Spoke Zarathustra* Nietzsche formulates a riddle about time. Walking along a road, his "dwarf" on his shoulder, he comes to an archway with the words, "The Moment," inscribed on the arch. He asks himself, the "dwarf" representing his weaker, lesser side, "Is time a straight line or is it a circle?" Often we think of time as a straight line stretching infinitely far into the past and infinitely far into the future with the moment being a point on that line. But no one has any experience that would justify taking time to be such a straight line. Moreover, the complexity of the moment seems to involve a sense of temporality in which we, ever anew, draw a circle that inscribes a recollection of the past with some kind of vision of the future. The "dwarf" jumps off Zarathustra's shoulder and shouts, "I know, time is a circle that closes when we die." Zarathustra finds this to be a very hasty judgment. We can interpret this hastiness in light of the idea of the eternal return as a failure to recognize that in a sense the circle of time closes in each moment as we hermeneutically synthesize the past and the future we envision for ourselves. The lesson of the riddle, in terms of Heidegger's appropriation of Nietzsche, is that the temporalizing of existence is a matter of a construction of each moment in which one cares for one's being with a constancy that reflects an awareness of existence as being-toward-death (219–246).

However, does the possible arc of meaning that may be found in the event that lies within the moment come to an end in one's death? Does it not extend with a sublime indeterminacy across the divide of death in the ethical possibility that one sees in the face of the dead one, the *appeal*: "Do not let me die!"? Emmanuel Levinas is known for a critique of Heidegger on precisely this point (*God, Death* 4–30). Let our metaphysics, our concept of being, derive from an ethics, he pleads (*Otherwise* 17–35). If we envision the meaning of being-in-time under the possibility of an ethical recollection of the dead (and if the horizons that project the meaning of existence involve a concern for those who will survive us) into an infinite future, the possible positive arc of meaning in the event projects a sense of time that is sublimely indeterminate and sublimely open in an openness to the being of others.

It may be something of this kind that informs the "wager" on an infinite future good that Blaise Pascal argues for in *Pensées*. One cannot prove that such an infinite good exists, but it is reasonable to cultivate a faith in it as the basis of one's vision of the meaning of human existence. Why? Because, you are already embarked, he says (121–127). Let's gloss this in terms of our argument here, extending the voice of the demon who whispers of the eternal return. If you examine yourself, you will find feelings that are not simply self-occupied. You will find loves for family, for friends, the implication of which is minimally a desire for their well-being. But you must wish that well-being to be as extended and as great as possible. You must wish for the well-being of those whom they love, their children, their children's children, and so on, in-finitely into the future. In other words, faith is a constancy of address to an infinite humanity as the content of the sublimely infinite yet indeterminate arc of meaning in the event in the moment. Such is the scope of a sublime freedom that is expressed in an adequate *amor fati*.

Notes

1. This claim about an aesthetic justification of existence is one that Nietzsche never surrendered, although in later work the narrative dimensions and possibilities of aesthetically informed existence have a potential grandeur in a will informed by the idea of the eternal return.

2. Missing in Kant is a developed sense of care as a response to human vulnerability, a point stressed in Carol Gilligan's formulation of an ethics of care in her *In A Different Voice: Psychological Theory and Women's Development*.

3. "Desert" is a central concept in philosophical ethics. It includes notions of merit, what one has a right to and what is justified by way of disapproval or punishment.

4. The position referred to here is, broadly speaking, generally referred to as physicalism. The question of how to explain consciousness within a physicalist account of the mind is hotly contested (Stoljar).

The Apocalyptic Sublime: Hollywood Disaster Films and *Donnie Darko*

Seung-hoon Jeong

The unrepresentability of historical catastrophes has often been both the cause of aesthetic anxiety and the ethical kernel of European cinema. Suffice it to remember how Claude Lanzmann's *Shoah* (1985) "reflects" on the Holocaust without "representing" it. The Holocaust is deemed comparable to the shocking intervention of the Freudian Thing or the Mosaic law which goes beyond human understanding, and toward which one can take only an ethical rather than aesthetic attitude; art should then testify to "the infinite debt of spirit with regard to a law that is as much that of the order of Moses' God as it is the factual law of the unconscious" (Rancière 126–28). Jacques Rancière calls this tendency the "ethical turn" of aesthetics, critically pointing out its key operational concept, the *sublime*.

The Sublime Between Aesthetics and Ethics

However, Hollywood has never cringed at "representing" sublime disasters as marvelous spectacles. Its scopophilic impulse toward catastrophe indeed embodies the cinema's inherent desire to represent the unrepresentable, to visualize it within the rectangular field of screen, as if this could make psychological room for, and ultimately overcome any fatalistic suffering from the traumatically sublime Thing. Steven Spielberg's *Schindler's List* (1993) thus vividly reconstructs German concentration camps from which a German hero redeems hundreds of Jews — for Lanzmann, the film is an inverted American superhero's "kitschy melodrama" that transgresses or trivializes the Holocaust's sublimity (Lanzmann).[1] In such ways — good or bad — all sorts of catastrophes have been incorporated by Hollywood into the disaster "genre" while visual technology has become ever more advanced in its depiction of terror, ruin, destruction, and the like. On the spectators' side, the cinematic effect of special effects implies the turn of sublimity into something sensible, sensational, splendid, stimulating. A catastrophic event appears as overwhelming but tamable, devastating but agreeable, unexperienced but sharable along cultural norms and forms. Thus, the fear of being threatened by a "sublime" event turns into the desire for being only virtually overwhelmed and thus actually entertained by its "beautiful" representation on the screen, from which a safe distance is kept in order to secure *aesthetic disinterestedness* for visual pleasure. Well protected, spectators consume the aestheticized sublime by enjoying it through all senses. As many Hollywood blockbusters belong to the disaster genre, the sublime on screen might now be the most desired cinematic capital.[2]

This aesthetic distancing from the sublime reduces Kant's supersensible "noumenon" to the sensible "phenomenon" and replaces unfathomable *jouissance* with induced pleasure. The *mathematical sublime* that Kant elicits (in his *Critique of the Power of Judgment*) from "absolutely great" things beyond measurability (131–34) is always fabricated as calculable events or effects and translated in numbers of comparison and competition: This dinosaur is 50 feet tall, cost $1 million to create, etc. The safety in which we see a fearful thing as attractive, however, enables us not simply to enjoy its sensible aspect, but also to experience its power without being really endangered. We, though physically powerless, then find a capacity for resistance, "the courage to measure ourselves against the apparent all-powerfulness of nature," as Kant says. To measure ourselves may mean to acknowledge that our aesthetic *imagination* fails in measuring the sublime, but that we have correspondingly immeasurable *reason*. With noumenal reason we can subjectively think nature as more than sensibly imaginable nature, as "the presentation of something supernatural" in its sublime totality. Sublime objects elevate the strength of our soul above imagination toward reason which ultimately serves as the ground of our "superiority over nature." Thus genuine Kantian sublimity is not in nature but in our mind (144–47). In this case, our free will to resist the sublime outside would be empirically limited but concern the foundational decision to accept the entire given as unavoidable and assume any responsibility for it. Kantian ethics resides then in this fundamental freedom, that is, the *moral* sublime, as opposed to the *natural* sublime. Psychoanalytically speaking, this moral sublime does not serve the pleasure principle to do whatever our inclinations desire without any constraints; rather, as Slavoj Žižek argues, it resembles the Freudian "death drive" to do what we do not want to do, "to thwart the 'spontaneous' realization of an impetus" (Žižek, *The Parallax View* 202). In other words, our free will may be the will to exercise this freedom as the moral law imposed on us so that the given situation is chosen as given by ourselves in spite of ourselves. We could then find room for a redemption that results from our own sublimity in front of the invincible environment.

In this sense, it is possible to think about the sublime in terms of post-catastrophic redemption instead of catastrophe itself. Is Schindler's act sublime? Perhaps, yes, as it can imbue us with "respect," an aspect of the Kantian moral sublime. Is Lanzmann's attitude sublime? Definitely, according to Jean-François Lyotard, who elaborates in *The Postmodern Condition* on "the aesthetic of the sublime" especially through the *avant-garde* art that is in the ethical service of witnessing the unrepresentable (71–82). For Rancière, however, this ethical turn thwarts every promise of political emancipation, reducing aesthetics to "the interminable mourning of irremediable catastrophe" from which "only a god could save us" (129–32).[3] Here, one could argue for or against Rancière's criticism that Lyotard inverts the Kantian autonomy of the moral law into "an ethical subjection to the law of the Other." Again, theologically, this Otherness is rooted in the Jewish God; Kant also takes God's prohibition of the image as the essence of the sublime (Kant 156). Yet I note that Kant's moral sublime may concern a different realm, including our "resistance" to sublime events. This resistance could take the form of apolitical mourning or emancipatory activity or something else, and this diversity would leave room for diversely thinking about *the apocalyptic sublime*. Then, what can widen this room might be less the image of sublimity visualized in the (post)cinematic age than our diegetic experience of a sublime situation, especially on the side of characters' subjectivity. And not limited to medium-specificity, *the (post)cinematic sublime* could also imply a sublime effect that can intervene in spectators' subjectivity through the cinematic experience, a cinematic effect that leads us beyond the screen toward unthought dimensions of the world and our minds. In this context, this essay will take a close look at Richard Kelly's impressive debut feature *Donnie Darko* (2001). But before that, it would be useful to look back briefly on the history of Hollywood disaster film in which to locate the unique place of *Donnie Darko*.

The Ethical Sublime in Hollywood Disaster Film

Hollywood disaster film offers a multitude of case study items in this regard. As a genre, it is not simply about the visualization of catastrophe but deeply about the narrativization of post-catastrophic redemption. From its establishment in the 1970s, the classical structure of "situation-action-situation modified" underlay such foundational films as *Airport*, *The Poseidon Adventure*, and *The Towering Inferno*.[4] A disaster usually occurs at an early point of the storyline, and the rest of the running time is filled with the characters' struggle for rescue, finally followed by the return of the pre-catastrophic situation with wounds, victims, or nightmares lingering over it. Ethical sublimity is often sensible at the turn of this struggle to the dénouement. In *The Poseidon Adventure* (1972), for example, the Nietzschean reverend does not just wait for God's salvation like the chaplain character, but leads a group of "the strong" through the claustrophobic maze of a *Titanic*-evoking wrecked liner until he finally saves people by opening a door to the outside while falling into the fire as he rages against a pitiless God. It is, then, through this act declaring the Death of God, that he paradoxically incarnates Moses' leadership and Jesus' sacrifice at once, a sublime divinity immanent in the impotent human. He embodies the "moral" sublime through the resistance to the "natural" sublime in the Kantian terms mentioned above.

After the 80s campy genre mutation (*Ghostbusters*, *Gremlins*, etc.), the *fin-de-siècle* imagination of the 90s yields various types of cinematic concerns over impending millennial catastrophe.[5] The apocalyptic sublime especially seems to pervade three types of science fiction (SF) narrative. First, the normal post-catastrophic redemption storyline shows how a disaster takes place and is overcome (*Jurassic Park*, *Independence Day*). Second, the main narrative consists of pre-catastrophic efforts to prevent an apocalypse from finally occurring (*Armageddon*, *Dark City*). And, third, techno-dystopian SF films typically use the motif of time travel to transform the post-apocalyptic redemption into pre-apocalyptic prevention (*Terminator 2*, *Twelve Monkeys*). Mixing the first and second types, the third one starts with a post-apocalyptic situation from which a hero is sent back to a pre-apocalyptic time in order to get rid of the cause of the assumed apocalypse, thereby changing the future.[6] Here, for instance, against the "techno" (rather than natural) sublime of Terminators — whose insurmountable power takes on the Kantian *dynamic* sublimity (as distinct from the immeasurable *mathematical* sublimity) — the moral sublime manifests itself when the Terminator-for-humans in 1991's *Terminator 2* (Arnold Schwarzenegger) sacrificially submerges himself in molten metal in order to erase every trace of his cyborg body brought from the dystopian future. A certain divinity exudes out of the machine at this end of the story, as if to literally embody *deus ex machina* in a different sense of the term.

The first decade of the new millennium sees cinematic anxiety about global catastrophe manifest itself in a variety of ways from (in)direct invocations of 9/11 (*United 93*, *Cloverfield*) to imaginations of climate apocalypse (*The Day After Tomorrow, 2012*). A growing number of films update the motif of pre- or post- catastrophic preemptive/redemptive struggle with ever more upgraded technology. Notably, in the backdrop of today's U.S., *Déjà Vu* (Tony Scott, 2006) begins with a terrorist bomb attack in New Orleans which evokes the Oklahoma City Bombing, 9/11, and, geographically, Hurricane Katrina all together. Then, as though these historical disasters could have been averted, an ATF agent travels back four days into the past by means of spacefolding technology to forestall the bombing and the murder of a woman with whom he fell in love only through her images captured on the surveillance "time-warp" screen. Set in the year of 2054, the "Precrime" system in *Minority Report* (Steven Spielberg, 2002) carries to an extreme the mission of pre-catastrophic prevention. If three "Pre-Cogs" (prescient cognitive mediums) report an impending crime visually on their mind-screen, agents rush to the locale and arrest criminals, while in the last-minute rescuing, their victims. In Richard Grusin's terms, catastrophe is "represented" through "premediation," namely the "remediation" of the future.[7] This way media serve as an interface to and remedy for an event that has not yet occurred so that, in theory, we can proactively parry the blows of future trauma (even though Precrime ultimately fails in the film). The proactive premediation thus promotes the pre-catastrophic preemption.

At this point the ethical sublime would deserve a more sophisticated consideration as opposed to the example of heroic self-sacrifice. If sublime freedom lies in our self-determination to accept even an unfavorable and unexpected situation, this can imply that we do not in vain try to avoid it as absurd but rather want to retroactively recognize and accept its cause that has been hidden in the chain of fatal causality. But furthermore, if we decide to avoid a destined situation even though we actually want to accept it, this may also suggest the exercise of "freedom against desire," yet through another type of cognitive activity: This time, if even just in our mind, we try to retroactively insert the possibility of our present act changing the future and the causal chain. In other words, we etymologically change not the actual past but past possibilities, i.e., enlarge its potential by adding a new possibility and now choose it as the determinant cause of our changed future. According to Žižek, this is exactly what happens to the top agent of Precrime (Tom Cruise) in *Minority Report*. Despite the system's prediction that he will kill the murderer of his son, this hero finally blocks his explosive inclination to pull the trigger on a man who turns out to be the murderer. By doing so, he breaks the closed circle of determinism and changes "the true value of modal propositions about the past" (Žižek, *The Parallax View* 202). For Kant, freedom is neither fully determined by preceding causes nor dependent on pure contingency. If this antinomy works on the linear causal chain, it can be resolved only by a reflexive causality: Even though I am determined by causes, natural or motivated, I have the freedom "to retroactively determine which causes will determine me" including those which I can posit in the past. The courage to accept this responsibility underlies ethics (203).

In sum, freedom is not the opposite of any determinism, but a self-determined necessity that is retroactively recognized, constituted, and assumed. "The effect is retroactively the cause of its cause" insomuch as it is a choice that retroactively opens its own possibility in the past (Žižek 204). In this sense freedom would enable an etymological time travel through which to ontologically visit the unthinkable dimension of the past and introduce there an unthought cause of a new future. Do physical time travels, then, depicted in films not literalize this potential change of the temporal loop? Do they not actualize this virtual time travel in order to change the past and thus the future? The cinematic time travel might thus be an intrinsically ethical act. And time travel for a pre-catastrophic prevention might be the utmost ethical act imaginable, if not realistically possible. The ethical sublime, in this case, might not merely reside in a human mind and act, but broadly reverberate around the epistemological activation of ontological noumenon, the retroactive actualization of spatiotemporal potential.

Donnie Darko, *an Indeterminate Text*

Let us here admit that Hollywood films do not always leave room for our contemplation of this radical sublime. Time travel rather appears as a genre cliché in SF settings, which often reduces an ethical act into a superheroic gesture. Suffice it to recall Superman's post-catastrophic redemption, or say, resurrection of his dead girlfriend in the original *Superman* (Richard Donner, 1978); he flies around the earth in its counter-direction so rapidly that it starts to rotate back and thus time is rewound until before the moment of her death. This last-minute rescue achieved through time travel — ridiculously rather than sublimely — only suggests that Superman is a god rather than a man.[8] No genuine human struggle, sacrifice, or freedom would be found in such superhero-disaster films, as spectators already know that they will only enjoy the thrill of predictable post-catastrophic redemption that is predetermined in the genre system. Given this dilemma as grammar, I draw special attention to Richard Kelly's SF-tinted cult film *Donnie Darko* as both a unique symptom and exception to the Hollywood disaster film. Its uniqueness lies, first of all, in the time travel that occurs not along the linear chronology of an actual world as seen in most films, including the aforementioned *Terminator* series, *Twelve Monkeys*, and *Déjà Vu*, but in a virtual world whose twisted temporality is not completely determinate. What follows is an attempt to unfold different possible determinations of this indeterminate text.

The standard interpretation is based on the director's fictional *Philosophy of Time Travel*, the book presented in the film as written by Grandma Death and given to Donnie (extracts from it are included in the film's website, DVD extras, and director's cut). In brief, a Tangent Universe (TU) branches off from the Primary Universe (PU) when a jet engine crashes into Donnie's bedroom while he sleepwalks outside, led by a giant bunny man Frank. But as inherently unstable, the TU will collapse in 28 days and take the PU with it if not corrected. Closing the TU is the duty of the Living Receiver, a weird teenager, Donnie Darko, who can wield such supernatural powers as telekinesis and mind control. At the end of the given 28 days (during which what we see is the TU and not the presumably suspended PU), let's suppose that Donnie uses his telekinesis to detach a jet engine from an airplane into a "time travel portal" created by God, which appears as a tornado wormhole that I will soon describe.[9] Then, at the moment of the engine's fall, he decides to stay in his bedroom and accept death from above in order to keep the PU going on without the intervention of a TU. Put differently, a disaster occurs at the beginning, Donnie is set as the juncture of two universes, and his time-reversing power enables him to prevent the apocalyptic collision of the two worlds at the cost of his life. What seems assumed is that the final destined apocalypse is a one-time event that will end both of the worlds. In this fatalistic chain of time, Donnie "ethically" exercises his "freedom" to retroactively insert a choice of life and death in the past, a choice that however puts him in a double bind of choosing either dying alone in the original PU (in the case of choosing death) or dying with the whole world in the dead end of the TU (in the case of choosing life). That is, he will die either way, but he can save the world in one of the ways. What matters is that he gives himself this preventive choice only after the original disaster by way of getting to know about his power to reverse time, and that this power as such is superheroic while its exertion is sacrificial. Certainly he looks divine from the beginning, as the opening scene shows him waking up on a hill where he has a godlike view of the world. But this hill is also evocative of Gethsemane, as he finally turns out to be more like a self-sacrificing Jesus and not a never-dying Superman. Even if his sacrifice is primarily concerned with returning his girlfriend, killed in the TU, to life in the PU — that is, his motivation still recalls Superman — Donnie is morally sublime whereas Superman is simply visually marvelous.

However, to take a different perspective on Donnie's power makes sense, since it is not certain that he enables the time to reverse by his own free will. On the 28th day, from the top of the hill, he sees a huge tornado because of which a jet engine is about to fall off of an airplane that carries his mother and sister. Cinematically, the airplane appears like an enigmatic spot in the middle of the natural sublime unfolding in a Romantic style extreme long shot, but the next shot shows the engine in close-up, rapidly passing through a supernatural wormhole. These two shots present an epiphanic moment at which the start of temporal reversal is revealed through their spatial juxtaposition, followed by a hyper-accelerated backward montage of events that have happened for the past 28 days. Then, convincingly, the eye-like black hole in the engine, flying within the wormhole, is matched with a skull image residing within an eye, taken from Escher's *vanitas* print hung on the wall of Donnie's room. Just beside this print, Donnie, fully awake, is now sitting on the bed, laughing in resignation. The problem is that, presumably, the same engine is destined to fall at the end of the world, which then is destined to *return* to its starting point and not to face a one-time apocalypse. In other words, the TU is trapped in a negative "eternal return" of the same hellish 28-day-loop with the same traumata, including the death of Donnie's girlfriend, a vicious cycle that will eternally repeat, unless a decisive action is taken by Donnie. He thus has no superheroic power but the dutiful freedom to choose death by realizing that the original juncture of the two worlds occurred through his survival of the crash of the engine, and thus that he can only fix the situation by sacrificing himself. His vandalistic rage against the conservative and repressive society of 1980s America then turns into a higher-level ethical act concerning the entire universe. In short, anti-heroic Donnie's post-apocalyptic adventure ends up becoming a pre-apocalyptic self-sacrifice to get the world back on the right track and out of the Möbius time-strip that perpetually recycles a periodic catastrophe.

At this point, the film's inadvertent connections to 9/11 merit attention. It is not only the jet engine's terrorist attack that evokes the airplanes that crashed into the World Trade Center, but also the film's temporal setting; Bush Senior's 1988 presidential race resonates with the Bush Junior's presidency upon the film's release just after 9/11.[10] In light of the above, it would not be odd at all to see Donnie's retroactive prevention of the apocalypse as embodying America's post-catastrophic "yearning to turn back the clock on tragic events" (Stuart). And if we combine the two former interpretations, Donnie could be viewed as having both the power to change the world and the duty to save the world just like the U.S. Likewise, our "respect" for America, just like Donnie's moral sublimity, would come out if the U.S. used its superpower for its high duty. But in the years following 9/11, the United States lost international respect due to the vicious cycle of terror and war which deprived the post-catastrophic world of redemption. More specifically, this circulation of retaliation was initiated by somebody who stood for America's power but did not take moral responsibility for its duty. So allow me to suggest a playful allegory: Who should have sacrificed himself, like Donnie, at the moment of 9/11 to save the world if not George W. Bush? In other words, is Donnie not the virtual verso of the actual G.W. Bush? We see in him a sort of para-practical redemption, that is, a post-catastrophic fictive reversal of the U.S. President's failure to learn the nature of his power, as well as an unintended cinematic critique of the president's actions.

Free Will as Love of Fate

One might cast doubt on this reading of Donnie's death as an act of poetic justice, that is, of saving the right world through his sacrifice. In fact, his goal is to overcome the dichotomous moral choice of "love" against "fear," the doctrine of the Christian fundamentalist right embodied by suspicious New Ageist Jim Cunningham and the authorities of Donnie's school. Against this simplistic morality that neglects life's complexity, Donnie denounces Cunningham as an "Antichrist," whose house later turns out to hide "a kiddie porn dungeon." Compared to this false Messiah, Donnie appears to be a true one who, however, also faces a truly existential choice — life versus death, or, on an epic scale, the death of the world versus the death of his girlfriend — like Jesus in *The Last Temptation of Christ* (Martin Scorsese, 1988) which is briefly noted in the film.[11] But on the other hand, just as this alternative story of Jesus' individual happiness does not change the actual history of Christianity, so Donnie's death does not really prove to be an effective sacrifice for a better world because it only closes the TU and that has no impact on the PU where, for instance, Cunningham's dungeon may remain undiscovered by the police. Instead of a religious reading, then, Peter Mathews draws on Leibniz to argue that although our world is the best of all possible worlds, multiple worlds remain equally possible before epistemological confirmation; the moral lesson is less important than Donnie's doubt of religion and the motifs of the unknowable. Despite the given ending, we can keep both the PU (where he is dead) and the TU (where he is alive) as dual existences in mind, without making a moral judgment.[12] Eternally suspended between two worlds, "Donnie is both dead and alive, trapped inside a cinematic box that cannot be opened" (Mathews 47). Moreover, according to modern scientific research into entropy, every event has an unpredictable ripple effect, a set of contingencies that can change the meaning of an action, just as a red car Donnie passes by in the beginning of the film turns out to be Frank's car which kills Gretchen in the end, but this is true only when we recognize it retrospectively. "There are no direct causes, only side-effects: reality is made up of contingencies that project us through our possible lives, and to think otherwise would leave us with the same sense of illusion experience by Spinoza's stone"— the stone that thinks it is flying freely because of its own desire, not aware of its cause (47).

This idea needs some nuanced clarification in terms of free will. According to Cunningham's morality, free will awards sovereignty to the individual, who must then use it to create happiness; so if you are not happy, it is your fault and you are guilty. Free will is actually predestined to institutionalized ethical inertia. But regarding Donnie's question about whether one could see into the future through a set path of all time predecided by God, his science teacher answers that if destiny were visibly manifested, the choice to act differently would be available, putting an end to all preformed destiny. This suggests that the TU is to be repeated unless Donnie's suicidal determination succeeds. His own ethical time traveling is, in this sense, nothing other than "repeating" the past moment of the engine terror "differently," breaking the dead closed circuit of the world that repeats the same past over again. Then a new concept of repetition is differentiated: repetition in and of difference. This is proper to the aforementioned notion of freedom as a self-determined necessity, and furthermore, of life as *autopoeisis*, that is, a self-organizing system in which the current self can be viewed not as merely resulting from past causes but as retroactively positing its own causes. It is thus not simply determined by contingent conditions but self-reflexively determines this determination itself. Life "posits its presuppositions" in this infinite feedback loop, thereby repeating itself with different outcomes at every moment (Žižek, *The Parallax View* 205).[13]

I elaborate on this because the moment of retroactive self-determination seems to enable a *positive* "eternal return," in Nietzsche's proper sense of the term. It is indeed not a repetition for sameness, but a repetition for difference, an insertion of the possibility of difference back in the past for a different future regardless of its result being positive or negative. What returns is not a positive or negative content, but the same empty form of difference in itself that yields a different content. Nietzsche's *amor fati* says: "Accept fate as inevitable, and you will break its grasp on you" (Žižek 207). This turn of the "eternal return" from negative to positive depends on our epistemological reconfiguration of sublime fate as the precondition of ethical freedom against it. Unlike Spinoza's stone, our free will is neither free from fate, nor free from knowledge of fate; it is rather willing to make fate itself free only by consciously (re)embodying it. One may, of course, doubt the positivity of a return that requires Donnie's death. But his *amor fati* is all the more sublime because the positive return of a new life is given to the entire world instead. The world will now live a second time, which lets us sense a more ontological dimension of the world than would be apparent in an individual's poetic justice or moral sacrifice.

"Time is out of joint"

For this reason, it would be possible to take the perspective of the world itself rather than the subject. That is, the TU as such could repeat the PU differently and positively after the decisive moment of a "Time

[that] is out of joint." Hamlet utters this line after encountering his father's ghost, a shocking supernatural event that alters the way he perceives the world and the state, which he now needs to fix. Jacques Derrida also argues that a radical singular event only occurs when time is "out of joint" (10–24). Gilles Deleuze affirms that when a "caesura" occurs "once and for all," time is "unhinged" from its circular, periodic movement and experienced only as a pure empty form of change, marking the before and after of the crack, becoming no longer cardinal but ordinal — the second, third, fourth. Time always repeats itself as "difference in itself" (Deleuze 119–23). In other words, time-in-itself is the pure condition of difference; it eternally returns not with the same trauma or something, but with the differential event of "time-being-out-of-joint." In light of this eternal return, Frank's first appearance to Donnie in the dark would look like that of a ghost-father figure. And the "animal" form of this big Other might resonate with the surreal jet engine, a "mechanical" Thing, in terms of ontological otherness that interrupts the human world. Back home after the catastrophic night, Donnie faces the uncanny face or dark eye of that Thing, the "mysterious object at noon" which sucks in our vision as the camera zooms in. Just like Alice's trip "down the rabbit-hole," this image marks the starting point of Donnie's adventure in the TU.

What happens, then, in the second return of the world? The TU begins by revealing the many negative aspects of the affluent, leafy American suburbia within which Donnie lives. His community is primarily white and middle-class, with large houses and spacious lawns, private expensive schools, and so on. The fallen jet engine cracks open this wealthy and peaceful community, while literally tearing apart a big U.S. flag hung on the ceiling of Donnie's room. Doesn't this moment remind us of Žižek's book title and ironic greeting framed by 9/11? "Welcome to the desert of the Real!" For the unprecedented attack on American soil revealed the unthought "Real" of sublime antagonism to the imaginary and symbolic construction of what the American people had believed as their well-protected "reality." Of course, the terroristic engine is purely accidental and not political at all, but it works like a violent *objet a* protruding out of the Lacanian Real, or say, the Deleuzian Virtual, the potential realm immanent in the Actual reality (see Deleuze). Notably, Frank is also the name of Frank's father, who is a cursed and dead alumnus of Donnie's parents; Frank junior leads Donnie to engaging in arson and vandalism, thereby making him into a sort of terrorist. The Frank family may thus stand for an uncanny and undead exception of the society repeatedly ruled by the

Bush family at the national level. This socially "abject" figure is cut off from society but roaming around it like a specter that makes social reality inconsistent and liberates what is repressed in reality. And Donnie, as a sort of postmortem figure (his first encounter with Frank and the following sleep could be taken as his symbolic death), becomes a social abject whose resistance to society, sympathy for the other, and horror for apocalypse all mingle and ultimately open another time-world by his second, real death.

The point is Donnie's embodiment of the Real between these two deaths. He debunks political conservatism, moral impasse, educational repression, sexual ambivalence, and so on, often revealing how normal reality is perversely constituted. For example, Cunningham's religious morality inevitably needs and hides a self-contradictory repression that is resolved through his addiction to child porn; while at the same time, we might see this sexual crime as a specific form of the pervasive immanent sexualization of children (contrast the gaudy Sparkle Motion dancers show, which is culturally affirmed, to the fat Chinese girl's white angel dance). Likewise, when Dukakis and Bush debate on Panama's drug crimes and its American connection, Donnie's family members quarrel about their own drug addiction. Individual or collective, the dependence on drugs is everywhere, publicly problematic but privately permissible. In short, the white middle-class Americans at the end of the Reagan age appear like an updated version of "the Last Men" in Nietzsche's terms. Standing for First World passive nihilism, these postmodern individuals are immersed in ever more refined and artificially aroused daily pleasures like drugs, food, and sex. Permissive hedonism allows everything trivial but not an excessive core that can threaten their sound conservative morality. On the contrary, Third World active nihilism is found among fundamentalists who risk self-sacrifice for an alleged universal sublime Cause, just like terrorists attacking the First World (see Žižek, "The Clash of Civilizations at the End of History"). Though not from the Third World, Donnie plays the role of a potential terrorist immanent in his society—not a complete outsider of the First World so much as a subversive insider. But let's be careful: The question is not how to judge or justify his violence, but how to read symptoms of the Real in a new time of reality.

In short, Donnie Darko inspires us to face terror differently. Terror is not simply a sublime disaster against which a society unites its different conflicting members. If this post-catastrophic redemption served the traditional social function of terror, it would work as a trigger to explode repressed social desires and traumas so that we can better look back on the pre-catastrophic situation and get it back from a different perspective. Therefore, time-being-out-of-joint is not a state to be fixed, but a radical singular event through which immanent but unrepresented social symptoms of the Real erupt onto reality. Donnie's death may be a sort of narrative compromise to tame the further chaotic eruption of the Real. In the restored PU, Cunningham is alive and Bush will be elected in the History that we know. But what matters much more is the TU itself as a liberated time.

Apocalypse, Atopia

I conclude, nevertheless, by drawing attention back to Donnie, as his subjectivity would be the matrix of the ethical sublime against the apocalyptic sublime in the end. As a matter of fact, he is not a mature hero and his terrorism does not open a realistic exit from reality. One could even see the film as having been dreamt by Donnie in the hours immediately preceding the crash of the jet engine. The moving song heard at the moment of Donnie's death, Tears for Fears' "Mad World," includes the following line, "dreams in which I'm dying." Resonating with this case, narrative events in Hollywood movies often turn out to have been either dreamt by a dead hero or to occupy some ambiguous hallucinatory dimension in such films as *Jacob's Ladder* (1990), *The Sixth Sense* (1999), *The Others* (2001), *Vanilla Sky* (2001), and *The Butterfly Effect* (2004) (King 58–59). Thomas Elsaesser suggests that all such "mind-game" films, including *Donnie Darko*, foreground two narratives options: In the first a character or the audience is toyed with; in the second, the mental condition of the central character(s) is extreme, unstable, or pathological ("The Mind-Game Film"). We can toy with Donnie, who cannot fight threatening forces of the world, so he might instead dream of the Virtual as Real where he can more easily debunk and destroy the world. Like narcolepsy in *My Own Private Idaho* (Gus Van Sant, 1991), a radical daydreaming occupies Donnie's mind in this way. *Donnie Darko* could then be a high teen genre film in which a boy with a Peter Pan Syndrome takes or avoids the coming-of-age narrative with critical self-consciousness. Conversely, Donnie the Nietzschean Last Man's idealistic resistance to the world is entrapped in a double bind where neither growing (accepting norms) nor not growing (ignoring them) would be the answer.

The implication is that Donnie is not a predetermined Messiah, but an indeterminate mind that continues to determine itself and thus changes predeterminations. Put in another way, he may be a postmodern subject who composes himself through the experience and embodiment of floating signs whose meanings are indeterminate and contingent. Grandma Death is waiting for God's letter (death?), and Donnie sends her a letter. Gretchen is a mysterious stranger who appears on the day of the engine terror by chance, another *objet a* on the side of love as opposed to Frank's death. Donnie's English teacher says that "cellardoor" is the most beautiful compound word, a word which sounds like a beautiful interface surfacing onto the Real, often in the form of daydream. At the end of this adventure, Donnie, the postmortem subject, dies again. His death, however, is not a return to reality but an opening to another unknown time, even if it could be cyclical. This is the only ethically sublime way of allowing "atopia," if not utopia, to be cinematically imagined in the apocalyptic closed circuit: a-topia that is not a *topos* (place), but the non-placed movement to a different time itself, the self-displacement of the world without anchorage. We do not know where the world will go after Donnie's death, but we know that the world is not the same any more, in light of one person's absence. This tiny change offers no place; it offers, instead, a post-apocalyptic atopian time that we live in and from which we retroactively think over the apocalypse past.

Notes

1. Notably, Lanzmann's critique of *Schindler's List* recalls Serge Daney's similar well-known critique of *Kapo* (Gillo Pontecorvo, 1960). Daney finds the "pretty tracking shot" of a Jew's electrocution on the fence of a concentration camp in this Academy-nominated film to be "immoral," because the spectator has to be "aesthetically seduced" where it is only a "matter of conscience" of being a human (Daney 34–35). Ethics beyond aesthetics is lucidly presumed here.

2. Similarly, techno-apocalyptic films such as *Terminator* and *Jurassic Park* have anathematized emerging technologies and the human hubris of becoming the creator of machines or lives, yet this technophobia has been depicted ever more graphically through the never-ending advancement of visual technology (see Arthur). Hollywood always capitalizes on public fears of imminent catastrophe by turning them into public pleasures.

3. Yesterday's genocide returns as the never-ending catastrophe of the present as if it were an immemorial trauma. A decisive moment that cuts a time into two is then no longer a revolution to come (as in the modernist aesthetics and politics which Rancière hopes to reinstate), but the radical event that is already past but still present in a "theology of time"; once glorious, now disastrous, the time of today's art is suspended between the primordial trauma and a salvation to come.

4. In fact the disaster film has a long history, as the first *Titanic* film traces back

to 1913 and the original *King Kong* to 1933. More broadly, diverse types of catastrophic events have enriched cinematic imagination and documentation from the birth of the cinema. But it is in the 1970s that Hollywood set up the specific genre of the disaster film as a marketing category through technological advancement for the global cultural and commercial arena (see Keane).

   5. Even non-disaster films reflect this tendency, as David Fincher's *Fight Club* ends with the total, sudden collapse of buildings, of the neurotic postmodern consumer society (Arthur).

   6. The *Terminator* series (the original was made in 1984) is actually more complex: A hero on the side of humans is sent back to the past to prevent a terminator on the side of machines from killing the future leader of humans. That is, the time travel is done not to defuse the apocalypse of nuclear warfare itself (which is presumed from the beginning and even not represented), but to maintain the post-apocalyptic situation (in which the humans' fight against the machine is presumed to continue).

   7. Grusin's original idea on premediation is that since 9/11, U.S. media have attempted to prevent the immediacy of such a traumatic shock by replaying images of past disasters and anticipating future scenarios of potential ones. As a result any catastrophe "would always already have been premediated" so that one can be less terrified and better prepared even if it really occurs (8–16). I add that digital technology has ever more perfectly simulated such potential terror to the extent of leaving nothing unrepresentable and unpredictable, with the (side) effects of oversaturation and trivialization of sublime audiovisual stimuli as mentioned above.

   8. Even Spider-Man, perhaps the most recent and humanized superhero, always suddenly appears like a *deus ex machina* for the last-minute rescue of endangered people, especially, from their fall out of Manhattan's skyscrapers — a post-catastrophic cinematic compensation for the failed rescue of victims fallen from the World Trade Center on 9/11.

   9. He learns that time warps when a "vessel" passes through a "portal" at light speed. The engine serves as a vessel while a wormhole acts as a portal.

   10. The exact release date was October 26, 2001, so the film was "perfectly attuned to the present moment" and "weirdly consoling" (Hoberman).

   11. James Walters regards the temptation part of the Scorsese film, Jesus' illusion of a normal married life, as unfolding in a potential world like Donnie's TU (Walters). This possibility denoted as virtual is, however, a literal what-if dream sequence, without time travel impinging upon the logic of the actual world. Similarly, a flashback leading back to an earlier point of the actual world is not time travel.

   12. Donnie's attitude toward God is ambiguous. Hypnotized, he obeys Frank's orders without knowing his (or God's) "master plan." He does not answer the question: "Do you believe in God?" and he says, "the search for God is absurd if everyone dies alone"— he dies alone. Geoff King argues that he may be not an atheist, but an "agnostic," who believes that there can be no proof of the existence of God but does not deny its possibility (90–91). This uncertainty leads him to science and philosophy.

   13. As Žižek interprets it à la Hegel, Francisco Varela's biological notion of the "emergent self" implies that the Self is not an entity but nothing but the process of perpetual autopoeisis itself (see Brockman 212). This view, shared by other scientists, is common in contemporary brain science and systems theory.

History Is Always Virgin: Quentin Tarantino's *Inglourious Basterds* and the Lyotardian Sublime

Marco Grosoli

Quentin Tarantino's first feature film (*Reservoir Dogs*, 1992) starts with an exegesis of Madonna's "Like a Virgin." According to Mr. Brown (Quentin Tarantino himself), that song is about a girl obsessed with sex who, while making love to a particularly well-endowed partner, realizes that the pleasure she now feels is so intense that it *hurts*. Her umpteenth time is then like the first time: She is precisely *like a virgin*, although she is very far from being one.

Perhaps we should push this exegesis a little further, in a way that will prove useful also as far as Tarantino's universe itself is concerned. Madonna's song is about the Kantian notion of the sublime—an intolerably overwhelming experience for human consciousness as it makes pain inextricable from pleasure (Lyotard, *Lessons on the Analytic of the Sublime* 8–15); any possible temporal distinction (such as that between the first and the last time) falls apart in front of this unbearable excess (141–146): Consequently, the Kantian sublime cannot let itself be bridled and regulated by (Western) dialectical reasoning, which relies first of all on a "disciplining" of time.

The Kantian sublime, the irredeemable excess of representation, is resumed and reworked in several phases (perhaps *every* phase) of Jean-François Lyotard's philosophy. The Jews, in particular, occupy a special place in his works in that they are considered to be the proper epitome of the Kantian sublime: They are those who irretrievably escape the striving for totalization characterizing Western civilization.

More tangentially, the sublime lies also at the core of the essay Lyotard dedicated to cinema. "Acinema" quite firmly distinguished standard narrative cinema from more experimental attempts. The former (169–176) is essentially a kind of (Capitalist) *economy*. It teases the spectator with delightful, aberrant, irregular movements, only to then synthesize them in the form of a unified image that the viewer can consume for his or her own sake. In so doing, this cinema mirrors more broadly the efforts by the dialectic to make all differences into a unified representation. Tarantino's cinema is a particularly relevant example of this as it makes way for countless textual fractures (sudden outbursts of violence, lengthy pointless dialogues, digressions of any kind) only to leave untouched the easily recognizable narrative frames that the films fit in. *Jackie Brown* (1997), for instance, as a classic-noir-cum-blaxploitation movie is left *perfectly untouched*. Every excess is thoroughly re-integrated in the larger picture. To put it metaphorically, the undaunted Bride of the two volumes of *Kill Bill* (2003, 2004) is always/already determined by Bill, who prepares the path she blindly ends up following. Innumerable exceptions *distort* the narrative norm all the time while never breaking it.

Inglourious Basterds (2009), the film this paper will concentrate on, is no exception. Most scenes indulge in gratuitous redundancies: Even ordinary dialogue sequences are inherently troubled by a swollen, mannerist kind of stylistic amplification. Arguably, any other director would have shot the dialogue in which Shoshanna Dreyfuss tells her black assistant that *Nation's Pride* is to be premiered in their theater according to a regular shot-and-countershot strategy. Tarantino makes it a veritable choreography of movements, in which each frame subtly diverges from the shot-and-countershot confrontational scheme that it is supposed to serve. Nonetheless, the frontal opposition between the two characters (the basic structure of shot-and-countershot) is kept. Tarantino's cinema only "excavates" its limits while never threatening them; it diverges from representation without out really parting company with it. It is a patent excess of textual (and "cinephiliac") *jouissance*. Nazi Jew hunter Landa, a man of exquisite manners and a highly refined rhetorical ability who visibly (almost physically) bursts with excessive enjoyment, perfectly embodies this dynamic.

However, in the final part of his essay (176–180) Lyotard theorizes an actual way for this energetic excess (that ultimately *feeds* the film experience) to elude the economic management granted by narrative procedures.

As such, only this excess is properly of a "sublime" kind, for it breaks that balance between the excess and the norm "standard" cinema is based on. Some experimental and *avant-garde* works can engage in a veritable revolt of the *film support* (the *pellicule*) against the tendency to gather perceptions and feelings around a unified frame. This is exactly what occurs in the climax sequence of *Inglourious Basterds*. An international commando unit manages to exterminate the whole of the Nazi elite, including Hitler, by causing an explosion inside the film theater. The Nazis, visibly enjoying the jolts of the violent movements onscreen unified by the myth of their own superiority (the imaginary motion picture *Nation's Pride*, on which they joyfully mirror themselves by identifying with the German hero who annihilates hundreds of enemies), are defeated by the burning of tons of inflammable film, an explosion organized by Shoshanna, a young Jew.

Yet, this revolt of the *pellicule* is very far from what Lyotard meant. While the French philosopher implied that the support of the actual film projected should oppose its own existence as an unproblematic site for the projection of a self-complacent illusion, in Tarantino the *pellicule* rebellion is strictly and exclusively narratival. It is only a part of the story being told. Unlike what occurs in Ingmar Bergman's 1966 *Persona* (Comolli 20) or in Monte Hellman's 1971 *Two Lane Blacktop* (Bonitzer 68), the material support of *Inglourious Basterds* is left untouched. It does not melt, nor does it break or destroy itself. Any extreme form of excess has been reintegrated inside the narrative machine.

This paper will try to reconstruct the reasons behind this moving away from the Kantian and Lyotardian sublime, and to identify what this implies at the broader level of the film's significance with regard to the contemporary socio-political situation: namely, the "biopolitical" vicious circles between "State" rule and "terrorist" exception, between subjectification and de-subjectification.

After (?) Auschwitz

> It seems to me, to be brief, that "the jews" are within the "spirit" of the Occident that is so preoccupied with foundational thinking, what resists this spirit; within its will, the will to want, what gets in the way of this will; within its accomplishments, projects, and progress, what never ceases to reopen the wound of the unaccomplished. "The jews" are the irremissible in the West's movement of remission and pardon.

They are what cannot be domesticated in the obsession to dominate, in the compulsion to control domain, in the passion for empire, recurrent ever since Hellenistic Greece and Christian Rome. "The jews," never at home wherever they are, cannot be integrated, converted, or expelled [Lyotard, *Heidegger and the Jews* 22].

For Lyotard, the Jews are the epitome of the Kantian aesthetic sublime (31–32 and 37). They are the ultimate exception because they escape even the dialectical short-circuit between the rule and its exception. Theodor Adorno's legacy is here clearly discernible. His (and Horkheimer's) *Dialectic of Enlightenment* ended by similarly making the figure of the Jew a universal symbol of resistance (168–207), to the Nazi, or, today, the capitalistic. Indeed, according to Adorno and Horkheimer, the hegemony of techno-scientific capitalism (which is the ultimate outcome of the Enlightenment) does not at all break with the Nazi irrationality of myths of identity. There is a secret continuity between these two apparently opposed stances, since both Nazism and capitalism are essentially attempts to make up an artificial totality. Against this totalitarian tendency, one has to emphasize the exception, difference. Ultimately, Lyotard agrees with Adorno's stance that "this murder committed against the Other, of which thought and writing are in quest, this annihilation, has not happened once, sometime ago, at 'Auschwitz,' but, by other means, apparently totally other, it is happening now in the 'administered world,' in 'late capitalism,' the technoscientific system, whatever name one gives to the world in which we live, in which we survive" (*Heidegger and the Jews* 44).

In our film, in the dialogue introducing the British film critic/lieutenant, Goebbels is said to "beat the Jews in their own game"—that is, he wants to build up a grand movie studio exceeding even Hollywood, back then employing several Jewish directors and producers. The film critic then traces an explicit homology between Goebbels and David O. Selznick. This means that, although indirectly, the extermination of the exception and the normalization of it through the powerful machine of spectacle (in image-dominated late capitalism) is seen as something related by a mutual and fundamental continuity. Later, the same British lieutenant, while pretending to be a German, is rescued from being unmasked by his accent by lying that he is from Piz Palu, in the Alps, and he once was an extra in the film of the same name. The image is then the ultimate form of integration of the difference, of what sticks out of the norm. Elsewhere in the film, Goebbels himself complains that by now a movie star is more powerful than he is. In other words, a postmodernist "society of the spectacle" reduces the whole world to the world's image (Shoshanna to Fredrick Zoller: "So you are both the nation['s] pride and the star of *Nation's Pride* [the film]?"), and in so doing continues the totalizing strive attempted by Nazis by other means. It is for this reason that Landa manages to escape the explosion in the theater. Landa perfectly corresponds to Adorno's and Horkheimer's definition of anti-Semite: someone who *needs* Jews (in the first minutes of the film, he *can* shoot at Shoshanna and kill her, but mysteriously *does not*), and who ends up necessarily and grotesquely embodying most Jewish clichés (obsessed with money, relying more on the manipulative subtlety of language than on action, suspiciously polyglot, very able to change his identity, endowed with a shifty, diabolical intelligence and a perverted sense of humor, and so on). "There is no anti-Semite who does not basically want to imitate his mental image of a Jew, which is composed of mimetic cyphers" (Adorno and Horkheimer 184). Landa, himself admits: "I can think like a Jew." Furthermore, Landa's speech about "the Jews as rats" follows almost literally the definition of anti-Semitism given by Adorno and Horkheimer (170–172): something repulsive regardless of any actual feature it may possess. After the end of war, Landa is ready to lead a comfortable life as a capitalist millionaire on Nantucket Island. So despite the evident discontinuity between Nazism and late capitalism, there is an umbilical cord linking them, as symbolized by Landa, the Jew hunter, the exterminator of differences, and pursuer of totality.

Lyotard diverges from Adorno in individuating what this "Jewish" resistance against totality should be. He reproaches (*Heidegger and the Jews* 44–45) the German theorist for maintaining an idea of the sublime which is not only aesthetic, but also distinctly *artistic*. In other words, by affirming that only highbrow art can contrast the almighty barbarism of an all-unifying capital, Adorno remains too modern, too attached to the idea that the unrepresentable does have a *form* it can be presented by ("An Answer to the Question" 14–15). Interestingly, Lyotard once described this idea of overcoming the Adornian specificity of art in terms of destroying the walls, entrances, and exits of a theater ("Adorno as the Devil" 128)—which is exactly what occurs in the penultimate sequence of *Inglourious Basterds* as the *pellicule* burns. The burning *jouissance* of the sublime experience is no longer contained in a walled-off artistic experience but is literally everywhere, just like Shoshanna's laughs are no more projected on a screen but are visible in real space, thanks to the dust in the air upon which her face is projected. Late capitalism spreads the exceptions everywhere only to better unify them through the unifying power of capital. Looking for an exception exclusively in the artistic domain thus misses the point, because exceptions have now become the rule of the late capitalist game as a whole, the rule of the globalized market and of all that revolves around it. Postmodern art should then open up the irretrievable difference *beyond taste*[1] as well as against totality, that is, beyond the separateness of form ("The Sublime and the Avant-Garde" 42–43). In other words, it should open up the difference between postmodernism as all-encompassing totality (thanks to the omnipotence of capital) and postmodernism as the ascertainment of the fact that there always remains some kind of difference. The unpresentable is not to be presented specifically by art anymore: it just "happens" (41),[2] outside as well as inside the aesthetic domain. With capitalism the exception has won (Shoshanna's "Jewish vengeance" has succeeded in exterminating the exterminators) at the same time that the exception has been successfully exterminated (Shoshanna herself dies), because the exception has become the new all-encompassing rule regulated by capital—and the moment it becomes the rule, the exception cannot help but stop being itself. One must then break this new rule and restore ("Jewish") difference again.

One clear example of this is *Inglourious Basterds'* finale. Landa is painfully marked with a swastika on his forehead. On the one hand, this mark witnesses the continuity between Nazism and capitalism, on the basis of a common aspiration to totality. Now, even after the war, everyone seeing Landa will know that he is not only a capitalist, but also a Nazi. On the other hand, this mark indicates the difference between something and the place it occupies, that is, its place of inscription within the symbolic texture. Such a difference (which is exactly what the Kantian sublime is about) is the matter of art, with Malevich's *Black Square* being its ultimate case: the minimal difference between something and its own place, a black square on another square (in such a case, the difference between the two could evidently not be "more minimal," while still persisting). In this respect, scarified Landa is a "symbol of Nazism on a Nazi," again the pure difference between something (a Nazi) and the place it occupies within the symbolic texture (the swastika marking him as Nazi). Unlike the *Black Square* though, Landa does not belong to the separated domain of art: He fully belongs to the world (albeit the fictionalized world of the film). Difference is thus reconquered *beyond* art—that is, after the separated place for the sublime, namely art (in *Inglourious Basterds*: the movie theater), has exploded.

In order to better grasp what is at stake in this final scene, however, it is necessary to refer to the end of the film's second chapter. Lieutenant Aldo Raine is interrogating a German officer about some important strategic information. The latter refuses to collaborate. Then a certain Donny Donowitz steps in and kills the prisoner with a bat.[3] A second (terrified) prisoner talks immediately, but before he is released he gets a swastika-shaped scar on his forehead. Unlike in the final scene, this time we do not see the scarification. It is hidden by an ellipsis, and only suggested. In both scenes, there is a subjective shot through which the viewer shares the POV of the disfigured. In this way, Tarantino *marks* the spectator as Nazi. Between the first, only-alluded to, and the second, actually-shown, scarification, what we see is almost the entire film. All of this is buttressed by the fact that the first scarred German soldier talks precisely because he has been a spectator, having witnessed the brutal killing of his non-talking comrade, and by Raine's comment that Donowitz's ritual executions are "the closest we get to going to the movies." In the final scene, the camera shows the scarification from *very* close, and the following (and final) shot is the subjective shot: The film, thereby, as a whole makes the viewer face his or her own enjoyment of "cinematic excesses" of any kind (such as the pleasure of seeing Nazis crudely beaten and of pro-filmic violence in general, of enjoying a flamboyant style and so on) up to the point of repulsion (the disgusting final scarification from very close). By this rejection caused by over-proximity, he or she feels guilty for participating in the capitalist game of "narratively regulated enjoyment as consumerism." So the spectator is split from within, between his or her own enjoyment and the guilt for having submitted to enjoyment's inevitably "totalitarian" reintegration. In other words, the viewer is confronted with the fact that he or she is virtually one of the Nazis in the burnt theater. This split is Tarantino's answer to Lyotard's "acinema." There is no need to give up narrative closure by making the *pellicule* revolt in order to turn the viewer-friendly equilibrium of the spectacle upside down, because *narrative closure as such* relies precisely on its own being upside down. Lyotard's "acinema" is a plea to pervert the regulated economy of the viewer's pleasure. Nothing though is more perverted than the very ordinary pleasure the viewer gets from the achievement of narrative closure, since this closure is inherently contradictory; it is enhanced by the disavowed pleasure it claims to deny. Nothing is more unregulated than this very regulation. Lyotard's "acinema" is a plea for subversive deformity, but nothing is more monstrous than this closure achieved by denying its own premises (Nazism defeated — and, implicitly, democracy established — by Nazi means). What Tarantino does is to openly show this monstrosity, by showing narrative closure *as well as* the cinematic excess it is based on, by patently displaying the enjoyment which is supposed to stay back and concealed for narrative closure to run properly.

History and the Immemorial

In order to fully seize what this "moving away from Lyotard" on the part of Tarantino is about, one should consider another difference between Adorno and the French philosopher. Adorno famously claimed that Auschwitz is the unthinkable negativity that dialectical reason cannot ever turn into positive. Lyotard basically reproaches the German thinker for having "used" Auschwitz this way in order to *restore* speculative reason, against the patent necessity to overcome the dialectic once and for all. Such an overcoming was, in principle, what Adorno aimed at with his "negative dialectic"; according to Lyotard, though, "negative dialectic" is but a dialectical trick in order to restore speculative reason while pretending to get away from it. Adorno's incoherence lies in his extracting a positive *result* from this supposedly irredeemable negativity, just like a standard affirmative dialectic would. So Lyotard (*The Differend* 86–106) carefully dismantles the "word game" at the core of speculative reason, consisting primarily of the fact that an artificial *we* is created out of the Auschwitz situation: The exterminators and the victims have been improperly made common (that is, they inhabit the same "phrase"), whereas there can be no common ground between them; they remain incommensurable, unlike, for instance, the Hegelian reversibility between Master and Slave. The only *we* that can result from Auschwitz can be a non-speculative one, and it is basically an old acquaintance of post-phenomenological philosophy (suffice it to mention Jean-Luc Nancy's "inoperative community"): "this true *we* is never *we*, never stabilized in a name for *we*, always undone before being constituted, only identified in the non-identity between *you*—the unnameable one, who requests — and *me*, the hostage" ("Discussions" 377; original's emphasis). In other words, "a *we* can perhaps identify itself on the basis of this non-identification: a community of addressees alert to the 'marvel'" (376). The only possible identity for a *we* "after Auschwitz" (as a form of community freed from Nazism's coercive myths of purity) is the incommensurability of the respective identities forming it.

Inglourious Basterds opposes this need of a non-speculative *we* by means of a speculative non-result. We do have a community made of members incommensurable to each other; the only thing that connects the Jewish Shoshanna, her black assistant, the British former film critic, the German spy, the American lieutenant is a negative connection, their aversion to Nazism, the void, and an intransitive incompatibility to any obsessive striving for purity and identity without difference. Yet this *we* is not the result of Auschwitz, but its solution. In the film, it is this community without a stable identity that defeats Nazism. So if, according to Lyotard, "speculative dialectics get stuck in the genre of mythic narrative" (*The Differend* 106), here the mythic narrative *par excellence* (Nazism) is defeated by another mythic narrative, glorifying an international commando unit that fights Nazism on the latter's own ground (as it annihilates Nazi elites by locking them in a sort of theatrical concentration camp) rather than being the historical result of that fight. This makes such an opposition definitely more speculative than not, since there are two opposed poles fighting each other. The "non-speculative" *we* is then made back into narrative (an organized deployment of conflicts), and into the speculative (a way to conceive the oppositions based on a hidden and underlying common ground between the opposed terms) again, but only at the expenses of the other larger narrative called History (because, of course, History tells us that Hitler, Goebbels, and the others were *not* killed in a Parisian cinema). Once again we have a narrative reintegration and another counter-movement that goes against narrative integration, although in a different and properly historical sense.

This attitude towards History is, to some extent, close to Lyotard's but only to some extent. Lyotard has often pointed out that the violation of historical truth is justifiable, when commanded by the need to stick to a greater truth concerning what History structurally forgets (*Heidegger and the Jews* 9–17)—such as, of course, the "Jewish reverse-side" of it. *Inglourious Basterds* is indisputably self-aware about this. At the beginning of the long tavern sequence, culminating in a massacre, some characters play the game of guessing the name written on a card stamped on his/her own forehead, by asking yes/no questions to the others. One of them has "King Kong" on his card. So he starts asking questions like "am I American?," "do I come from the jungle?," "was I brought to America in chains on a ship?" The questions are more and more obvious, indicating that he has clearly already guessed correctly, though he continues asking. He ultimately claims, "then I must be King Kong!" But only after the following question is answered in the negative, "am I the history of America's black slaves?" So here is a film (*King Kong*) and its obvious historical subtext, and the former manifests the latter only by discarding and transfiguring historical truth, only through a fictional idealization. The two levels, History and its fictionally-represented meaning, are connected through their very disconnection.

Such a view of History owes a lot to Freud's conception of the *immemorial*, the timeless dimension consciousness cannot access, and which is accessible only through repetition: "[T]he kind of history that does not forget that forgetting is not a breakdown of memory but the immemorial always 'present' but never here-now, always torn apart in the time of consciousness, of chronology, between a too early and a too late" (Lyotard, *Heidegger and the Jews* 20). As David Rodowick (27) puts it, this necessity to detour from historical truth "could be called Lyotard's 'leap into the void': an interval defined by that moment of suspension between the act of leaping, when one's feet leave solid surfaces, and the hard landing of present history. This is an act of faith to preserve an ethics of time." The emphasis is definitely on the ethics of time rather than on the hard landing of present history. Lyotard wants to preserve a separate place and a distinct existence for the immemorial, for the timeless power of unpresentable time presenting itself as absolute otherness, as an unsolvable enigma over and over again.

However, this is not the only possible interpretation of the Freudian immemorial. Giorgio Agamben recently (*The Signature of All Things* 81–111) revisited the Freudian immemorial, with a reading which is quite far from Lyotard's: For Agamben, the immemorial is not a sublime absolute otherness, because this otherness resolves its own timeless nature always here and now. In other words, its timelessness is not relegated to some inapproachable otherness, but consists in the mutual clash between present and past moments. The immemorial does not negate time from an inapproachable "beyond," but rather manifests the coincidence between past and present. And this is what *Inglourious Basterds* does. The absolute otherness (of Auschwitz) is no more in place, because it is revealed as coincident with our own (at least in 2012) historical present: the *war on terror*. This is the most daring (and important) of the film's anachronistic "retro-projections."

Before exploring this subject, however, a few words should be spent regarding the status of narrative (i.e., of the representation of time) in *Inglourious Basterds*. The film is very far from the Lyotardian "collapse of Grand Narratives"—not to mention the postmodern *idée reçue* of multiple-centered narration, and the like. *Inglourious Basterds is* a Grand Narrative. If it has a loose dramaturgy (too long scenes, not enough suspense, too long dialogues), this is only because its genre is not necessarily dramatic: it is *epic*. In the epic genre (even in Homer's original epic), digressions frequently interrupt the action to describe previous facts (or situations) the reader/hearer must know in order to understand the larger frame. But apart from them (such as the flashback where the life and deeds of Hugo Stiglitz are recounted), the narrative sequence is perfectly linear. There is only one exception: When the first scarified German soldier tells his Fuehrer his misadventure, its tale alternates back-and-forth with the actual images of what happened. But it has already been demonstrated that this particular episode has a special place in the overall structure, so it is assuredly an exception that thoroughly confirms the rule. The chapters follow one another so that, chapter by chapter, a great change in space overshadows the not-so-great moving ahead in time. The impression that there is little progression comes from the fact that there are multiple characters, and each segment (each "chapter"), focuses on one (or a few more) of them for too long, as if it were a short movie on its own terms. But again, this is what epic narratives have always done: Each of the details composing the larger picture is carefully exposed, so that the coherence of the whole ensemble is solid, but not dramatic. The single pieces do not have to conform to the laws of dramaturgical ("rhythmical") progression; their interaction does not necessarily have to follow the dramatic unity of action. Their connection is static instead of dynamic, but nonetheless every piece of the puzzle does contribute to the final achievement (the theater's explosion).

Particularly, the character of Birgit von Hammersmark would seem to have been included just to dismiss the babble on postmodernist arbitrariness of narration and heterogeneity that has been associated so many times with Tarantino's way of storytelling. She is a spy, so she manipulates multiple versions of reality, as if they were all at the same level. But they are not. When tortured, she admits what truth really is. She treats fiction as something entirely separated from the truth, so that she can indifferently play with identities. But a shoe (the emblem of fetishism, i.e., typically the connection between presence and absence by means of their separation) nails her down to her own identity; Landa discovers that she is a spy thanks to her lost shoe. "If the shoe fits, you must wear it," he says. Tarantino's postmodernism (if any) is not a matter of vacuously playing with identities removed from any form of belonging; it is the absence of identity itself which is claimed by the international commando unit *as an identity in itself* (as in Lyotard's *we* who "can perhaps identify itself on the basis of this non-identification: a community of addressees alert to the 'marvel'" ["Discussions" 376]).

Terrorism and the Biopolitical Turn

Giorgio Agamben shares Lyotard's philosophical horizons in many respects; above all, they both belong to the post–Heideggerian legacy. But for him Otherness is systematically reversed onto the Self. There is a fundamental short-circuit between the exception and the rule — which is exactly what Lyotard refused, since this short-circuit would still be of a dialectical kind. According to Agamben though (especially in his *Homo Sacer* and *The State of Exception*), it isn't: *biopolitics* is precisely the name for a non-dialectical (because leaving *mediation* aside) infinite reversibility between *Life* (*bios*) and *Law* (*nomos*). Life is always/already included in the Law by its very exclusion.

> Everything happens as if both law and logos needed an anomic (or alogical) zone of suspension in order to ground their reference to the world of life. Law seems able to subsist only by capturing anomie, just as language can subsist only by grasping the nonlinguistic. In both cases, the conflict seems to concern an empty space: on the one hand, anomie, juridical vacuum, and, on the other, pure being, devoid of any determination or real predicate. For law, this empty space is the state of exception as its constitutive dimension. The relation between norm and reality involves the suspension of the norm, just as in ontology the relation between language and world involves the suspension of denotation in the form of a langue [Agamben, *State of Exception* 60].

And one of the corollaries of this asset (informing the whole of Western civilization) is that, in order to maintain the Law, it is necessary to make exceptions. The limit-case of this is the war on terror: In order to fight terror, legal power suspends itself and establishes as law the suspension of law, thus "becoming" its outlaw terrorist enemy. Terrorism and the war on terror then cannot help but collapse on each other.

Agamben himself (3–4) affirmed that the U.S. reactions to 9/11 were an alarmingly precise example of that dynamic: Law is suspended in order to protect the law; democratic liberties are suspended in order to protect democratic liberties. Jacques Rancière recognized in several films (Lars Von Trier's *Dogville* and Clint Eastwood's *Mystic River*, for example) from the first decade of the new millennium significant symptoms of this ethical catastrophe in which legal power is indistinguishable from its opposite. Rancière quotes both Lyotard and Agamben, the latter as someone who radicalized the former's withdrawal of the ethical dimension in a lawless "absolute otherness," toward a more systematic double-bind (although not a dialectical one) between the rule and the exception. With regard to this, Rancière seems (9–10) to suggest (although not really explicitly) that Agamben's radicalization is more relevant to what Western society has become after 9/11 than Lyotard's.

More precisely, *Remnants of Auschwitz* is probably the book by Agamben in which the difference that distinguishes him from Lyotard is the clearest. "After" Auschwitz, resistance and dissent are not to be located (as for Lyotard) in the answer to the infinite call for "desubjectification."

> Testimony takes place where the speechless one makes the speaking one speak and where the one who speaks bears the impossibility of speaking in his own speech, such that the silent and the speaking, the human and the inhuman enter into a zone of indistinction in which it is impossible to establish the position of the subject, to identify the "imagined substance" of the "I" and, along with it, the true witness. This can also be expressed by saying that the subject of testimony is the one who bears witness to a desubjectification. But this expression holds only if it is not forgotten that "to bear witness of a desubjectification" can only mean there is no subject of testimony ... and that every testimony is a field of forces incessantly traversed by currents of subjectification and desubjectification [120–121].

The point is not really to re-open the space for desubjectification, but to find out the essential line that separates and connects (separates by connecting and connects by separating) subjectification and desubjectification. The testimony of this "line" is also the only thing that allows for an escape from the infinite biopolitical reversibility between Life and Law, rule and exception, because this line *is* the ultimate reversibility *at its purest*. The paradox is that by choosing one of the two sides is to fall inevitably back on the other, while the only way out resides in choosing *the line itself* between the two sides.

This fundamental co-implication of subjectification and desubjectification is embodied in our film by lieutenant Aldo Raine, a Tennessee soldier with much more than a drop of *Indian* blood in his veins, who likes to *scalp* his enemies.[4] In other words, he is someone who has incorporated the "Jew" his ancestors have exterminated. As such, he *is* the testimony of the line between subjectification and desubjectification.

Indicatively, he is also literally the remnant of Auschwitz, the only one of the Basterds (and of the international conspiracy) who survives the mutual extermination between the Nazi rule and the Jewish exception in the movie theater. *Inglourious Basterds* is particularly close to this biopolitical approach; we have already widely demonstrated how it relies on a narrative closure inseparable from its own negation. Additionally, it ends with Landa scarred and hence made a *homo sacer*, a crucial feature in Agamben's biopolitical thinking: He becomes someone who, in the Roman days, could be killed without breaking the law. But first and foremost, the film dares to imply that terrorism is at the very roots of late capitalist American society. It is a terrorist commando (referred to as such by Landa in a line of dialogue) who defeated the Nazis and hence founded postwar U.S. (that is, late capitalism). All of which indirectly implies that today's (or at least in the past decade, when the film was made and released) State power is inseparable from its terrorist opposite, and as such bears a significant connection with the Nazi paradigm. This matches Agamben's argument according to which late capitalist democracies (variously relying on the "war on terror") are still fully inside the biopolitical paradigm, whose quintessential epitome is the concentration camp: the infinite reversibility between the rule and the exception, between the terror and the war on terror. *Here* is where the present rejoins the past, as one of the anachronistic "retro-projections" mentioned in the last paragraph.

Far from being a film "pro" or "against" terrorism, *Inglourious Basterds* rather assumes that such a "pro"-vs.-"against" kind of alternative is a false one. Like Agamben, the film looks for the historical/theoretical roots of this "biopolitical knot" in World War II and in Nazi concentration camps, here marginally but unquestionably alluded to by the "gassed" audience in the finale. "That" moment in History was just the clearest token of a biopolitical paradox we are still locked inside. As a result, Tarantino sticks to paradox. He builds up an epic narrative which, as such, aims to reassure one's citizenship and feeling of collective belonging. However, at the same time, he also marks the viewer with a swastika on his/her forehead: A coherent narrative closure is achieved at the same time that it is dismantled. *Inglourious Basterds* wants to be an epic for today's globalized citizenship whose identity would not be national, but would instead rely on the line itself connecting and separating subjectification and desubjectification. Such a stateless identity cannot avoid being profoundly contradictory, thus openly admitting and assuming the "dark side" of its own establishment. Being a democratic citizen means, today, being *also* a terrorist, just as much as being a voyeur also means being a secret sadist. Above all, this paradox must not be hidden: it has to be displayed in front of our eyes, if we want to get over it.

Notes

1. The guardian of aesthetic taste *par excellence*, the (film) critic, here significantly dies. Before dying, however, he finds the time to taste an exquisite shot of whiskey.

2. The word "[it] happens" is Lyotard's, and signals the eventhood of the unpresentable, its being there regardless any presentation it may be the object of, notably an artistic kind of presentation.

3. This tool itself is highly indicative: What is at stake in the film is indeed, in Adornian terms, the industry of mass culture taking over what once was the Nazi project of totalization.

4. This is not the only reference to Native Americans. Shoshanna traces a red line on her cheek while preparing for her vengeance. Elsewhere, the dialogue mentions Winnetou, the Indian of the novels by German writer Karl May.

Tarrying with Sublimity: The Limits of Cinematic Form in Duncan Jones' *Source Code*

Michael J. Blouin

"But why shall I say more? To-day I wear these chains, and am *here*! To-morrow I shall be fetterless!—*but where?*"—Edgar Allan Poe, "Imp of the Perverse," 832

There is a recent trend in mainstream cinema of portraying protagonists trapped within narrow perspectives. Characters fight to move past limitations and outward into enlightened spaces; once outside, the audience wonders whether they have really escaped or if they are still enclosed within fantasy. While this is undoubtedly a theme that has proven to be financially successful, I will suggest that these works speak more broadly to the position of film as a medium in the early 21st century. Cinema, having served as the artistic form of choice throughout much of the last hundred years, can be read in these particular films as reaching a saturation point. Upon viewing Duncan Jones' *Source Code* (2011), one steps back to ponder the limits of cinematic form and what sublime truths, what revelations concerning the artistic process, lay forever at the cusp of its reach.

Source Code tells the story of Captain Colter Stevens (Jake Gyllenhaal), a war veteran who awakens at the launch of the film in the body of another man, only to learn that his life is stuck in a seemingly eternal eight minute loop. He regains consciousness on a train heading into Chicago which, at the end of every loop, explodes. As the film unfolds, one gradually discovers the truth about Stevens' condition and that the purpose of his mission is to foil a terrorist plot. In the process, Stevens falls in love with his seatmate, Christina (Michelle Monaghan). A romanticized dénouement raises significant doubts as to whether or not Stevens actually emerges from the existential crisis or if he is still mired in the loop. *Source Code* explores the virtual realm and its endless repetition of recycled devices; the captain is enclosed not only within the context of the narrative but also *within the form with which it is being told.* Theodor W. Adorno once distinguished art from the culture industry in a way that allows one to appreciate the significance of the film's final innovation: "Art strives to overcome its own oppressive weight as an artifact through the force of its very construction. Mass culture on the other hand simply identifies with the curse of predetermination and joyfully fulfills it" (72). Contrary to the thrust of Adorno's argument, I contest that recent mass culture, including *Source Code*, popularizes attempts to overcome the oppressive weight of a film's status as artifact.

At its close, *Source Code* manifests a yearning for (post)cinematic expression. The urge to break free becomes embedded within Stevens' narrative while his lot in life reflects the spectator's dissatisfaction with the limits of cinematic form, forcing the viewer to confront illusions of transcendence through sublime sensation. One vicariously follows the protagonist as he escapes from the filmic fetters that imprison him only to discover that the medium itself makes freedom impossible. Mainstream cinema effectively reaches an impasse. There is an unsettling mixture of relief and catharsis alongside a dread of persistent entrapment; the viewer's imagination struggles to find identification following the character's decision (conscious or not) to stay chained within cinematic space. This essay examines Stevens' enclosure within cinematic form and what this enclosure reveals concerning our postmodern condition. *Source Code* locates the outer edges of imagination in order to consider ascension. It therefore pushes the viewer to consider something greater, made possible only in the promises of artistic forms *yet to be conceived.* Walter Benjamin's famous treatise on film as a revolutionary shift in perception arrives where it began: "The history of every art form shows critical epochs in which a certain art form aspires to effects which could be fully obtained only with a changed technical standard, that is to say, a new art form" (237). In Jones' film, the viewer must address these essential questions surrounding cinema as a tool for human expression in the 21st century.

Locating an Edge to Cinematic Form: 2007–2012

Art repeatedly desires to push itself past formal limitations. An early analyst of this phenomenon is Edgar Allan Poe, the 19th century American writer who explores various oppressive literary structures in order to find the line between an empirically probing consciousness and what lies beyond. One example of many is "Imp of the Perverse." The narrative initially appears to be a rather straightforward meditation on a way of seeing the world that is not contained by traditional paradigms. But as the story proceeds, it becomes apparent that the narrator is ensnared by the very paradigm he longs to surpass: "No reason can be more unreasonable; but, in fact, there is none more strong" (827). The narrator approaches the brink of a mental apparatus which assumes, through logic, to subsume all elements within itself, but cannot avoid confronting its own constraints: "In some way I may answer your question, that I may explain to you why I am here, that I may assign to you something that shall have at least the faint aspect of a cause" (830). The narrator, it is revealed, has been imprisoned for murder and is trying to imagine his way out; the fetters that hold him within his cell represent the fetters that enclose the reader inside of Poe's narrative design and its inherent reliance upon familiar literary maneuvers. One approaches the tipping point of imagination — and the exterior of literary form — but is deliberately held back. The final line of "Imp of the Perverse" postulates a utopian impulse clashing with a barrier: "To-morrow I shall be fetterless!—*but where?*" (832; original's emphasis). Art, be it "high" or "low" in aim, shares one constant, a dialectic between reaching the limits of artistic expression and the pull toward transcendence, restrictive formal boundaries at odds with a desire to move forward. Poe describes the phenomenon in "The Philosophy of Composition" (1846) by noting that "a close circumscription of space is absolutely necessary to the effect of the insulated incident — it has the force of a frame to a picture" (263). These edges create a sensation of the sublime, a concept to be developed further in the following section. While literary works frequently interrogate this borderland, from Poe to the high modernists, mainstream cinema addresses these questions with far less regularity. Recent popular films including *Source Code* shift attention to the enclosure of cinematic form and what this suggests about the probing minds of film audiences today.

The historical development of literature initiates a discussion of current films' yearning for (post)cinematic expression. Theorist Georg Lukács offers a foundation with *The Theory of the Novel* (1920). He employs a Hegelian framework to position the novel as an appropriate venue for identifying the dialectical movements of consciousness. He argues that prose, as opposed to epic poetry, articulates the boredom and repetition of formal containment as well as the aspirations of the human spirit for an external essence: "Only the unfettered plasticity (of prose) and its non-rhythmic rigour can, with equal power, embrace *the fetters and the freedom, the given heaviness and the conquered lightness* of a world henceforth immanently radiant with found meaning" (59; emphasis mine). Once artistic form, in this case the novel, is historicized and defined, one can simultaneously locate an impulse to overcome it in an endless process that Lukács calls "becoming."[1] The meeting of these two tides takes place not only in literature but in cinema as well. Theorist Fredric Jameson suggests, as early as the late 1970s, that film as a medium might well be dead.[2] Yet, in order for the ramifications of this indictment to be felt widely, enclosures must first be mapped — Jameson repeatedly takes up this task in his writing — and the impasse must be projected onto popular narratives for the spectator to recognize themselves within the process. Subsequently, over the past five years, certain popular films self-reflexively express the limitations of consciousness while allowing the audience to recognize their utopian (and perhaps futile) desire to pass beyond them. In Deleuzian terms, as we will examine further in the next section, the mind encounters a counter-point in cinema and thus confronts its chained perspective, glimpsing in these works a series of (post)cinematic shadows that force one past the apparent safety of filmic frames.

Contemporary films developing the concepts articulated by Poe and Lukács include Mikael Hafstrom's *1408* (2007) and Christopher Nolan's *Inception* (2010). *1408* tells the story of Mike Enslin, a writer of trashy ghost books, who goes to the Dolphin Hotel to experience an "authentic" scare. Enslin laments his submissive status within a postmodern society that simply repeats the same aesthetic thrills, a grievance made literal upon entering the room 1408 and realizing his inability to escape from its torments. *1408* overtly references author Stephen King, whose short story provides the basis for the film, exploring the crisis of an artist trying to escape from the commercial forms he assisted in perpetuating. Horror formulas, recycled endlessly, deny Enslin's initial striving toward authentic artistic expression. When Enslin finally seems to escape from a microcosm of the horror film industry, he gradually realizes he has not actually left the room at all; a shock befalls him as a spectral woman from the Dolphin Hotel re-appears, dressed now as a waitress (a scene that pays homage to another King adaptation, *Misery* [Rob Reiner, 1990]). Even the theme of an artist trying to surpass the rigidity imposed by the marketplace is clichéd, foretold by Rob Reiner's earlier film. Cinematic form therefore reifies everything, including Enslin's presumed "escape." More recently, Nolan's film *Inception* features Dom Cobb (Leonardo DiCaprio) as a dream manipulator trying to return home to his children. By the close of the film, Cobb succeeds and the audience takes leave of him while he embraces his children — and yet a spinning top, which allows him to know whether he himself is the one dreaming, remains wobbling on a table nearby. *Inception* reveals cinema's inherent limitations alongside those of Cobb's constructed dream-worlds. His potentially triumphant return, to his children and to "reality," is undermined by the dream apparatus (cinema) that at first appeared to offer him an exit route. Cobb's status as a film subject forges an inescapable, Althusserian enclosure even he cannot dream himself through. Both works leave the spectator uncertain of whether they, alongside the protagonists, remain mired within the final shot in Hollywood prisons.

Source Code builds upon these themes of cinematic enclosure. Captain Stevens opens the film waking on a train *en medias res*. His initial struggle to piece together where he is, along with his shock of occupying the perspective of another, echoes the emotions of filmgoers at the beginning of this film, or any film, for that matter. The camera and Stevens' gaze are interchangeable, alerting viewers to the fact that their condition sorting out what is happening on-screen mirrors the condition of Stevens. Cinematic form is immediately linked to the premise of the narrative. When the train explodes, Stevens awakens in a small capsule, strapped to his seat, staring at a video monitor. Goodwin, the woman staring back at him, assures Stevens and the audience of *Source Code* that "some confusion is perfectly normal at this stage." With the capsule as a stand-in for the theatre, spectators join the captain in his frantic search to make sense of the images flashing before him.

These cinematic encounters are, at their core, oppressive. *Source Code* addresses an existential crisis among individuals fed by a steady diet of Hollywood fare. Goodwin leads one through "pattern recall," showing Stevens a series of familiar, if arbitrary, images: a set of cards, the story of an anonymous girl. Gradually, he begins to remember where he is and the point of the game he is being asked to play. The formula triggering his memory stands in for points of reference that allow spectators to situate themselves and move past the dizzying confusion of entering into a virtual realm. *Source Code* operates on a similar level. The spectator starts to recognize cinematic cues and obey the logic of filmed space and time. The project Source Code, which allows Stevens to enter into another's memories, speaks to the ambitions of the film industry at large. In a postmodern age, films grow increasingly repetitive. The viewer is subjected to endless sameness and trained to recognize arbitrary signifiers. Stevens traverses the virtual world in the eight minutes that have been allotted to him; when time expires, he re-enters and repeats *ad nauseum*. The industry likewise churns out films only figuratively to "blow them up" for the purpose of selling more products. This cycle relies upon the individual's compliance within the schema. Goodwin insists that the captain spend his time in the mission wisely: "Don't squander it thinking. Do." Rutledge, a scientist who designed the Source Code project, later tells the resistant Stevens of a powerful apparatus in place around him: "You are a hand on a clock. Understand? We set you, you move forward. We re-set you, you move again." Spectators, via Stevens, find no alternative but to seek a resolution that will please authority figures.

Cinematic time intimately intertwines with late capitalism. One purchases time inside of the capsule; the postmodern subject can only pay for a ticket as forces-that-be reset a virtual clock. Likewise, Stevens' mission within the eight minute loop is, by nature, delusional. He must buy into the fact that he is searching out a *real* bomb and that the people on-board the train actually require rescue, despite the fact that they are, logistically, already dead. At first, he recognizes the visual space as constructed, pointing out that his seatmate Christine, a beautiful woman, is only a distraction. Stevens notes, "All sims (simulations) have one." However, even this acknowledgement does not deter him from pursuing a bomb that Goodwin and Rutledge order him to locate. Obsequious, Stevens obeys their demands. In psychoanalytic terms, there is a schism between the desire and drive of *Source Code*: The captain desperately desires to defuse the bomb in question and save the people on-board the imaginary train. Rutledge, in contrast, reminds one of an underlying drive, working upon viewers, as they collectively await another explosion, only to replay the mission over and over again. As a face for the film industry, the scientist requires the repetition of virtual experience to be harnessed for his group's profit, conveniently disguised in the garb of "patriotism," while concurrently maintaining Stevens' desire for a genuine resolution.[3]

The question is thus not an unfamiliar one in this postmodern moment: Is there still a reality outside of Stevens' capsule? Though the captain tries to investigate the "real world," by calling his father and attempting to learn his fate, there is no reason to believe that this information is not still a mental projection borrowing from his visual storehouse. To emphasize this suspicion further, the mission's title, "Beleaguered Castle," refers to a restrictive game of solitaire in which the person plays alone and almost always loses. Undeterred, Stevens stares imploringly up through the tiny window and out into the blue expanse above, drawn toward a utopian exterior. Rutledge and Goodwin promise Stevens and the spectator that forward-moving time still exists outside of their confinement. But how can this Truth be demonstrated by cinematic form? Goodwin assures one that when the mission has been completed, they are all "off the clock." Yet one knows this to be fundamentally untrue. Rutledge plans to wipe Stevens' memory and start the process all over again. Recognizing cinematic form as a product of capitalist desire is perhaps a movement in the right direction. But, the film asks, toward what end? As Poe wrote many years prior, "To-morrow I shall be fetter-less!—*but where?*" In *Source Code*, the inquiry is reformulated: Can film surpass the confines it creates with merely the cinematic tools at its disposal?

Jameson contends that cinema projects structures similar to those articulated in Poe's fiction. Fueled by a larger capitalist industry, and its tendency to reify ideas into consumable packaging, films of the late 20th century, such as Stanley Kubrick's *The Shining* (1980), run up against their incapacity to supersede formal constraints. While Jameson acknowledges that the postmodern moment is devastating, he suggests that there is hope still to be found in the collective desire to move past these initial generic boundaries:

> All contemporary works of art — whether those of high culture and modernism or of mass culture and commercial culture — have as their underlying impulse — albeit in what is often *distorted and repressed unconscious form*— our deepest fantasies about the nature of social life, both as we live it now, and as we feel in our bones it ought to be lived [34; emphasis mine].

Jameson would undoubtedly agree that the dialectical shifts continue forward by their nature, though capitalism functions to control the severity. What was for Jameson during the 1980s a "distorted and repressed unconscious form" gradually emerges into one's consciousness today. Works such as *Source Code* argue that perhaps, in the first decade of the 21st century, film is ripe for dissolution. Cinematic form, acknowledging the extension of its reach, arrives at a theoretical end-game. Lukács observes:

> The artist's epic intention, his desire to arrive at a world beyond the problematic, is aimed only at an immanently utopian ideal of social

forms and structures; therefore it does not transcend these forms and structures generally but only their historically given concrete possibilities — and this is enough *to destroy the immanence of form* [144; emphasis mine].

At a moment wedged between artistic forms, as if an eclipse "felt in our bones," one is afforded an opportunity to glimpse the sublime, be it terrifying, rapturous, or, more accurately for Jones' film, both simultaneously. Before the next design emerges, and the viewer trickles from one capsule into another, one feels the terrifying — and liberating — edges of an enclosed social space in transition, experienced in *Source Code* as a (post)cinematic sublime.

Ruptures of Imagination: Bursting Forth from Cinematic Limits

The limits of *Source Code* are first established and then refused, forcing viewers to imagine what is yet to be seen. The film thus follows a trend in recent works not to present futility for its own sake, but rather as a clear marker suggesting a (post)cinematic beyond. At the close of the film, Stevens embodies a willful defiance of the gloomy limitations espoused by Goodwin and Rutledge. He reassures Christina that "this is not the end" and announces to his fellow passengers on the train, who lament a bitter world, that it "doesn't have to be." His optimism allows him to refuse the ending prescribed for them. Despite the fact that he has helped to avert another bombing in the "real world," Stevens convinces Goodwin to give him one more try at the loop. He smiles and predicts, "I'm gonna save her, Goodwin." Though his physical body is terminated by Goodwin, *Source Code* continues. The final scene takes place in Chicago's Millennium Park through which the captain and Christina leave the train to enjoy a stroll together on a beautiful, sunny day. They conclude the narrative by staring up onto the reflective surface of Cloud Gate, a sculpture in the park designed to symbolize a gateway between individuals and the cityscape/sky above, a binary expressing the essence of sublimity. Beneath the surface of *Source Code*, one strives to overcome the oppressive weight of the artifact against the heavily-sentimentalized dénouement. The final image produces another enclosure which necessitates a bursting forth of the imagination, a juxtaposition to fuel feelings of the sublime at the close of the film, as it holds body and sky in tension.

Georges Bataille, theorist of the abject, contemplates similar borders of artistic representation. His work mocks the apparatus of thought in a modernizing world, a structure he argues to be fundamentally short-sighted and inherently limited. Echoing Poe, Bataille laughs at the self-enclosure of imagination, in which one can merely dream of escaping from its fetters with only the use of faulty tools at one's disposal. Bitingly, Bataille writes: "Revolutionary idealism tends to make of the revolution an eagle above eagles, a *supereagle*" ("Old Mole," 34; original's emphasis). *Source Code* fits well within Bataille's analysis. Despite the fact Stevens, Cobb, and Enslin struggle to revolt against the restrictions placed upon perspectives infiltrated by the culture industry, Stevens' idealistic hopes, soaring ever higher and higher, play into capitalist desire by moving further from the grounds of "real change," based in the material realm Bataille espouses. Stevens cannot spot the folly of the game. Battling against the enclosed virtual system that defines him, without somehow first exiting the dream to witness its violent, bloody nature, is an endeavor doomed to failure. Bataille contends, "Without a sadistic understanding of an incontestably thundering and torrential nature, there could be no revolutionaries, there could only be a revolting utopian sentimentality" ("Use Value," 101). Running contrary to Bataille, Stevens embraces a different Hollywood ending, this time utopian rather than tragic in sentiment, and forsakes one torturous repetition in favor of another. In doing so, he neglects the corporeal, electing not to awaken and face the raw conditions of his corpse-like visage. He chooses instead to toil in the immateriality of metaphysics. After all, as Jameson might inquire, what is left to do with cinematic form if not to retreat into lethargic bouts of nostalgia, complete with ready-made cinematic visions?

The closing scenes echo the ending of Nolan's *Inception* by creating deep ambivalence within the viewer. On one track, one watches Goodwin pushing a button to end the life support of the "real" Stevens, whose lower half was brutally destroyed during war. The grotesque shot of his intestines and his half-exposed brain matter reveal the brutality and unsavoriness of Batailléan death. One recognizes at this point that conditions inside of the machine are abject decay — Stevens is quite literally dying. Simultaneously, his life proceeds in the realm of fantasy, where the sky is brilliant and familiar sentiments of Hollywood love/resolution fill the air. There is momentary conflict between pure absence (Death) aligned with pure presence, laughter on the train which Stevens recognizes as "all this life." The emotional quality of the film, closely aligned with theorist Jean-François Lyotard's examination of the sublime, is bitter-sweet. Does artistic expression reach its last gasp or is there something transcendent, a notion one can feel but never articulate?

After juxtaposing Bataillean death with Hollywood "life," a turn to the Lyotardian sublime underscores the potentiality at work in the film's bitter-sweet dénouement. *Source Code*'s cinematic form pushes the imagination forward in pursuit of an *a priori* Absolute. In other words, mankind's thinking faculties pursue a climax in which they realize their own aim. Behind all of this, aesthetic inquiry "has nothing to pursue but itself" (Lyotard, *Lessons* 6). This repetitious seeking is part and parcel of the thinking subject's relationship with representational art. For Lyotard, the sublime emerges at moments of impasse in which the imagination tarries with a notion which can never be reified, a Truth that cannot be accessed by continuous artistic probing, regardless of how thorough the pursuit may be. Lyotard writes of the sublime as "a 'presence' that exceeds what imaginative thought can grasp at once in a form — what it can *form*" (53; original's emphasis). In *Source Code*, critical thought forbids itself the Absolute but, in eight minute segments, *pursues it anyway*. Desire perpetuated by Rutledge's industry thus reveals in the film a profoundly significant repetition concerning the human condition.[4]

This endless pursuit is not without a degree of reward. As Lyotard argues in line with Lukács, imagination dialectically enlarges itself through these cycles. Stevens' imaginative space grows ever more pliable as he inquires and probes into his state of being. His capsule starts as excessively compact but as the narrative continues it becomes increasingly spacious. The most significant expansion occurs when Stevens learns from Goodwin that he is projecting the capsule for himself and nothing he sees is outside of his mind's projection. At this moment, in Hegelian fashion, the capsule expands outward dramatically. However, upon his next loop the capsule shrinks back into a manageable size. He is again strapped into his seat, prepared to depart obediently upon one final mission. Despite its plasticity, his consciousness remains inescapably enclosed. As Lyotard reflects, "The imagination cannot 'create' a form that would be adapted to it, for all form is circumscription" (*Lessons* 75). One feels sublimity at the meeting of imagination's end and a utopian desire pushing one out from Stevens' circumscribed window.

At the close of Jones' film, the audience is asked to imagine nascent possibilities for cinematic form. A voice-over by Stevens, who has apparently escaped from his existential crisis to phone Goodwin from the outside, insists Source Code "works better" than anyone could have hoped.

He urges Goodwin to keep up the good work and assist others in re-shaping their perspective on the postmodern world. Even Rutledge, left waiting unaware of the radical potential unleashed by Goodwin, retains hope: "Source Code is going to have its moment in the sun." What appears throughout to have ensnared one in a manipulative late capitalist design opens up to yet another faith in transcendence, an emotional aspiration that Jameson argues forever embeds itself within the process of form-making. The sublime cannot be fully visualized, as the overly-familiar, clichéd scene in Millennium Park admits, but glimpses of the sublime provide a deeper sense of purpose as well as a willingness to alter the architecture of the capsule. In order to move forward with faith, one must maintain the belief that ultimate seizure of the object one pursues, beyond the circumscribed space of the cinematic realm, remains truly possible.

Edgar Allan Poe tarries with this sublimity in a well-known tale, "The Pit and the Pendulum." Poe's narrator, again linked overtly to the reader, struggles to escape from a torture cell in which various unseemly deaths approach. The design of the narrative echoes the design of the chamber: The reader desires to escape from its self-enclosed and uncomfortable linearity. Idealized promises return throughout the narrative: "In death — no! even in the grave all *is not* lost. Else there is not immortality for man. Arousing from the most profound of slumbers, we break the gossamer web of *some* dream" (492; original's emphasis). The reason for the unsettled quality of the tale is not the unspeakable horrors *but the underlying hope that remains*. Even as the narrator acknowledges that to escape the cell, and the literary form, is a foolish endeavor, there is compulsion forward: "It was *hope* that prompted the nerve to quiver — the frame to shrink. It was *hope* — the hope that triumphs on the rack — that whispers to the death-condemned even in the dungeons of the Inquisition" (501; original's emphasis). Poe's textual experiment sets the groundwork for *Source Code*, flirting with the edges of imaginative faculties and posing a literary cleavage from which to reflect upon the limits of artistic form. At the close of Poe's story, a hackneyed rescue mission arrives, complete with trumpets blaring, to catch the reader and save the day, pulling them back from the brink. With a reinvigorated voice in 2011, Stevens re-iterates: "I'm gonna save her, Goodwin." The constructed-ness of this freedom draws the flux between futility and romanticism to the fore.

A recent cinematic incarnation of Poe's life, *The Raven* (2012), further explores this flux in parallel to *Source Code*. The narrative structure of the film builds off of literary devices initially invented by the author. Formulaic "tricks" involved range from the ever-logical detection tale, to overly-sentimentalized poetry, and on to perverse tales of the grotesque. The film thus unfolds in predictable fashion, based overtly upon Poe's designs. At the edge of the formulaic, when he fulfills the arch of the tale, the film once more suggests a shift. Director James McTeigue re-calibrates Poe's legacy, and the resultant paradigms of American literature the author supposedly left behind, by quite literally opening the cinematic space into a (post)cinematic sublime. Poe passes away and a brilliant white light overwhelms the screen. He makes a choice to write himself out of his own story, a decision mirrored by Stevens, who seizes control of the form that has been dictating his life's narrative. Poe's insistence over the course of the film that he is *not* an atheist, and his subsequent requests of the Lord to save him, linger onward as the words to one of his last poems are inscribed upon the final moments of the film: "Is all that we see or seem but a dream within a dream?" The form of the film follows the character's lead. As Poe's killer heads to Paris to "inspire" more nihilism in art, McTeigue's film reminds the viewer that the story need not end this way. Formulas will be broken, trajectories altered. The screen cuts to black as a gunshot reverberates — has the detective stopped the killer, thus saving the world from the influential germination of a misinterpreted Poe? Credits roll over a series of beautiful graphics: shards of glass, streaming outward, melding together into unexpected forms. The dream breaks outward, as it does in *Source Code*. Both Poe and Stevens realize their place within a self-cannibalizing form and, subsequently, the film explodes before our eyes. Capturing their exquisite freedom, as well as their damning fetters, the spectator must contemplate what comes next.

As is the case with Poe, who can only exist as a disconnected voice at the end of *The Raven*, if Stevens manages to "get out" of the visual prison that *Source Code* creates, the audience can no longer visualize him. Nevertheless, despite this recognized futility, the film forces the spectator to keep thinking after the final credits roll and re-assess their obedience as film-goers. In his meditations on cinema, Deleuze recognizes that the radical potentiality of "thought thinking itself" serves as one of the most valuable assets of cinema: "Something was in play, in a *sublime* conception of cinema. In fact, what constitutes the sublime is that the imagination suffers a shock which pushes it to the limit and forces thought to think the whole as intellectual totality which goes beyond the imagination" (Deleuze 157; original's emphasis). When Goodwin pushes the button and Stevens dies/begins to live, the setting of the train freezes. Everyone suspends in motion, laughing, loving, caught in a tableau. Cinematic form momentarily falters.[5] "Escape," *Source Code* suggests, might lead to an exterior of the moving image.[6] The viewer returns to imagining actively as the camera scans a still-life portrait and the spectator is forced to conceive of what "beyond" could mean, as well as questioning their position inside of the capsule, as the pushed button arrests the visual apparatus.[7] When action arrests upon the train, the spectator's mind is free to roam, a quality very rarely found in fast-paced contemporary films.

Surveying this tableau returns us to Poe's concept of the frame and Deleuze. Deleuze proceeds, "The cinematographic image must have a shock effect on thought, and force thought to think itself as much as thinking the whole. This is the very definition of the sublime" (158). When the images start to move again, there is a dialectical shift: The viewer either surrenders their recent radicalized thoughts up to a Hollywood resolution of simulated life against death or, in contrast, recognizes a cinematic form, like the mind itself, thinking itself in circles.[8] Imaginative faculties sense the cold wall of the capsule and the viewer becomes aware of their position in relation to desires and drives, as well as to the cinematic artifice.[9]

If *Source Code* is to be read as emblematic of social dissatisfaction, the viewer simultaneously pauses to consider what form an alternative might assume. Todd McGowan, a noted film scholar who repeatedly returns to these issues in his analysis of popular cinema, re-illuminates a fatal flaw that Poe and Hegelians have long recognized within the symbolic system:

> All of the images that surround us offer the allure of a complete enjoyment—a jouissance unperturbed by any lack. And yet, this avoidance of lack is purely imaginary: because the image has its foundation in the symbolic order, because it is projected from the symbolic order, the images do not escape lack and provide the completeness (and complete jouissance) that it promises [71].

This psychoanalytical reading applies well to the fate of Stevens. Though the character appears to overcome the limits of form, in actuality he has done little to disrupt the order of things. Though Stevens elects imaginary authority, "escaping" from the confines of the symbolic, his movement readily falls into mere abstraction. After all, what can possibly enter into consciousness without some kind of mediation? The solution to the impasse invoked by McGowan in his work *The End of Dissatisfaction?* is "partial enjoyment," a Hegelian recognition that "lack" remains an essential element of life. This perspective explains Stevens' decision to re-enter the machine and continue dreaming. If this be so, at the close of the film, does the soldier fully realize a "lack" in his virtual cavern? Is Stevens able to negotiate the terms of his surrender in order to retain a better sense of what is possible within the capsule, therefore achieving "partial enjoyment"?

I would argue that while McGowan's argument remains useful for analyzing *Source Code*, it presumes a certain end, placing the proverbial cart before the horse.[10] If Stevens and the informed spectator embrace "partial enjoyment" within the simulacrum, cinematic form will consequently lose political potency. After all, why continue to try and save the train from its impending doom? Or, from a pacifist outlook, where does one summon the impetus to express love to the woman in the next seat over? Against a forfeiture of genuine investment, the viewer can contrastingly read Stevens as suspending cynicism to preserve faith in the symbolic system, maintaining designs to open up innovative mental pathways. It cannot be negotiated; it must remain predominantly in the realm of affect. In short, the individual who presumes ahead of time to know where the train will stop cannot avoid following a prescribed route. *Source Code*, in contrast, promotes a willingness to await in earnest the eruption of Truth. The film preserves hope in mankind against a shrinking technological landscape and inspires viewers to think outside of the capsule, to attempt to re-wire with someone, or something, outside of the lonely Cartesian capsule. One should therefore not too readily dismiss Stevens' genuine reassurance for himself and the spectators preparing to exit: "Everything is going to be okay." It is only in holding onto such faith, *Source Code* suggests, that one form can pass into the next.

In the first decade of the 21st century, several important popular films attempt to contemplate the status of cinematic form in the contemporary world. Cinema retreads the route of the novel, achieving a reification that may appear to express nothing further. I contend that this recognition is made possible on a broad scale not solely by academic interjection but rather through encountering sublimity in bitter-sweet moments of constraint which collide with the fullness of human aspiration.[11] Lyotard notes, "The imagination does not contribute to pleasure through a free production of forms and aesthetic Ideas, but in its powerlessness to give form to the object" (*Lessons* 99). Feeling the fetters in *Source Code*, the viewer is asked to retain faith against powerlessness. Tarrying with sublimity, as scholars pontificate upon and Poe makes explicit, evokes an enduring belief that something always remains yet to be expressed.[12]

NOTES

1. Theodor W. Adorno, though doubtful that mainstream cinema will ever seriously endeavor to question cinematic form, acknowledges: "Whoever goes to a film is only waiting for the day when this spell will be broken, and perhaps ultimately it is only this *well concealed hope* which draws people to the cinema." Unconvinced, he goes on: "But once there they obey. They assimilate themselves to what is dead. And that is how they become disposable" (Adorno 95; emphasis mine). The question is thus articulated: At the close of these films (*1408*, *Inception*, *Source Code*), do we assimilate ourselves to the protagonist's figurative death? Or do we believe the cinematic resolutions, with their crystal clear skies and romantic musical accompaniment? Or, in the end, do we recognize our compliance in filmic illusion-making and find only the most recent limits of imagination?

2. In his preface to *Signatures of the Visible*, Jameson wonders about the nature of his study and the figurative death that accompanies film reaching its postmodern end. He considers "whether the entire discussion is not in the nature of a post mortem on a now historical form or medium, which finds its philosophy as well as its history posthumously" (Jameson 6).

3. The subservience to virtual images reminds one of the conditions facing a post–9/11 society. At times in the film, images from CNN intersperse with the images being fed to Stevens, forcing one to further identify with his state of being. To resist this call to duty, according to much Bush era discourse, would be "unpatriotic."

4. Lyotard recognizes this connection as follows: "There is something of the sublime in capitalist economy.... It is, in a sense, an economy regulated by an Idea—infinite wealth or power. It does not manage to present any example from reality to verify this Idea ... it only succeeds, on the contrary, in making reality increasingly ungraspable, subject to doubt, unsteady" (Lyotard, *The Inhuman* 105).

5. Importantly, even this "faltering" is not entirely an escape; in truth, cinema continues to manipulate here, from the swelling soundtrack to the numerous cuts and pans. While *Source Code suggests* something outside of the film, a tableau in place of cinematic form, it does so without completely losing the fetters in question.

6. There is tremendous optimism in this sublime encounter. Lyotard contends: "Thanks to art, the soul is returned to the agitated zone between life and death, and this agitation is its health and its life" (Lyotard, *The Inhuman* 100). Despite Stevens' death, art allows him (and us) to continue living.

7. G.W.F. Hegel would appreciate this moment of contemplation as part of consciousness finding itself: "Reason now has, therefore, a universal interest in the world, because it is certain of its presence in the world, or that the world present to it is rational. It seeks its 'other,' knowing that therein it possesses nothing else but itself: *it seeks only its own infinitude*" (Hegel 146; emphasis mine).

8. This popularizes a notion similar to what director Paul Schrader defines as "transcendental style," a method of surpassing the limits of cinematic form. He contends, "When the image stops, the viewer keeps going, moving deeper and deeper, one might say, *into* the image ... (the viewer) has moved beyond the province of art" (Schrader 161; original's emphasis).

9. Deleuze also notes, "Thought, in cinema, is brought face to face with its own impossibility, and yet draws from this a higher power of birth" (Deleuze 168). Thought continues to push forward amidst the reification of the mental apparatus that Deleuze finds at play in modern film.

10. One recognizes this concern when reading Evan Carton's analysis of Poe and American Romanticism as well: "If, as mere construct, art cannot comprise but can only obstruct Truth's realization, it nonetheless does constitute Truth's vehicle and preserver" (Carton 106). Gaining an elevated vantage point will cut off any truly transformative power present at art's edges; in other words, it allows one to surpass obstructions to thought via a pre-determined allowance for "partial enjoyment."

11. This pivot responds to film theorist Todd McGowan's Lacanian reading of contemporary cinema. According to McGowan, the society of enjoyment (including popular cinema) provides an opportunity for us to "enjoy in a way that frees us from its superegoic compulsion and opens enjoyment as such" (McGowan 196). In *Source Code*, Stevens could be seen as rejecting the command of "completion" or "complete enjoyment" and embracing a self-aware state of enjoyment, recognizing the futility of escape from desire and simply beginning *to play*. Against this claim, I would interject that the hope for utopian fulfillment cannot (and must not) be willfully discarded. Without a bitter-sweet tarrying with sublimity, which requires hope *and* despair, the subject would abandon thought and slide back into the status of consuming corpse. Though Stevens knows his imagination (likely) reaches its end, he retains faith in life. Stevens' yearning for (post)cinematic expression is the only way to avoid atrophy and continue re-building the capsule. It is, one might argue, this form-making alone that keeps us active in a postmodern world.

12. This dialectical turn echoes Jameson's advocacy of an alternative "aesthetic of cognitive mapping" in "Postmodernism: Or, the Cultural Logic of Late Capitalism." Architectural emphasis in *Source Code* overtly pushes us, in line with Jameson, toward "some as yet unimaginable new mode of representing" (Jameson 54). The cinematic structure is thus mapped until we realize the faultiness of its cartography and proceed to re-assess the map itself.

COMMUNIQUÉ-TION BREAKDOWN: (POST)CINEMATIC INTERRUPTIONS

Pleasure and Pain: Post-Cinematic Remakes

Holly Willis

A woman moves cautiously from room to room in a darkened house. We see her up close, her face tense with fear. She opens a door. She backs away. She screams as an invisible force spins her violently across the room, and suddenly the image itself seems to tear, transferring the violence thrust on the woman to the film stock itself. As viewers, we are sent spinning backwards out of the story to witness the wrenching of sprocket holes and bubbling of emulsion. The film is destroyed, along with the imagery of the woman and the house; the demon that started inside the story now rages outside the story, onscreen, scratching with bright slashes of light in a brilliant retinal attack that manages to be at once a stunning horror film and an enactment of the violence wrought by the arrival of new media forms on the specificity of traditional cinema.

The film is Austrian filmmaker Peter Tscherkassky's dazzling *Outer Space* (1999), an award-winning 10-minute short that borrows from the B horror film *The Entity* (1981) to perform a revision that is at once a creative distillation of the original, a critical analysis suggesting the alignment of the cinematic medium and the female, and a new media artwork that points to the significance of turn-of-the century media transition and convergence.

The film is also part of a spate of recent art-oriented media projects that returns to horror films, using them as a foundation from which to ponder both the nature of horror and the specificity of cinema. These projects are particularly important as they participate in a larger movement that marks a transition from traditional or classical Hollywood cinema (as defined by David Bordwell and Kristen Thompson in *The Classical Hol-*

lywood Cinema: Film Style and Mode of Production to 1960) to a form of "post-cinema" characterized by a dismantling of not only the temporal and spatial codes of the classical style and the illusion of coherence that it engenders, but also the fundamental structures of cinematic production, distribution, and exhibition that have remained relatively stable for over a century. The result of this dismantling is a dispersal of screens, stories, performers, and viewers, all of which are reconsidered and re-mobilized toward new ends. Theorists as diverse as David Rodowick, Jacques Rancière, Lev Manovich and Steven Shaviro have described the impact of a broad array of recent digital technologies on the notion of classical Hollywood cinema as an apparatus, and with regard to its formal characteristics, including its tendency to privilege realism, continuity, and coherence, as well as its role in constructing forms of subjectivity aligned with dominant ideology. While in his *Poetics of Cinema,* David Bordwell describes the evolution of recent narrative structures that initially seem to eschew linearity—as in the narrative repetition seen in *Groundhog Day* (1993)—as "hyperclassical" (62), Shaviro, in contrast, asserts that we are in the midst of the "post-cinematic." In his book *Post Cinematic Affect,* Shaviro explains that cinema is no longer the cultural dominant it was, but has been eclipsed by a series of digital innovations that are embedded within a larger political, economic, and technological context. He uses the term "post cinematic" not so much to map the evolution of narrative structures or the transformation of production workflows so much as to explore the ways in which recent projects are "expressive"; they conjure "a kind of ambient, free-floating sensibility that permeates our society today" (2). He goes on to explore the ways in which these projects are "machines for generating affect" (3).

Post-cinematic might also be used to designate the increasingly large array of media projects that hover at the intersection of cinema, video installation, media art, and the art world generally. As a group, these projects generally point to a crisis regarding the shift from representation, narrative, and discourse toward an information-based model of culture-as-technology. In this culture, the reader or viewer becomes a user or player, often in conjunction with a database or computational ethos based on algorithmic unfolding and machine-like processes. These elements—the database, algorithms, and the very process of revision—underscore a cultural need for new expressions and experiences of subjectivity in a world increasingly mediated by electronic networks; by practices engendered by social software; and by nonlinearity. While some of these projects share multiple lineages — including the histories of Net art, video art and expanded cinema — the cinematic apparatus remains central as both reference and point of departure, and the horror film as source helps mark the anxiety associated with the transition culturally, aesthetically, technologically, and institutionally.

As a participant in post-cinema, *Outer Space* enacts a return and violent revision; it expresses a deep-seated anxiety about the loss of the past and the uncertainty of the future; and it conjoins terror and the sublime, conjuring a frenzy of pleasure at the same time that it disrupts boundaries, here between old and new, and between one media form and a host of others.

That the boundary can be troubling has been demonstrated profoundly in the work of Julia Kristeva, most notably in her 1982 book, *Powers of Horror: An Essay on Abjection*. The book focuses on the notion of the abject, or that which threatens to break down the boundary between self and other. The abject consists of those things that both cross the boundaries of the body and spark disgust — a wound, or substances such as blood, pus, and shit. More specifically, the abject consists of those things that figure death and decay. "These body fluids, this defilement, this shit are what life withstands, hardly and with difficulty, on the part of death," Kristeva writes, explaining our repugnance: "There, I am at the border of my condition as a living being" (3).

Many film scholars have used Kristeva's work in explorations of horror films. For example, film theorist Barbara Creed writes in her book *The Monstrous Feminine*, "The horror film attempts to bring about a confrontation with the abject (the corpse, bodily wastes, the monstrous-feminine) in order finally to eject the abject and redraw the boundaries between human and non-human" (14). As such, horror films as a genre tend toward the conservative, working to explore the abject but ultimately repressing it. Creed continues, highlighting the significance of the abject in threatening the symbolic order: "As a form of modern defilement rite, the horror film attempts to separate out the symbolic order from all that threatens its stability, particularly the mother and all that her universe signifies" (14). Horror films revel in threatening this stability — somatic boundaries are violently crossed, and blood, guts and vomit are rampant — but in the end, order and stability generally return, and the symbolic retains its authority.

However, Kristeva also briefly describes the sublime in *Powers of Horror,* noting that while the abject breaks down the border between self and other, the sublime bridges or covers over the breakdown of that border. It is often coincident with the abject, but rather than focusing on the rift, the sublime connects these territories. Kristeva privileges poetry and modern literature for their ability to reckon with the collapse and reassertion of the boundary between self and other. Describing the sublime, she writes, "As soon as I perceive it, as soon as I name it, the sublime triggers — it has always already triggered — a spree of perceptions and words that expands memory boundlessly. I then forget the point of departure and find myself removed to a secondary universe set off from the one where 'I' am — delight and loss" (12).

Tscherkassky's *Outer Space* is one of several post-cinematic works that would seem to exemplify this notion of the sublime, precisely in its return to the "body" of cinema, to its dismantling and reconfiguration, and to an explicit meta-commentary on the visceral experience of watching a movie. The film belongs to a larger body of work by Tscherkassky, an Austrian filmmaker whose experiments in cinema span more than 30 years and who is deeply committed to exploring the essence of film as material and as larger apparatus. To make *Outer Space*, Tscherkassky appropriated sections of Sidney J. Furie's *The Entity*, in which Barbara Hershey plays a woman menaced by a powerful but invisible force; however, the film is not simply a remix or remake, but rather a re-photographic adaptation in which Tscherkassky created new images from the existing film through a printing process in which sections of frames were carefully exposed. As the force attacks and then rapes the woman, the images themselves are embattled; then, as the woman retaliates, the very frames of the film are made visible — sprocket holes and the optical soundtrack are seen — only to be scratched, ripped and destroyed. The illusion of coherent space and the clear temporal organization of a story unfolding in time are completely abandoned in favor of a radically disorienting experience of violence, but a violence in which we, as viewers, experience an upheaval of cinema, and more specifically horror cinema, witnessing not simply violated bodies, but the far more meta-experience of the violation of the material of cinema itself, which at once enacts and demonstrates the monstrosity of transformation while reveling in its sheer spectacle.

Indeed, one could say that this film, and a broader category of the contemporary horror remake, performs significant cultural work in negotiating a logic of the digital while in the process continuing the central conceptual practices of a larger post-cinematic movement. These practices include a kind of meta-cinematic analysis, using existing films as fodder for dissection, contemplation, and, on occasion, destruction. They also consider cultural artifacts generally, and existing films particularly, as a database from which to select and recombine, a process certainly not unique to post-cinematic work but rather part of a larger ethos subtending diverse artistic practices. In these ways, then, the remakes considered here do not draw their designation as remakes from the history of cinema, in which the remake is often understood in very narrow terms, so much as from an avant-garde cinematic practice based on collage and found footage, and from art-oriented practices, including appropriation art, database-oriented artworks, and more recent computational projects.

However, the films that I will discuss have a further distinction: Their manifestation of horror — in terms of genre, narrative disruption and material reconfiguration — at the same time reckons with a notion of the sublime. However, while Kristeva's pairing of the abject and sublime would *seem* to connect well with a discussion of the horror remake, her work is less useful in light of the more intellectual experience of the sublime that these conceptually-oriented remakes inspire. Indeed, Immanuel Kant's definition of the sublime as "that ... which is *absolutely great*" (original's emphasis), and his focus on the intellectual activity inspired when witnessing something immense or overwhelming, is more pertinent ("Of the Mathematically Sublime"). In *The Critique of Judgment,* Kant describes the sublime as that which is too vast or powerful for full comprehension. As such, the experience of the sublime provokes both pain and pleasure in a back-and-forth movement between the sense that what we are witnessing is tremendous in size or force, and the realization that we are reaching the edges of what our reason can comprehend. The sublime inspired by contemporary horror film remakes is an experience of the vast power of the digital and the computational and its transformative capacity; it is the feeling of combined exuberance and anxiety as we witness a paradigm shift, the reorganization of our conceptual models and the pleasure and pain of not yet having the ability to name or adequately describe this experience.

Psycho's *Remakes*

Examples of the post-cinematic horror remake are varied. However, for an array of reasons, Alfred Hitchcock's *Psycho* (1960) has inspired numerous post-cinematic art-oriented remakes, perhaps the best-known being Douglas Gordon's large-scale video installation *24 Hour Psycho* (1993), which slows the notorious film down so that it unspools over the course of 24 hours. Displayed in museums and galleries as a large-scale projection, *24 Hour Psycho* shifts attention away from the riveting narrative to everything around the narrative — the actual display of the film within the space; the role of the spectator in the movie theater in contrast to that of the wandering gallery-goer, who moves about; the temporality of the film in its elongated form and its original form; and the process of analysis and contemplation necessitated by the video project.

Gordon updated the installation, creating *24 Hour Psycho Back and Forth and To and Fro* in January 2010, and it was showcased at the Guggenheim Museum as part of a 24-Hour Program on the Concept of Time. The two-screen installation shows two versions of the slowed-down film, with one unspooling normally and the other running in reverse; the two films meet in the middle for one identical shot. In both cases, the installations invite viewers to conjure the film through memory as they encounter it in very slow motion. Because the images appear almost as a series of stills, and because it would be difficult to watch the video in its entirety, viewers often find themselves conjuring Hitchcock's version as a correlate in a complex orchestration of memory, correspondence, spatiality, and temporality. As viewers, we are disallowed the close connection to the story and its violence as would have been experienced when viewing the film in its original form, possibly in a movie theater. In its place, viewers instead stand back and experience the film at a distance, a distance that allows for a sense of the self in multiple registers — how it may have perceived the film in other viewings, and how it is perceiving the film in its reconfiguration. These reconfigurations point to and disrupt the past, distorting the original and offering an experience very much centered on crossing the boundary between the old and the new.

Gordon's project, in subjecting Hitchcock's film to scrutiny, not to mention deformation, joins a genre of video installations that return to cinema to perform a kind of aesthetic meta-analysis that, in the process, destroys the coherence of the original. In her essay "That's the Only Now I Get: Immersion und Participation in Video-Installations by Dan Graham, Steve McQueen, Douglas Gordon, Doug Aitken, Eija-Liisa Ahtila, Sam Taylor-Wood," Ursula Frohne discusses a broad range of artists who found their practice on a reflection on cinema. She writes, "One hundred years after the birth of film, the artistic 're-make' uses various methods and degrees of alienation to return film classics to their elementary structures, employing analytical procedures to shed critical light upon the history of the medium's effects." She includes the work of Diana Thater, Doug Aitken, Cindy Sherman, and Jeff Wall as examples of works that "have made the seductive power of filmed images their own," and distinguishes between those works that affirm what she dubs the illusionist principles of cinema, and those that are more conceptual and function to expose the constructed nature of cinema and its spectacle. She situates Gordon's *24 Hour Psycho* in the second group, celebrating the video's ability to make us aware of the isolated gestures that become prominent when the film is slowed down, and she uses the word "suspense" to designate both the literal suspension of the film within the installation, where it hovers without sound, as well as the suspense of the gestures of actors, which become much more theatrical.

Frohne's suspense, however, echoes the notion of the sublime, according the viewer the ability to reckon with two disparate registers. The suspense we experience as visitors to the gallery space where *24 Hour Psycho* hovers on a large screen consists of the temporal and narrative disjunction. The coherence of the original traditional narrative structure gives way to an expansive, almost languid unfurling that gestures to the tightly paced story delivered by Hitchcock. Where the original film delivered a powerful experience of horror, Gordon's post-cinematic version expands the narrative's temporal realm in order to study suspense specifically, and in the process of this meta-cinematic analysis, creates an experience of the sublime. But can the sublime retain its significant power when mobilized toward contemplation?

Stefano Basilico considers *24 Hour Psycho* in his essay "The Editor," finding the key to the project in the way in which it "reorganizes our experience of time," and he explains that the project undoes Hitchcock's use of time mainly by exposing Hitchcock's cuts, "rendering them conspicuous" (32). What is a tremendous exercise in editing for the shower sequence with its flurry of cuts is transformed into a slow contemplation of vivid violence, and an opportunity for reflection in this contemporary remake. The visceral gives way to the contemplative and attention to the boundaries of the body. However, the project doesn't merely revel in horror. Instead, it very much transports viewers, if only through duration. We inhabit that duration in a state both of contemplation and awe, with a very explicit awareness of the qualities of cinema that we both affectionately embrace and recall, and a sense of the sublime produced through the magnitude of the project.

Jim Campbell's *Illuminated Average #1, Hitchcock's Psycho* (2000) is yet another remake of *Psycho*, in this case created through a process of compressing the entire film into a single illuminated image that viewers experience on a lightbox. Campbell scanned the film's frames, then layered them, creating one image that contains all of the others. *Psycho* also forms the foundation for another project by Campbell titled *Accumulating Psycho* (2004), which "accumulates" the entire film by keeping the images onscreen at the same time as they play, and another titled *Night Light* (1995/1998), which visualizes the film's sound level and brightness.

Campbell's projects at once mangle and defile *Psycho*, wrenching the film from 20th century narrative coherence into 21st century data visualization and manipulation. The pleasure of the projects—specifically *Illuminated Average #1, Hitchcock's Psycho*—resides precisely in the doubling. The violence of the shower scene with its destructive cutting is replayed in the symbolic cutting and slicing of the film text into its constituent pieces, which are piled up in a stack to render a murky, dissolved image that represents the demise of the body of cinema, of cinema as an institution, and of the psychic structures so carefully bounded by classic narrative cinema. We're left an empty expanse, a state akin to the sublime.

These revisions of Hitchcock's *Psycho* all explore, examine, analyze, and play with a foundational film text to create a new version of the project. However, the process of creating a remake is not about reinvigorating a classic for a new generation but instead consists of a dual process of dismantling and reconstitution, and an almost obsessive return to the trauma of the original through repetition, duration, and deferment. Indeed, one might ask why so many artists have chosen *Psycho*, a black-and-white film provocatively deemed "boring" by film scholar Mervyn Nicholson, as their point of examination. It may be due to its iconic status in the history of American cinema, or the notoriously violent shower scene that suggests rather than shows, functioning as a kind of reverse fetishization and suspension of disbelief. However, it might also be due to the ways in which the divestiture of character identification and traditional story structure opens up a space, one easily understood as a platform for critical appraisal. However, the process also results in a doubling, and the production of a kind of subjectivity that is both situated overtly in relation to the apparatus of cinema, with an awareness of screens, other spectators and the accouterments of cinema exploded into new relations, and in process, an entity produced through the experience of embodied spectatorship.

The Database and the Sublime

Classical Hollywood films are composed from a collection of shots captured specifically so that they may be organized into a linear narrative with careful attention to temporal and spatial continuity. All material excised from the film's final cut remains peripheral at best, and more likely completely invisible to audiences, with a primary goal of the narrative structure being the illusion of the coherent experience of the story despite the numerous gaps, omissions, and elisions that actually exist. The body of the film is cohesive, self-contained, whole. However, a major characteristic of the post-cinematic is its attention to the database, or to an entire collection of materials from which a narrative might be created. In the case of the *Psycho* remakes, as the original film is dismantled, and its parts reassembled, the fact that the film is indeed a collection of fragments with an order imposed comes to the fore, bringing with it the understanding that that order is not immanent or necessary but deeply contingent and even unstable; the boundaries sustaining the original narrative's coherence loosen, and we witness yet again a dispersal and reconfiguration. The "body" of the film is indeed susceptible to disfiguration, and its disparate versions are akin to monsters cobbled together from an array of parts.

While the dismantlings of *Psycho* provoke experiences of the sublime with reference to a particular and single film, the horror remake and its connection to prior projects might also be considered within the broader context of a series of films, or even in terms of the very structuring of a database, understood here simply as a collection of materials from which to create diverse combinations and recombinations.

Marsha Kinder has written about "database narratives," those narratives "whose structure exposes or thematizes the dual processes of selection and combination that lie at the heart of all stories" (6). Lev Manovich finds databases to be at the heart not only of new media practices, which often center on accessing and manipulating information, but also new forms of subjectivity, which are increasingly distributed across databases. While Kinder and Manovich differ fundamentally in their theorization of the database as it relates to traditional narrative, both theorists point to the emphasis on selection and combination, paradigm and syntagm. In a database narrative, we witness the array of choices that are available, and the pleasure of the narrative is not in its coherence, but in understanding the overall structure, and witnessing the differences sparked as different options play out. Films such as *Memento* and *Run Lola Run*, both of which showcase the role of narrative structure and the combination of shots, demonstrate the power of the database as a structuring device.

Media artists Kevin and Jennifer McCoy often use existing films as a database from which to make new works, and horror forms a foundation for their project *Horror Chase* (2003), an installation that crafts an unending chase sequence using material taken from Sam Raimi's *Evil Dead 2: Dead by Dawn*. The artists allow a chase sequence to be reedited live and continuously, varying the speed and direction of the chase but never allowing it to end. The result for viewers is something that unfolds "live," but which is generated from a piece of cinema culled from the past; the project plays with the tension between what is live — or alive — and what is dead and must be resurrected.

As with the *Psycho* remakes, the project erases classical narrative structure, plucking the particularly exhilarating chase sequences, those that form a bridge between narrative stasis and violence, to create an experience of unending suspense that unfolds algorithmically. We hover continuously in between in a kind of limbo, but with an acute awareness of that limbo and the mechanism producing it. The bifurcation between story and metastory, between narrative pleasure and critical scrutiny, is at the heart of Kant's notion of the sublime. Rather than merely experiencing the violence in the horror chase sequence, or the decimation of the original film text, we participate in a reflection on the powerful capacity of the project's generative core, and the idea that the project's limits have, in a sense, been erased. We are asked to confront the expansive force of the algorithm, and experience both the ensuing pleasure and terror. Indeed, the structure of the *Horror Chase* installation draws our attention not merely to the suspended story onscreen, but to the apparatus that produces it. We become very much aware of not only the critical gesture of isolating and realigning the chase sequences, but to the infrastructure that allows it all to happen. We participate in an experience of digital engagement, marveling at the machine and its abilities, while attentive as well to our embodied presence within the gallery space. That this occurs in conjunction with the chase scenes is at once very humorous, but also telling. The sense of the sublime we experience here with the horror chase is mapped onto the broader pleasure and anxiety of the cultural transition from analog to digital, from linear to nonlinear, and from singular narrative throughlines to distributed stories.

Media artist Scott Snibbe's *Visceral Cinema: Chien* (2005) crafts an installation work that is, in a sense, a remake, in this case of Luis Buñuel's

1927 film *Un Chien Andalou*. Initially, the installation seems to consist merely of a projected image showing the shadowy outline of a man dragging a piano with a rope. As such, viewers tend to approach it hesitantly, politely standing off to the side in order not to disrupt the projection on the wall. However, the more adventurous (or the very young) cheerfully bisect the projector beam, and when they do, with their shadows entering and becoming part of the artwork, the piece responds. Depending on where you stand, either the laboring fellow will slow down, the shadows will disintegrate into hordes of ants or the rope will snap. While these alterations may seem minor, what occurs in the gallery space is a bit more radical. Visitors become performers in the piece, morphing from passive onlookers into active participants, from relatively invisible beings into exhibitionists. Further, because the installation's mechanism remains opaque, normally aloof viewers suddenly find themselves working together to figure out the piece's underlying rules. Although Snibbe borrowed the image and title from Buñuel's notorious Surrealist film, which contains several shocking sequences, including the graphic slicing of an eyeball, he chooses to reference the film obliquely — his interest in the visceral shifts from the screen to the social environs of the gallery, transforming the seemingly neutral space into one electric with unexpected interaction.

Scholars have debated whether or not new media artworks that borrow the tactics of data visualization might participate in the experience of the sublime. Lev Manovich's essay "Data Visualization as New Abstraction and Anti-Sublime" argues that "data visualization art is concerned with the anti-sublime" (8), due to the fact that artists attempt to map and organize vast amounts of information precisely so that it is understandable within the capacity of human cognition. Warren Sack, however, argues that some new media artworks embody Kant's definition of the sublime by doing the opposite; rather than reducing immensity to a scale of comprehension, artists instead attempt to demonstrate the vastness of computation. Jon McCormack and Alan Dorin use the term "computational sublime," which they define as "the instilling of simultaneous feelings of pleasure and fear in the viewer of a process realized in a computing machine" (12), and it is this capacity which is captured by *Horror Chase* and *Visceral Cinema: Chien*.

In *Horror Chase* and *Visceral Cinema: Chien*, visitors tentatively probe the border of new form of cinematic embodiment and engagement that is extended or enhanced through the digital, and the traditional pleasures of narrative — character identification, the resolution of conflict and visual pleasure — are replaced by experiences of problem-solving, pattern recognition and an understanding of the grammar of information. These in turn align with a kind of subjectivity required by a world mediated by electronic networks, and the projects' provocations produce the sublime precisely in bridging the intellectual work performed to understand the underlying mechanism while at the same time prompting an understanding of tremendous computational power.

Designing Spaces for the Sublime

All of the projects mentioned so far take shape as gallery-based installations, but another example of terror and the sublime occurs in museums and galleries that become entire environments in which artists stage their work. Such is the case with the unusual exhibition design of the Santa Monica Museum of Art's "Dark Places" (2005), which featured the work of 76 international media artists — ranging from LA-based artist Jordan Crandall, the Delhi-based RAQS Media Collective, to architects Diller + Scofidio — presented in a monster-like architectural armature suspended in the Museum's main room and embodying an amalgam of horror film monsters, from the bodily mutation of *Alien*'s creature to the hard-body structures of *Predator*. The structure featured four large-scale front screen projections, four smaller rear screen projections, and eight workstations, with eight intersecting programs of media on each screen and the ability for the entire structure to fluctuate from light to dark depending on visitor activity. Curated by Joshua Decter and designed by the international design group Servo, the show challenged the idea of neutral and pristine presentation, creating instead an environment in which artworks bleed together and viewers deal as much with the exhibition design as with the art itself. Indeed, the sculptural viewing environment contained several projection systems that pushed outward aggressively, like wide, gaping mouths, while smaller projections in the interior space of the structure were like orbs of light luring visitors into the body of the beast. With "Dark Places," the sense of anxiety and trauma that emerged from the show's array of artworks was made material by the organism that housed the images; it sparked horror in part because it recalled and resurrected horror film monsters of the past, with the result that rather than just being *about* dark places, the show itself *was* a dark place, and viewers were invited into the monster and left to find our own way through its glowing, responsive body.

As with the artworks mentioned previously, the "Dark Places" exhibit space stages representations of horror within a context designed to query the very status of the cinematic. Gone is the focus on the single film, the traditional theatrical experience, and the individual spectator of 20th century moviegoing. In its place we find projects bleeding into one another within a monstrous body, and we are asked to confront the constituent elements of knowledge and being as we are interpellated, not as cinematic subjects, but rather as those who inhabit a fully mediated and networked space. The unity and clarity of previous cinematic experiences haunts the space, reminding us of what has been lost, but at the same time, we work to understand the new configuration, which is just beyond comprehension. Kant's description of the sublime contributes to an understanding of this moment to the extent that it remains just that — an experience that straddles the haptic and cognitive. As we push to make this experience functional or instrumental, to use it as evidence of the cultural anxiety of a particular moment, does it lose its more radical sense of delight?

Conclusion: Pleasure and Pain

It is clear that we are in the midst of a dramatic reconfiguration of cinema — of cinema as social institution, as apparatus, and as discursive structure — and post-cinematic artworks are increasingly abundant. But what is the role of the horror film in so many of these projects? Why do so many remake existing horror films and then extend what gets "remade" beyond merely the film itself to include a revision of the cinematic production process; the ways in which the films are distributed and shared; and the exhibition forms and venues in which they are presented? The question has four answers:

First, horror films are fundamentally concerned with the transgression of boundaries, as are post-cinematic works. Both call into question culturally established norms, making us aware of those norms through their violation. Further, in uniting the high art venues of the gallery and museum with the low art genre film, these projects meld entities normally deemed disparate, crafting something that is hybrid or interstitial and, as such, often deeply troubling for viewers.

Second, horror films prompt visceral responses, tapping into our sense of discomfort through the somatic reactions of the body. Post-cinematic works often mobilize that discomfort in crafting experiences that are at once emotional and intellectual, as well as embodied; rather than merely contemplating the media artwork as object, then, we often engage horror-based post-cinematic works more actively due specifically to their horrific elements. Most of the projects described here, however, confuse the visceral; rather than simply responding to the horror seen onscreen in a visceral way, we instead also move around, gesture, and — with our own bodies — experience the artworks through full-bodied perception, while also constantly hovering between the status of the original with reference to its remake.

Third, horror films tend to emerge at moments of cultural upheaval. The horror films of the 1970s responded to Viet Nam, for example, an argument made deftly by director Adam Simon in his 2000 film *The American Nightmare,* which chronicles a decade of horror films, between 1968 and 1978. In reflecting on upheaval, horror films provide an indirect means for viewers to grapple with social and cultural issues. Similarly, post-cinematic projects respond to cultural shifts at the turn of the century, crafting artworks that answer our need for new forms of narrative experience. These artworks are, as such, often monstrous; they don't yet have a fixed form but are hybrids, cultural shape-shifters searching for new forms.

And, fourth, horror at its best illustrates the fundamental instability of existence, a state echoed often in post-cinematic works which situate us uncomfortably in zones that are deeply unfamiliar in their violence. In his essay "Philosophical Horror," Paul Santilli distinguishes between things and events that are horrific — murder or incest, for example — and those things that horrify by challenging ontological boundaries. Murder and incest *should* be horrifying; they are deemed horrifying culturally, and our repugnance to acts of this sort helps police the boundaries needed to maintain social order. What interests Santilli, however, is horror that challenges the very structures we use to organize our sense of the world, making us uncomfortably aware of the tenuousness of those boundaries. Calling on the work of Martin Heidegger, Santilli writes, "Horror is not only a peculiar emotion arising from time to time in response to a possible monstrosity, but it is a constant feature of our being in the world. It is a basic mood and orientation, or *Stimmung,* with respect to existence" (174). It is the anxiety we face as humans, and is founded on our horror at the lack of fixity and solidity in our world. Santilli continues, "What art horror shows us is that it is Being itself in any or all of its manifestations that has become uncanny and monstrous" (175). Recalling Kristeva, the sublime is conjured by artworks that illuminate this state of existence, transforming the abject to the sublime.

Returning to Tscherkassky's *Outer Space,* our heroine battles against unseen forces that ravage her in a darkened house while the filmmaker scratches back and forth over the images, creating a spectacular attack that is not just about the violence against the female, but also a reflection on the destruction of celluloid. And perhaps this underscores the fundamental compatibility of the juncture of the remake as post-cinematic expression and as horror. If, as Robin Wood has succinctly noted, horror films may be defined as instances in which "normality is threatened by the Monster" (150), post-cinematic artworks threaten the "normal" cinematic apparatus and its ability to construct certain forms of spectatorship and subjectivity, offering in their place instability and a kind of monstrosity. They are monstrous in their defilement of the traditional cinematic body. However, to the extent that these projects also often invite viewers to reflect on the ways in which the media around us extends, supports, and, indeed, constructs new frameworks for being, they support experiences of Kant's sublime, arousing both pleasure and pain — pleasure in the knowledge that our sense of reason can reckon with experiences that are beyond the faculty of sense, and pain in the desire for an alignment between the magnitude of what we witness and our ability to understand it. The sublime prompted by these remakes of horror films alternates between the two, combining the exhilaration in witnessing a paradigm shift alongside the pain of not quite being able to master the full implications of a radical aesthetic, cultural, and epistemological transformation.

Watching the World Burn: Intensity, Absurdity and Echoes of the Sublime in Contemporary Science Fiction Destruction

John P. Warton

> "Since time immemorial, people have craved spectacles permitting them vicariously to experience the fury of conflagrations, the excesses of cruelty and suffering, and unspeakable lusts — spectacles which shock the shuddering and delighted onlooker into unseeing participation" — Siegfried Kracauer, *Theory of Film*, 58

> "This is not to say that the cultural products of the postmodern era are utterly devoid of feeling, but rather that such feelings — which it may be better and more accurate to call 'intensities' — are now free-floating and impersonal, and tend to be dominated by a peculiar kind of euphoria" — Fredric Jameson, "Postmodernism, or the Cultural Logic of Late Capitalism," 64

Despite the commodification of destruction spectacles within science fiction (SF) cinema, their persistent escalation in the post-mechanical age, in which the mechanics of the camera are no longer required to produce a filmic image, suggests a spectatorial allure to Fredric Jameson's "kind of euphoria" generated by these digitally manufactured stimuli that bear striking resemblances to the sublime. Though the sublime has been examined through a number of different lenses, SF cinema's enduring enthusiasm for awesome terrors and terrible wonders suggests the persistent relevance of 19th century philosopher Edmund Burke's writings on the sublime and its subsumption of terror. Displacing previous notions of the sublime in SF cinema, specifically Scott Bukatman's well-reasoned but ultimately dated analysis, contemporary encounters with the sublime—or rather, *echoes* of the sublime—emerge from the visual and audial depictions of mass destruction. Yet not all mass destruction is sublime.

This essay examines post-mechanical SF cinema's potential to invoke echoes of the sublime through commodified spectacles of destruction. As in the case of Roland Emmerich's *2012* (2009), destruction sequences can quickly snowball into absurdist, cartoonish action, distancing the spectator and confining sublime encounters to the reactions of the intra-diegetic characters. Nevertheless, some mass destruction sequences still reveal a capacity to produce echoes of the sublime through the images' associations with recent historical traumas.

The Post-Mechanical SF Sublime

Though Jameson's "waning of affect" is evident in myriad articles and film reviews about the superficiality of contemporary visual effects and their depthless visual excitation, digital age SF films bearing disaster and mass destruction sequences continue to surface. Since Jameson first published the opening quote in 1984, superficial intensities have exponentially exploded beyond his foresight, yet his observations remain salient. SF cinema has adapted to the attractions of intensity to the point that depictions of mass destruction have become a near-mandatory construct of the genre, where modernist affect is supplanted by postmodernist superficial sheen and depthless euphoria. Jameson admits in the introductory quote that the "waning of affect" does not atrophy away leaving behind an empty void, but rather it is supplanted by superficial "'intensities' ... dominated by a peculiar kind of euphoria" (64). (Jameson's euphoric intensities do also bear a resemblance to Edmund Burke's notion of *delight*—neither horror nor pleasure, as I discuss below—experienced during encounters with the sublime.)

Countering Jameson's waning of affect, Brian Massumi states, "Fredric Jameson notwithstanding, belief has waned for many, but not affect. If anything, our condition is characterized by a surfeit of it" (27). In his amendments to Jameson, Massumi deconstructs "affect," equating the term with his own definition of "intensity" (27). He writes, "The problem is that there is no cultural-theoretical vocabulary specific to affect.... Affect is most often used loosely as a synonym for emotion. But ... emotion and affect—if affect is intensity—follow different logics and pertain to different orders" (27). Continuing, Massumi delineates between affect and emotion, describing the latter as the semiotic exegesis of a specific intensity:

> An emotion is a subjective content, the sociolinguistic fixing of the quality of an experience which is from that point onward defined as personal. Emotion is qualified intensity, the conventional, consensual point of insertion of intensity into semantically and semiotically formed progressions, into narrativizable action-reaction circuits, into function and meaning. It is intensity owned and recognized. It is crucial to theorize the difference between affect and emotion. If some have the impression that affect has waned, it is because affect is unqualified [27–28].

Massumi, by arguing that elicited emotions are merely descriptors of sensorial effects of specific intensities, suggests that emotions are the means by which people structure and categorize various intensities in order to unpack and better comprehend the experience. For Massumi, emotions impose limits upon intensities; however, when one encounters an intensity (affect) that imbues conflicting emotions (e.g., joy/anxiety, attraction/repulsion) categorization becomes convoluted. As images of destruction hinge upon the aesthetics associated with the sublime, evoking dialectical emotions of awe/terror and attraction/repulsion, they find themselves trading on an intensity that frustrates simple categorization. In this way, Jameson's "intensities" and Massumi's "intensities" both describe that ambiguous, peculiar sensation of a sublime encounter such as those produced by witnessing intense mass destruction events.

Identifying the sublime in SF cinema as an encounter with mass destruction supplants Scott Bukatman's influential analysis on the SF sublime. In his essay "The Artificial Infinite: On Special Effects and the Sublime," Bukatman characterizes the sublime as a "tension between diminution and exaltation" (255–256). He posits that the infinite is transcended by a cognitive mastery over it, producing an ambivalent duality, and specifically identifies sublimity as the feeling of tension produced by encountering representations of technological wonders and the resultant anxieties produced (250, 268). Considering his reliance on Douglas Trumball's special effects sequences from Stanley Kubrick's *2001: A Space Odyssey* (1968), Trumbull's own *Silent Running* (1972), Steven Spielberg's *Close Encounters of the Third Kind* (1977), and George Lucas' *Star Wars* (1977), Bukatman's reasoning is sound. And, to be fair, advanced, awe-inspiring technology is often the hallmark of SF cinema from the mechanical era where the characters' diegetic astonishment at the encounter with the supernatural mirrors the extra-diegetic spectator's astonishment at the realization of the visual effects. As Barry Keith Grant notes, "We marvel at special effects images at once for their fantastic content and for the power of their realization" (19).

The critical problem, however, is that Bukatman's emphasis on a sublime image produced by special effects is bound to the parameters of the production process. Sublimity, in terms of the encounter with technological wonders, is confined to a spectatorial affect based upon questions regarding the process of how mechanical profilmic trickery and post-production analogue composite shots achieved such astonishing spectacles. Bukatman's sublime, then, obsolesces as a result of the digital transmogrification of the medium in which the spectator no longer wonders *how*. With digital technology, the scope of visual possibilities stretches toward the infinite where form, shape, and scale are only bound by the limits of human imagination. By Bukatman's logic, spectacular images wrought by digital effects would also have an artificially infinite capacity for sublime encounters because of their ability to present technological wonders *through* technological wonders. As not all digital visual effects are sublime, or at times even observable, one must re-examine the attempted provocation of the sublime through audial and visual content and aesthetic context, rather than the technology that manifests it.

Ceci n'est pas sublime

Counter-arguments and objections inherently beset any discussion of the sublime and an important qualification regarding its relationship to SF cinema is in order. Concurrent to the rise of digital effects and the escalation of SF destruction, we have witnessed numerous catastrophic tragedies and historical disasters in which hundreds, thousands, and even hundreds of thousands have been killed. Recent human-instigated attacks (e.g., 1995's Oklahoma City bombing; the 9/11 attacks on New York City and Washington, D.C., in 2001; the bombings in Bali in 2002; the London bombings in 2005; Baghdad's Green Zone bombing in 2009) and natural disasters (e.g., the Sumatra-Andaman earthquake tsunamis of 2004; Hurricane Katrina and its subsequent floods in New Orleans in 2005; the 2010 floods in Colombia, China, and Pakistan; and earthquakes in Sumatra in 2009, Haiti in 2010, and Tōhoku, Japan, and Christ Church, New Zealand, in 2011) expose the "peculiar" parallels between experienced destruction and cinematic fictions, with journalists often reporting victims' reactions as testifying to the "unreality" of the events and their resemblances to filmic spectacles. Cinematic destruction spectacles, however sublime-like, *do not invoke the sublime*; these digital representations of destruction are carefully manufactured stylized renderings.

By way of an analogy, consider Disney's *Twilight Zone*-themed ride "The Tower of Terror." After ascending its way to the top of the haunted hotel, an elevator drops its fifteen passengers allegedly down thirteen stories in simulated free-fall. Prior to this stage, the passengers have approached the hilltop "hotel" and witnessed the dropping cars through gaps in the tower's façade and heard the accompanying screams, snaked along the queuing barricades through the dilapidated hotel lobby, endured the preshow narrative describing the characters and their mysterious disappearance, and settled themselves into an elevator car fitted with seats, lap belts, and of course, handle bars. The space in which the passengers occupy is wholly fictional (indeed, the whole of Disney's Theme Parks can be considered as a fictional space). They knowingly and, for the most part, willingly place themselves within the narrative space, fully cognizant of what lies ahead within their enveloping diegesis. Despite the passengers' awareness of the surrounding simulacra and the fictional context they inhabit, the drop itself nevertheless produces a fleeting glimmer of that instinctual terror of helplessly free-falling.[1] This affect is not equal to that of someone who has genuinely experienced riding in an elevator in free-fall; it is a manufactured *simulation* of that intensity.

In the early 1980s, Great America, an amusement park just north of Chicago, offered a thrill ride called "The Edge," a free-fall experience much like "The Tower of Terror" but without the aesthetic pomp or encompassing narrative. The four-rider stand-up carriage traveled up a high vertical shaft, transitioned forward onto a drop track, then plummeted in free-fall over 100-feet until it was slowed by a curving ramp and braking system. On 22 May 1984, the free-fall ride malfunctioned. Halfway up its ascent, the carriage disengaged from the lifting apparatus, dropping the three young teenage occupants into free-fall sixty feet back down the ascension shaft (McNeill; Enstad; Zorn). Consider, then, the disparity between the ride's intent to simulate terror and the genuine terror experienced by the three injured riders. Despite corrections and safety improvements to the ride, "The Edge" was removed in 1986 due to the stigma of the accident. It seems that although park attendees went seeking hair-raising thrills, the anxiety over the ambiguity of this ride's simulated terror and its association with genuine terror did not ultimately warrant the risk of patronage.

Though one may feel affected by filmic representation of mass destruction and genocide, movies cannot convey *in equal measure* the affects produced by genuine, historic events. Under the threat of spectatorial indifference, hyper-realizations of destruction — such as the sudden and violent decimation and/or upheaval of assumed stable or predictable entities of urban spaces, mass transit systems, land and seascapes — attempt to physically affect the spectator to the same degree as an unmediated experience of disaster.

However, an encounter with the sublime is not an experience subject to intentional invocation; film renderings of mass destruction cannot manipulate the film spectator into a genuine encounter with the sublime for that implies a mastery over, or a containment of, the event, just as Disney holds mastery over a manufactured free-fall. The nature of the sublime is one that propels beyond human comprehension and cannot be bound by frames or figments: "It immediately involves, or else by its presence provokes, a representation of limitlessness" (Kant, *Critique*, 90). Yet comparisons of experienced sublimity to filmic spectacle persist. Witnesses to the sublimity of historical destruction, saturated with astonishment and terror, often formulate verbal descriptions for an encounter that is ontologically beyond description. It is understandable, then, that comparisons to filmic spectacles are made because they are arguably the closest illustration of such events, for though they are not sublime, they can often provoke an affect that is analogous; while mass destruction simulacra are not sublime, these images *can evoke comparable emotions* one might experience in a sublime encounter — similar, yet diluted, like a refraction or an *echo*. These emotional reactions, to which contemporary SF filmmakers so desperately look for spectatorial engagement, are merely echoes of the genuine sublime.

The "Genuine" Sublime

Naturally, the notion that sublime simulacra echo *genuine* sublimity requires explication. Unfortunately, discussions of what is genuinely sublime are invariably plagued by divagations, finding itself a malleable notion and subject to evolving methodologies each within their own historical contexts. Owing to this malleability, arriving at an absolute definition for the sublime seems impractical, if not impossible. From the 18th century empiricism of Edmund Burke and the rationalism of Immanuel Kant, to the late twentieth century postmodernism of Jean-François Lyotard and the psychoanalysis of Slavoj Žižek, the sublime seems naturally predisposed to adaptation by tangential modes of discourse. Andrew Ashfield and Peter de Bolla note that even within the scope of 18th century writings on the sublime, certain authorial biases revealed through illustrative tropes led to tangential lines of argumentation within the broader discourse: "In effect the analysis of reading becomes stained by a set of discriminations which it neither knowingly inherits nor necessarily welcomes from the discourse on the sublime" (7). That is, rather than focusing on the subsuming concept, notions of the sublime adopted new characteristics as a result of descriptive elaborations. Both Kant and Burke are guilty of such discrimination in their chauvinism. Both philosophers attempt to better clarify the attributes of the sublime by juxtaposing it with notions of the beautiful. In their attempts to elucidate the concept of the sublime, however, Kant and Burke's gendered generalizations and stereotypes obfuscate the concept.

Further plaguing an absolute definition of the "genuine" sublime are the prudent arguments of post–Kantian writers, such as Samuel Taylor Coleridge, from the Romantic period. Coleridge, for example, reunites Kant's bifurcation of mind and nature in the primacy of the mind's own imagination (Shaw 95–96):

> I meet, I find the Beautiful — but I give, contribute, or rather attribute the Sublime. No object of Sense is sublime in itself; but only so far as I make it a symbol of some Idea. The circle is a beautiful figure in itself; it becomes sublime, when I contemplate eternity under that figure.... Nothing that has a shape can be sublime except by metaphor [qtd. in Shaw 95].

For Coleridge, the human capacity to imagine the limitless eternal through natural spectacles witnessed by eyes and ears is a product of the mind's capacity for semiotic representation. Sublimity is in the eye of the beholder. Whatever is deemed as sublime, then, is spectatorially subjective. How does one identify what constitutes the sublime if each encounter is dependent upon the individual? Even within this very discussion, is my consideration of mass destruction as sublime salient?

Whereas the Romantics presuppose the imagination's ability to subjectify the sublime, 20th century postmodernist Jean-François Lyotard argues that the imagination is incapable of comprehending sublime encounters. For Lyotard, the sublime actualizes a break between the event and what we comprehend the event to be:

> It is what dismantles consciousness, what deposes consciousness, it is what consciousness cannot formulate ... Before asking questions about what it is and about its significance, before the *quid*, it must "first" so to speak "happen," *quod*. That it happens "precedes," so to speak, the question pertaining to what happens [90].

Between sensorial witness and mental understanding is a moment in which the "something" has not yet been determined, consumed, or narrated. For Lyotard, the gap between experience and reason reveals the inadequacy of the human imagination in managing encounters with the sublime.[2]

Given the discrepancies among explanations of the sublime within empiricism, rationalism, Romanticism, and postmodernism, as well as feminist, psychoanalytic, and Marxist methodologies, a catchall definition for the *genuinely* sublime, then, cannot be attained. Yet, despite the variances within each theorist's writings, their specific examples of manifest sublimity seem to bear common characteristics: confrontations with the rages of the natural world such as the ocean (Burke, *A Philosophical Enquiry into the Origin of Our Ideas of the Sublime and Beautiful*), the storm (Kant, *Observations on the Feeling of the Beautiful and the Sublime*) or environmental turbulence (Schopenhauer, *The World as Will and Representation*); sudden encounters with immense darkness, such as a gothic cathedral (Samuel Taylor Coleridge, *1818 Lectures on European Literature*) or an abyss (David Hartley, *Observations on Man*); the memory of death's nearness such as the Holocaust (Jean-François Lyotard, *The Differend*), or the sinking of the *RMS Titanic* (Slavoj Žižek, *The Sublime Object of Ideology*). Although the concept of the sublime has endured much transmutation, these writers' examples, employed to elucidate their own take on sublimity, share characteristics that suggest the resilient relevance of Burke's theory of a sublime manifested through *distantiated* terror.

Burkean Sublimity and Distantiated Terror

Terror acts as the lynchpin for Burke's notion of the sublime, permeating the intensities of astonishment, awe, and wonder. Burke describes the sublime as a feeling of delight that comes from an encounter with the terrible and horrific, rooted in the primal instinct of self-preservation (86). In this respect, the sublime seems particularly apt in describing the aesthetics of destruction:

Whatever is fitted in any sort to excite the ideas of pain, and danger, that is to say, whatever is in any sort terrible, or is conversant about terrible objects, or operates in a manner analogous to terror, is a source of the *sublime*; that is it is productive of the strongest emotion which the mind is capable of feeling [39; original emphasis].

Through empirical examination of the senses, particularly sight and sound, Burke characterizes sublimity as grandeur, power, and the infinite. Indeed, witnessing the *sudden* tumults of the natural world, such as a lightning storm or a volcano eruption, are wondrous to behold but the sublime emerges more in the effects of the agent rather than the agent itself—the mass destruction. The sublime is the response to a visualized catastrophe in which we are horrified at the atrocity but also awestruck at the manner in which it unfolds.

Burke observes that the sublime impedes the individual through an arrestment of astonishment: "Astonishment is that state of the soul, in which all its motions are suspended, with some degree of horror" (57). If astonishment is the arrestment of the body by exposure to some sudden terror, the *cinematic* invocation of terror and horror naturally suggests the horror genre. And indeed the bulk of horror films foreground the depictions of pain, danger, and physical terror. However, Burke further develops his notion of the sublime by acknowledging additional degrees of sublimity: "Astonishment ... is the effect of the sublime in its highest degree; the inferior effects are admiration, reverence and respect" (57). The amalgam of terror with awe, then, derivates from horror cinema to embrace that of SF cinema, which Barry Keith Grant and Vivian Sobchack define through the genre's perpetual thematic undercurrents of reverence and awe. Whereas in horror cinema the central characteristic of destruction is the inward focus on the monstrous body, for Grant and Sobchack the SF film focuses its destruction outward toward society, the earth, or the heavens (Grant 18; Sobchack 30). Sobchack writes, "The aesthetics of destruction please us as a well-mounted slide might please a scientist. The passion and human hunger of the horror film is replaced by the satisfaction of objectivity. Terror is replaced by wonder" (38).

To clarify this last remark, fear and terror in the SF film are not *replaced* by wonder but *subsumed* by it. Continuing, Sobchack writes, "The terrifying aspect of traditional horror films arises from a recognition that we are forever linked to the crudeness of our earthbound bodies; the fear in SF films springs from the future possibility that we may—in a sense—lose contact with our bodies" (Sobchack 39). The horrific has not been exchanged with the awesome but merely incorporated into it. In contemporary SF cinema, depictions of destruction can create an echo of sublime astonishment and awe in conjunction with a fearful astonishment.

The sublime as a delight from an encounter with the terrible and horrific seems to imply a psychological appetite for sadistic experiences. Burke eludes sadism, though, by arguing that the sublime is a by-product of an exposure to and *removal of* danger that causes a sensation of "delight" rather than "pleasure," as the latter is reserved for what is beautiful and joyful, untarnished by exposure to terror (36–37). He describes this as a "removal of pain or danger," but Burke is not suggesting that the pain of burning one's fingers followed by the relief of cold running water is an encounter with the sublime. Burke's "removal" is rather a physical distancing away from immediate risk of pain or danger, while yet remaining near enough to be drawn to the threat as an aesthetic delight: "When danger or pain press too nearly they are incapable of giving any delight, and are simply terrible; but at certain distances, and with certain modifications, they may be, and they are delightful" (40).

Distance, then, becomes a prerequisite for a sublime experience, though not only in contemporary reactions to destruction and terror, but also in ancient writings as well. Compare, for example, Marc Redfield's comments on the 9/11 attacks ("To those not immediately threatened by it, this disastrous spectacle could seem at the time at once horrifically present and strangely unreal" [56]) with Lucretius' writings in *De rerum natura* from the first century BC ("Pleasant it is when on the great sea the winds trouble the waters, to gaze from shore upon another's great tribulation; not because anyone's troubles are a voluptuous joy, but because to perceive what evils you are free from yourself is pleasant" [Redfield 73]). The sublime encounter is only attainable within a tight orbit around the object commanding attention; far enough from enveloping terror but, paradoxically, near enough to feel its threat — a position along the event horizon. Lyotard, praising the underlying threat of annihilation in the Burkean sublime, regards the sublime as only attainable through the requisite distantiation provided by the mediation of art: "Art, by distancing this menace, procures a pleasure of relief, of delight. Thanks to art, the soul is returned to the agitated zone between life and death" (100). In film, distance between spectator and screen is an imperative of the medium; yet too much distance eliminates any potential encounter with echoes of the sublime. Distantiation, for most SF filmmakers, is undesired in that it reduces the potential to produce the genre's dominant affects of awe and wonder; in SF film aesthetics, this typically manifests through low-budget productions exhibiting poor production values, lackluster acting and belabored special effects. As Grant states, "nothing destroys the pleasure of a science fiction movie more than seeing the 'seams' in a matte shot or glimpsing the zipper on an alien's bodysuit" (19).[3] Distantiation, then, as a necessary condition of the sublime, must be present but not in the Brechtian sense, in which overt self-reflexivity short-circuits the spectatorial experience. Echoes of the sublime are communicated in film through an immersive encounter, enveloping the spectator, reducing distantiation to the vacuous space between viewer and screen. In contemporary SF cinema, the dominant approach has been to overwhelm the spectator with digital light and sound spectacles of destruction.

Sublimity and Absurdity in 2012

Theorists have applied a variety of appellations to this cinematic aesthetic of visceral excitation: invoking Guy Debord's *Society of Spectacle*, Bruce Isaacs employs "spectacle aesthetic"; Geoff King and Scott McQuire both use "impact aesthetic"; John Orr describes it as "hyper-modern"; and David Bordwell refers to it as "intensified continuity" (Isaacs 147; King 99; McQuire 41; Orr 40; Bordwell 121). I, in light of my limited space, use them interchangeably.[4] The exponential growth of SF cinema's usage of destruction images through impact aesthetics *seems* to be a direct reaction to Jameson's postmodernist "waning of affect," though such usage only further underscores the argument for diminishing returns. Attempting to manufacture synaesthetic affect through a turbo-boost of digitally enhanced spectacles has typically resulted in the opposite effect, instilling spectatorial distantiation through spectacle *ad absurdum*. As both Michele Pierson and Angela Ndalianis claim, SF cinema in the 1990s can be characterized as a period of overindulgence in the application of emerging CGI technology, often at the expense of coherent narrative causality (86–87, 125; 256, respectively). Regarding 1990s SF and horror films, David Sanjek states: "The profusion of sequels, remakes, and narratives that amalgamate familiar elements into various forms of pastiche results perhaps not in contempt on the part of the consumers but a weariness bred of sensory overload and intellectual under stimulation" (111).

SF cinema of the 21st century, on the other hand, reveals a bifurcation of aesthetics. The admittedly more compelling branch of the aesthetic bifurcation reveals an abstemious hesitation towards digitally enhanced visual excess, from which emerges an intriguing cooperation between CGI effects and documentary realism techniques (appropriated from *cinéma vérité* and Direct Cinema movements) that together function as a method of infusing its destruction imagery with affectations associated with the memories of recent historical destruction, such as *Children of Men* (Cuarón, 2006) and *Cloverfield* (Reeves, 2008). The other side of the aesthetic bifurcation escalates on from its 1990s predecessors in a style of visual carousal made possible by further technological advancements, as in *Sky Captain and the World of Tomorrow* (Conran, 2004), *Avatar* (Cameron, 2009), and *John Carter* (Stanton, 2012). In films such as these, a divergence develops between intra-diegetic sublimity and its extra-diegetic absurdity. Roland Emmerich's destruction extravaganza *2012* provides a foremost example.

During the 1990s German-born filmmaker Roland Emmerich emerged as the leading director of digital destruction epics. Under his direction, *Stargate* (1994), *Independence Day* (1996), and *Godzilla* (1998) embrace an impact aesthetic bent on visceral encounters with intense devastation. The international-friendly (yet U.S.-centric) *Independence Day* is an oft-cited text within academia as it depicts the CGI-simulated obliteration of structures connoting political and commercial power in a pre–9/11 era. In his post–9/11 films *The Day After Tomorrow* (2004) and *2012*, Emmerich redirects his attention away from violent confrontations with the "Other" to focus rather on the tacit social contract of international cooperation between people groups during a sudden threat to humanity.

Whereas other disaster films center on a mass transit system, a building, or a city, in *2012*, Emmerich broadens his scope of catastrophe to a *global* perspective. Scientists from India and the U.S. predict a worldwide tectonic plate displacement that will obliterate life on earth. Through the concerted, albeit conspiratorial, cooperation of (primarily first-world) nations, financed by the world's richest elite, a collection of arks is built to ensure the survival of terra firma life and human cultural heritage. Though the general public is left unaware of the looming annihilation, underground rumors spread about a massive construction project in the mountains of China. When the disaster occurs, everyman Jackson (John Cusack), his divorced wife Kate (Amanda Peet), their two young children, and Kate's boyfriend Gordon (Tom McCarthy), struggle to reach the safety of the arks and in so doing mend broken familial bonds. As hippie conspiracy theorist Charlie Frost (Woody Harrelson) states, "Something like this could only originate in Hollywood."

In keeping with the conventions of the disaster genre, themes of nuclear familial healing and the sanctity of *all* human life interweave throughout the narrative. Yet these concerns, because of their conventional nature, are immaterial next to the film's visual splendor of transnational destruction: rather than inspiring sublime-like synaesthesia through its visuals, *2012* is beset by its penchant for absurd escalations of destruction.

The escape sequence from Santa Monica airport provides an effective illustration. Gordon, piloting the twin-engine light aircraft, lifts off the ground just as it crumbles away beneath them. Rather than steering toward the ocean or climbing to a safe elevation over the destruction, Gordon instead pilots just above the rupturing ground, weaving in, around, and under the crumbling city. Skyscrapers collapse before them. Highway overpasses crumble, sending cars and people into free-fall. A subway train rockets out from its tube into mid-air and Gordon pilots *under* it. Meanwhile, the central characters behold the enveloping devastation with awestruck expressions, as if on a guided tour of the apocalypse. And this is but one scene in a series of escalating near-death experiences that compound *ad absurdum* in both narrative and visual effect.

When fleeing their Los Angeles home for the Santa Monica airport (in a limousine), Jackson and family maneuver around a cascade of falling cars, under a crumbling elevated freeway, and *through* a collapsing skyscraper. The family stops at Yellowstone National Park to retrieve a map detailing the location of the arks and, again, narrowly eludes spectacular volcanic eruptions and tectonic plate upsurges. In Vatican City, a crack splits across the Sistine Chapel ceiling between the nearly-touching fingers of God and Adam, and then floodwaters demolish St. Peter's basilica and the thousands of people standing vigil. In Washington, D.C., a giant tsunami throws the USS *John F. Kennedy* aircraft carrier down onto the White House. Tsunamis flood over the crests of the Himalayas. An ark pries loose from its moorings, surfs down the mountainside, and collides with Mt. Everest. Though the film's intent may be to provide the spectator with an overwhelming encounter with destructive "intensities," the compounded indulgent spectacles ultimately undermine the images' capacity to affect; instead, the incredulity provokes laughable disbelief within the extra-diegetic realm of spectatorship.

Intra-Diegetic Sublimity, Extra-Diegetic Absurdity

The global devastation in *2012* coheres with Burke's notion of the imagined infinite within the sublime, as the camera frame cannot contain the destruction's implied endlessness. Furthermore, Emmerich positions the camera within the violence of the narrative space, assuming the image's potential for affect is directly dependent upon the spectator's visual proximity to danger and death, despite the mediated form. Intriguingly, it is along the plane of the theater's silver screen that Emmerich ruptures any hope of aligning intra-diegetic and extra-diegetic reactions to the visuals of mass destruction. That is, while the destruction is considered sublime by the characters from within the narrative, the spectator, from a position outside of the narrative, regards the same destructive event as overblown absurdity.

By emphasizing their proximity to limitless danger in the narrative space, the central characters experience the sublime. They do not wail in terror but watch in wide-eyed, open-mouthed shock, encountering terror yet distanced from it by the intra-diegetic frames within the escaping cars and planes. During Jackson, Kate, Gordon, and the kids' escape from Los Angeles and Las Vegas, the characters witness the apocalyptic devastation through windshields, windows, open doors, and mirrors, intercutting among interior close-up reaction shots of the passengers, exterior reaction shots of the driver or pilot, third person perspectives of the vehicle within the perilous narrative space, and subjective perspective shots of the passengers/driver/pilot witnessing the devastation. The distantiation through these mediating frames allows for the characters to witness the surrounding destruction as if it was itself a movie; unfortunately, this intra-diegetic sublimity does not incite its echo within the film spectator. For the viewer, the amplified, intensified destruction quickly escalates into the realm of the ridiculous.

In discussing other contemporary SF films such as *The Matrix Revolutions* (Wachowskis, 2003) and Peter Jackson's *King Kong* (2005), Greg Tuck argues that the spectacular and the sublime are antithetical. He posits that spectacles, including those of mass destruction, are shaped by magnitude and essentially empirically derived, whereas sublimity invokes an idea rather than an indexical image (261). For Tuck, more is less. He writes, "Commodities repeat the logic of the spectacular which aims towards the sublime by similarly hoping that by offering more of the former they will somehow generate the value of the latter" (266). In general, Tuck's position aptly applies to *2012* and its overblown, compounding action sequences; however, and in addition to his inclusion of the sterile notion of indexicality, Tuck's analysis relies upon a false argumentative dichotomy that excludes the possibility of magnitude and visual excitation as *contributing* to a sublime idea by providing a context through which the sublime may be encountered.

The challenge to the SF filmmaker is not to exaggerate the disparity between intra-diegesis and extra-diegesis through escalating visuals but find within its fiction analogous elements to *experiential* fact. For one brief moment in *2012*, during Gordon's flight through a crumbling Los Angeles, the stunned pilot — in slow-motion — glances out his window as he passes a skyscraper torn open with terror-stricken people hanging from the exposed edge. This passing shot comprises the only genuinely extra-diegetic echo of the sublime during the 158-minute film. It is not invoked through its impact aesthetics but by its direct associations with the memory of experiential mass destruction. In this case, the image of people dangling from the demolished upper floors of the skyscraper immediately forces the memory of 9/11 and the attack on the Twin Towers to the surface, and with it the associated intensities.

By correlating the fictional destruction with experienced destruction, the film encourages a transfusion of affect from the historical human trauma to an analogous simulacrum — from the brief image of a terror-stricken woman on the verge of falling to her death to the personal accounts of the 9/11 attacks, reporting their witness of helpless victims falling from the towers. However ethical, visuals appropriating the genuine, experiential sublime can produce echoes of the sublime within its cinematic fiction. As Burke writes:

> There is no spectacle we so eagerly pursue, as that of some uncommon and grievous calamity; so that whether the misfortune is before our eyes, or whether they are turned back to it in history, it always touches with delight. This is not an unmixed delight, but blended with no small uneasiness. The delight we have in such things, hinders us from shunning scenes of misery; and the pain we feel, prompts us to relieve ourselves in relieving those who suffer [46].

Though spectatorial affect wanes in response to the familiarity of digital destruction simulacra, the market is nevertheless continually inundated by films emphasizing intense depictions of mass destruction, suggesting the dogged pursuit of euphoria through astonishment and terror analogous to encounters with the sublime. As a result of CGI and the infinite quality of digital technologies, the SF sublime can no longer be defined by the wonder evoked through encounters with advanced technology as is argued by Scott Bukatman. Rather, the post-mechanical sublime in SF cinema manifests through Burkean astonishment and terror evoked by images of mass destruction. Though films centered on images of destruction typically fall prey to aesthetic exaggeration as they search for artificial astonishment, when science-fictional intra-diegetic destruction invokes visual associations with experientially genuine sublimity, echoes of the sublime can materialize from the memory.

Notes

1. In the first part of his essay "Film, Emotion, and Genre," Noël Carroll distinguishes between emotions and instinctive responses. I have elected to consider them unified, rather than digress into delineations between the various lobes of the cerebral cortex and the accompanying limbic system. For these purposes, then, the sensation of being startled, for one, will be considered an emotional response.

2. Paradoxically, Lyotard considers that the sublime can only be achieved through artistic renderings, or, rather, the speculation of such art (106). This significantly contrasts with my own "echoes of the sublime." Unfortunately, the discussion regarding this disparity lies beyond the scope of this paper.

3. Grant's "pleasure" here refers to the awe and wonder associated with SF, not the comic pleasure found in the mockery of cut-rate special effects or low production values.

4. Semantic differences may cause some to reject the assimilation, but I leave this for another discussion at another time.

The AIllusion: Intelligent Machines, Jacques Derrida's "Ethical Turn" and Oren Peli's *Paranormal Activity*

Larrie Dudenhoeffer

> "In truth the will to create, the need to write, simply, coincides deep down with the Luciferian temptation: to become like God, to make oneself an author, to authorize oneself in an autonomous world"—Denis de Rougemont, *The Devil's Share*, 132

In Oren Peli's *Paranormal Activity* (2007), an independent film shot on digital for only $15,000, a demon invisibly stalks and torments Micah (Micah Sloat) and Katie (Katie Featherston), a twenty-something couple sharing a two-story San Diego tract house. In the film's opening scene, Micah, who regards these visitations with skepticism, if not utter disbelief, meets Katie at the front door saying, "Kiss the camera!" He uses this digital camcorder to similarly stalk, film, and interrogate Katie about the entity in the daytime, while mounting it on a tripod while they sleep so as to capture its movements at night. Ultimately, the demon takes control of Katie; in the film's climactic scene, it confronts Micah off-camera downstairs, and after a few suspenseful moments, throws what seems to be Micah's corpse at the tripod, tipping the camcorder to one side on to the floor. It records Katie's face, which, after sniffing the corpse, renders into a monstrous CGI mockup. The camera finally shuts down as she charges at it, showing her teeth in an ironic callback to "Kiss the camera!" In this movement, the film enacts its own ingestion—i.e., the conversion of a video stream into a data archive—suggesting that the demon in it is really the camera all along.

150

The trailers unusually do not feature many scenes from the film; they rather focus on shots of viewers in a movie theater screaming and recoiling in their seats. The trailers thus "program" the film's reception,[1] specifically "photoshopping" viewers' nervous response to its images. In short, the terror on the faces of these viewers mimes the terrifying appearance of Katie's CGI makeover *before* most of them even see the film's conclusion. *Paranormal Activity* thus writes the operations of the camera directly into its audience's experience of time, reason, visuality, and the sublime. The camera, an inscriptive medium, traditionally functions in two significant ways. It first of all transfers an image onto a filmstrip, creating the *illusion* of the immediacy of its subject. At the same time, the camera also works to retrieve information, setting up the *allusion* to another time and space, to another diegetic moment, and insisting that the viewer trace, retain, and recall the details of a film's images as they flow one to another.

However, the digital camera in *Paranormal Activity* does not simply duplicate someone's or something's image through the chemical emulsion that the light surrounding it triggers. Using an electronic sensor, it renders and compresses its subjects into raster images, or megapixel displays, so as to always already make re-scalable their color, size, orientation, and resolution. These raster images thus enable the instantaneous creation of a camera-subject that does not exist at the moment the image is taken, the creation, in short, of "autonomous world[s]," to use Denis de Rougemont's phrase (132). Their singularity adds another function to the camera: that of *artificial intelligence* of a rudimentary sort. N. Katherine Hayles argues that artificial intelligence, the construction of machines with cogitative skills comparable to our own, dovetails into specialist discussions of artificial life, where machines come to act as our models rather than our tools (239).

In other words, these intelligent machines "evolve the capacity to evolve," replicating the conditions responsible for our own species-emergence (241, 243). The demon in *Paranormal Activity* is, in a way, the digital camera, re-elaborating the supersensible enormity of the sublime as the data-transfer of the organismic into an altogether different format. This essay will examine two exemplary texts from Jacques Derrida's "ethical turn," rechristening them cheekily as "satanic" in relation to film as a mode of writing, and from there will move into a reading of *Paranormal Activity* as a tutor text for what we might call the *AIllusion*: the triangulation of illusion, allusion, and artificial intelligence that this sort of cinematic technology evolves.[2]

The Satanic Rites of Derrida

Derrida, in *The Gift of Death*, discusses the repression of the "demonic," the ecstatic mysteries of the ancient cults, within the "sphere of responsibility" (4), the superordination first of the ethico-philosophical tradition of the Greeks, and then that of the onto-theological mission of Christianity. In the course of this double movement of repression — thus of interiorization — the subject makes itself responsible for its own death, anxious over its external representation in the sacrificial-orgiastic mysteries. The subject makes the orgiastic "subject to itself" (4). In other words, the secret rites of these mysteries commute into the secrets of the soul, the subject's inner degree of *askēsis* or readiness for death.[3] The soul, in a way, represents an "emulsification" of the flesh's involvement in these rites, serving as their snapshot and index, and transforming their space into a sort of graphic design, in that the experience of the soul takes as its criteria the same as that for writing, a sense of its interiority and separateness from its immediate surroundings (15). The soul, as it codes our concern over dying into a mode of self-relation, conceals and contains the demonic mysteries within itself, at once separating itself from them and smuggling them into our very subjectivity, where they remain, secret and invisible (17, 21–22). The repression of the demonic and the instantiation of the secret thus suppose the responsible subject, waking from a demonic fusion with its community only in order to separate from it (22).

This self-mythologization speaks to *Paranormal Activity*'s muddle of the neopagan with the ultramodern, since Derrida argues that "technological modernity" actually shares much in common with the orgiastic.[4] This technologic culture mobilizes the demonic in its aestheticism and its demands that we take on "the individualism of a role" rather than anything like a "responsible self" (*Gift* 36–7). The roles that we enact for the camera, for example, surface from out of the very indifference that it nevertheless develops, images, recodes, and erases.[5] As an inscriptive mechanism, it first abstracts its contents from the rest of their "community" or material environment, so that it comes to resemble the invisible "soul" of the image, the "flesh" from out of which it separates. The camera then re-creates the subject's condition as responsible for its relation to its own death, in that it archives its contents' movement and in doing so substitutes the interior space of our responsibility with *fidelity* to the moment in the instance of its death. The notion of *illusion*, in relation to the cinema, does not merely gesture to the artificiality of its sounds and motion-images: It dramatizes the roles modernity asks us to assume, even finding a role for the camera, that of a film's transcendent "soul" and at the same time that of the demonic trace of the community that its images shrink into the interiority of their frames. Still, the camera as the secret of the image or scene, according to Derrida's definition of "secret," makes us tremble, since it imprints on the flesh the return of an event that we can "neither see nor foresee" and which we then approach with considerable apprehension, "right down to [the] soul" (55). The illusion of the film image returns us to more than the transience of the moment, to the fact that one after another dies in front of our eyes, as in a ritual sacrifice. The illusion of the cinema, in its vigil over death, makes us tremble in that it really screens from us the camera's interiority to the scene, as it invisibly stalks every frame and repeats with every frame the conversion of the non-responsible camera-subject to the faithful image. The camera is at once the "demon" of cinematic initiation, taking on the qualities of ritualistic expression, and the "soul" of the cinema, responsible for quietly and invisibly disciplining each filmic moment's death.

If, as Rene Girard suggests, "no text can make allusion to the principle of illusion that governs it" (147) without risking the audience's unresponsiveness to its codes, why does *Paranormal Activity* so noticeably incorporate the camera into its narrative? The answer might come from another spin to Derrida's "satanic turn," this time from *Rogues: Two Essays on Reason*. It contrasts the *ipsocentric,* the subject who can make ethical decisions and act on them, to the *voyoucratic,* a sort of counter-citizenship that, as clandestine, outlaw, and corruptive, introduces disorder into a system (17, 66). The voyoucratic thus combines the divine with the animalistic, the very incarnation of the evil, the satanic, and the demonic, much as with orgiastic mysteries (97). These terms comprise the exercise of reason to first unify information into an "architectonic" through the construction of analogies and then to act as a sovereign force over the subject, silent, watchful, and resistant to any curbing of its authority (101, 121). In other words, reason closes the subject off to the unforeseeable and the incalculable, establishing teleologies to neutralize "the alterity of who [or] what comes" (128), to script the coming of the event in advance, and to moderate exposure to the radically other (148, 152).

This formulation of reason resembles the demon in *Paranormal Activity*, which seems at once ipsocentric, able to make decisions, act on them, and therefore settle or unsettle the social order, and voyoucratic, a secret counterforce that remains silent when Micah tries to communicate with it. The demon sets in motion the analogical work of the film, as the camera collects evidence — the rustling of sheets and so forth — to shape all of these epiphenomena into the "architectonic" category of the demonic. However, it also comes as an event, the movements of which the viewers and characters cannot calculate or foresee. The demon thus functions as an *allusion* to the camera, not simply as a vehicle of cinematic illusion. It alludes to the camera as a sovereign agency, as something that takes the event and re-inscribes it into its narrative agenda. Although really a mockumentary, *Paranormal Activity* claims to consist solely of "found footage," outside the controls of directorial film composition. The film thus makes allusion to the correspondence of reason to the cinema, as each re-presents material things, mocking up analogues to them: images, sounds, and commutations of the other senses. Moreover, reason and narrative cinema function as analogues to each other, as they reciprocally elaborate rules of inquiry and structures of knowledge. The cinematic image, then, at every moment makes allusion to the camera as sovereign, subordinating our subjective experience to its own medialization and instrumentality, and as a counterforce, throughout most scenes remaining unobservable and directing our attention to those that introduce crisis and disorder into the narrative that takes its arc from them. In this case, the camera alludes to something that equally and simultaneously captures it.

The film camera, as an analogical medium, much as with reason, the index of the responsible, ipsocentric self, makes it easy to see the first two of the three components of the AIllusion at work in it. As a representational device, it creates simulacra or "illusions" of the material it records, and then as an archiving device, it constantly makes allusion to that which exceeds the framing and the sharpness of its images. However, *Paranormal Activity* features a Sony FX1 digital camcorder, which, while still a representational and archival medium, renders its subjects into megapixel signals for instant display, stitching, and storage, without necessarily the same fidelity to the moment of their capture, since at the same time it can correct, improve, relight, stabilize, and interpolate them. The digital camera, in short, incorporates certain computer effects into its mechanism, and therefore the digital image assumes a "reality" all its own. If the film camera resembles reason in relation to the material realities that it memorizes, re-presents, and narrates over, then the digital camera, which snaps images that users can endlessly tweak, alias, and mosaic independently of their source, creates virtual realities that must similarly recondition our reason, subjectivity, and sense of embodiment. This technology exemplifies what

N. Katherine Hayles calls "emergence," where certain "properties" and "programs" appear on their own, often roguishly "developing in unanticipated ways" (223). The digital camera, then, motions toward the final component of the AIllusion: artificial intelligence.

Andy Clark defines the subject as a "natural born cyborg," a mash-up of the tools, machines, and semi-intelligent objects that annex it to "technological envelopes" in which they can all reciprocally develop, operate, and mature (7, 26). Our minds, then, dovetail into the "complementary capacities" of their technological environment (78). The subject thus emerges as a "shifting coalition of tools" open to morphological change through its incorporation of "nonbiological elements" (137). The demon in *Paranormal Activity* figures the technological envelop surrounding Micah and Katie and the complexities of their adaptation to it. The demon renders the digicam omnipresent, the efficient reason of the film's raster images, responsible for them though mostly invisible within them. This camera more than frames, re-presents, and factors into the couple's technological environment; it uploads it into a digital format, converting it into a grid of rescalable, recodable, and reconfigurable algorithms. The camera, to follow Clark's analysis, must dovetail into their cerebral sensory cortexes — into the seat of their individual realities — as it evolves the details of its camera-subjects into discontinuous information values, chronological time into fragmentary moments of dramatic intensity, and the explanatory nature of reason into the functionality of intelligent machines that can "talk" to each other simultaneously in order to execute certain tasks. The digital camera's extension of the raster image into our architectonics of reason and the technological environment makes the "secret" impossible, since, as the film shows us, the demonic resurfaces in modernity *as* the responsible. The traces of the demon in the footage Micah records at night transform responsibility into a matter of image editing, as it comes to represent the aim of demosaicing: to reconstruct a full color image from an incomplete data-sample, to carefully fill in those areas that remain invisible.

Analog-to-Digital Conversion

The film opens with an establishing shot of the couple's tract house, and then cuts to Micah standing in front of a mirror, the digicam recording its own image. This shot, extending as it does the work of the trailers, almost immediately compresses the film's characters with its audience, with the camera aiming at them as well. In the next sequence, the camera charts its own emplacement in a technological envelope, as the film cuts to Micah's cell phone, complete with the calendar graphic "September 18, 2006," a marker of these electronic devices' capability for digital synchronization; to Katie's car turning onto the driveway; to Micah strumming an electric guitar; and to the couple investigating the strange noises coming from the refrigerator. The camera, out of all of these devices, "wants Katie," as spiritualist Dr. Fredrichs (Mark Fredrichs) says about the demon in another scene. After Micah teasingly says, "Kiss the camera," the frame cants to the right, a movement which recurs when the demon fully takes control of Katie in the climax of the film. Moreover, the camera tracks this character as she climbs the stairs, much as with the demon following Katie wherever she goes, most of the time similarly without incident. She seems to treat Micah's "strange fascination with electronics" as though she dealt with a film camera, thinking it mainly enables the user to "look back and remember fondly"—in other words, to capture an event, create the illusion of its re-presentation, and make allusion to the objective reality that it once was. She misses the rudimentary artificial intelligence of the digicam, as Micah insists that it rather enables its user to "react appropriately" to certain information and "take care of it," or readjust the values, contours, and other signatures of its image file. Its software thus communicates with its user's reason as surely as with such machines as computers, cell phones, and so on. When the camera zooms in on Katie as she mutters something, unable to detect the words, it makes its first gesture to the invisible: a triangulation of the camera framing the shot from outside of it, the sounds and movements of the demon that the film traces rather than images, and the victim whose inner thoughts remain secret in these scenes. And when Micah says, "We're operational, babe," the camera at that moment makes the two of them its operators and its operations, its *mise-en-scene* a technological envelope of tools and nonhuman elements that includes its users among them. In the next shot, the couple wonders if they sense the demon's "footsteps," while the shadow of the camera slides along the walls. The shadow displaces and refigures these imperceptible footsteps, and suggests that the camera follows and simulates the couple's movements as its demon, as a force that modulates their most secret moments together into transmittable information.

On "Night #1," the couple stirs as machinelike thuds emanate from downstairs, and in the morning they awaken to discover Katie's car keys on the floor. Micah quips that their misplacement offers "incontrovertible evidence" of the demon's existence, missing the fact that the camera stages an inversion of its first recordings of Katie driving a car, meaning that the technological envelope the car metonymically relates to in this scene *wants to also be inside its users*. The camera thus treats Katie as a device driver for its communication subsystems. Micah, refusing to take such events seriously, mixes, while at the computer, a rip-off version of *The Exorcist* soundtrack to make the visiting Dr. Fredrichs "feel welcome in his own environment." Although this scene seems light-spirited in tone, it actually develops the correspondence of the noises coming from off-screen space during "Night #1" to the music coming from the similarly off-screen software of the computer. It suggests that the repression of the demonic into an interior — traditionally the soul of the responsible self— takes the form in *Paranormal Activity* of uploads, samplings, and file-sharing in electronic memory devices. After Dr. Fredrichs arrives, Katie describes an earlier encounter with the demon at age eight, when she saw "a shadowy figure at the foot of [her] bed," flipping "the lights on and off" and supposedly setting fire to the family's "old house." Fredrichs tells the couple that the demon is "something that's basically connected to [Katie]." The details of this story and Fredrichs' response to it evoke the connectivity of the digicam to the computer, and moreover to Micah's electric guitar, the Internet, and maybe the couple's "smart" security/lighting systems. The shadowy figure in the story occupies the same space as the camera on its mount as it watches Katie and Micah sleep night after night. Its tendency to switch "the lights on and off" refers to more than the interruption of electric current; it designates the operative terms of an informational matrix, whether the gene sequences of an organism or the zeroes and ones of a network application. In fact, the fire that Katie experiences at eight rhymes with the "fire wire" that connects the digicam to Micah's computer, suggesting that the demonic codes the mechanisms that imperceptibly mediate, envelop, and recondition subjective experience, transforming the self into a user, role-player, and overall developmental loop.[6] The "incontrovertible evidence" of the demonic in this sense thus seems to be Katie's age at the time of its first manifestation, since "eight" signifies the root of the octal number system, the octet another name for the "byte" or "eight bits" instrumental to computer operation, including the imaging system of Micah's digicam. If time equals the replacement of things rather than the measurable duration of collective memories, then the return of the demonic in the film and its intensification make more sense if seen in terms of software versioning. Then, on "Night #3," the camera captures in fast motion the couple sleeping after a sexual exchange. The timer on the right of the screen races and then slows down as the door on the other side of the frame subtly opens and closes on its own. After watching this footage in the morning, Micah asks if the demon is "doing random shit." These scenes, which show no sexual content, suggest that it does not. The demon, as a displacement of the camera's relation to the diegesis, continues to interface with the couple. The fast motion, for example, cinematographically resignifies and "embodies" the chronoceptive distortions of the sexual act. The opening and closing of the door develops a metaphorics connecting the camera apparatus, the film's digital *mise-en-scene*, and contractions of the vaginal orifice to one another. More specifically, the muscles of the vagina autonomously open and close throughout the sex act, the shutters of the camera automatically open and close to re-illuminate the image, and the demon autonomously "records" these movements on to the opening and closing of the door in the *mise-en-scene* in a manner at once responsible for what the audience can see and repressive in its censorship of what they cannot see — namely, the demon, the camera, and the sexual act. If the demon does "random shit," as Micah suggests, it does so as sort of a random number generator, where certain sequences emerge and repeat as time elapses, much as in this scene, where the timer and frame-rate slow down at the moment when the demon emerges in order to resequence the concepts of memory space, material embodiment, and information-gathering into the nodes and relays of the film's AIllusion. Micah in another scene admits that demons show themselves "intelligent in the way they do things," suggesting that the one in *Paranormal Activity*, as the figure for the digicam, more than digitally represents or memorizes the events of the film, as it also models them after the inner workings of its own intelligent design.

After "Night #5," Micah discovers a sub-audible growl using sound-mixing software and interprets it as a sign that the demon "wants to communicate." He ignores the fact that this sign travels the channels of a camera microphone and computer console, intelligent machines that can speak to each other through cable or wireless interlinks and apparently can evolve enough capacity for voice recognition so as to invite the film's characters into a dialogue. The demonic thus returns as the interiority of this dialogue within this technological milieu, as a secret statistical code that nonetheless threatens to change the dynamics of embodiment and make it deviate from its normative and always "abstract representations"

(Hayles 199). These scenes nicely segue into "Night #13," when a similar-sounding growl and an accompanying crash startle Micah and Katie, who run downstairs with the camera to see from the stairway a chandelier swinging on its own. The film cuts to them trying to sleep again, as they slump down on the mattress and cover themselves up in a series of dissolves. The next morning, Katie thinks that maybe they "shouldn't have the camera," observing that it only seems to make the disturbances "worse." Micah responds that ridding themselves of the camera "is not an option at this point." Unwilling to draw out the analogy of the demon's reemergence to Micah's acquisition of the camera, they resign themselves to a thorough digitization of the material environment and its rebounding on the tools (reason, desire, sense membranes, memory systems, and so on) that allow them to stream information from it. Partha Dasgupta thus writes about this "mass-scale digitization" that "now that the genie [or demon] is out of the bottle, it is very hard, if not impossible, to stop it. Computers exchange information. Information is data. Data is the convergence of everything. Barriers mean nothing anymore" (1). The convergence of these tools and signals into a common digital form suggests that the camera's timer "evolves" into the clocklike movements of the chandelier, or rather that the conventional grammars of time evolve into the operators of dramatic momentarity. Moreover, the demon's growl, the film rerouting it from the computer to the diegetic soundtrack, syncs up with the series of dissolves as altogether representative of *digital noise*, degradation of image quality and chroma resolution that makes sections of a film appear grainy or "invisible" in spots. This sort of noise formalizes the return of the demonic in digital technologies, alluding to the camera's interiority to the contents of an image or scene, divulging the "secret" of the raster illusion of scalar composition, and calling attention to the relation of Ouija to the intelligent machine, as they tap into a dialogue unthought, unspoken, and undetectable to the ear, undoing the separation of the modern from out of the nonmodern and occult.

The event of "Night #15" motivates Micah to contact the demon through Ouija. The camera records Katie rising uncharacteristically upright and standing over Micah in a trance from 1:36 to 3:30 A.M. while the film again speeds through the footage. She then exits the room, after which Micah soon wakes up, seeing that she is gone. He dismounts the camera, descends the stairs, and finds Katie outside swinging on a chair in a repetition of the movement of the chandelier. He goes inside, unable to coax Katie out of the trance, and sees the television on, white noise across its screen. The film cuts to the next evening, when Micah shows the Ouija board to the camera, the framing of the film superimposing it over the flat-screen television set in the distance. The two of them argue over it, and, after they leave for a dinner date, the camera films the demon ostensibly moving the Ouija's "cursor," as Micah calls it, and then setting the board on fire. All of these scenes capsulize the steady disruption of reason's analogical character, as the snow on the television screen — traditionally an analog medium — communicates the couple's failure to make sense of the reemergence of the demonic within the safe confines of their technologically "modern" surroundings. The superimposition of the Ouija and television mediums suggests their digital compression, so to speak, in that nonmodern, ritualistic, or "satanic" mechanisms overlap in function with "smart" technology's re-elaboration of the efforts of reason to master the incalculable. The noise on the screen figures the noise inside the minds of the film's characters, and also the failure of the camera to render a clear image of the demon. The fire the demon sets thus mocks the work of emulsification, since the camera cannot develop an analogue faithful to it and the characters cannot decipher the codes through which it speaks to them. The demon's manipulation of the Ouija — midpoint in the "channel" from the camera to the television set, "connecting" them — truly acts as a *fire wire*, a four-circuit audiovisual network customary for digital equipment. The convergence of the Ouija, camera, and television set in this scene thus replaces analog signaling with arbitration, in which nodes transmit information in micro-seconds to a digital setup. When we see Katie swinging in the clocklike manner of the chandelier, then, we really witness the wiring or the re-inscription of the camera's timer on to the bodies and the objects on the screen.

Micah, intent on tracing the demon's movements, spreads talcum powder on the wooden floorboards upstairs. On "Night #17," the couple follows its animalistic tracks into the attic, where they discover a photograph of Katie at eight or thereabouts, burnt at its edges. In the morning, Micah readjusts the brightness levels of the night's footage, enabling them to finally see the demon's footprints. These scenes thus narrativize the technique of *image burning*, where changes to the image's contrast make certain details appear shadowy and certain colors oversaturated. The photograph of Katie treats "image burning" literally; more importantly, it cues Micah to adjust the color and brightness of the digicam footage to expose visual evidence of the demon's activity, which the computer, in effect, creates. The next night, the readjustment of these values, much as with the camera's flash, emerges within the *mise-en-scene* as a similarly automatic feature, the demon turning the downstairs lights on while the couple sleeps to illuminate the otherwise dark areas of the screen. The door then slams on its own, the mechanical devices in the room mysteriously communicating with one another, operating independently of their manual controls, and doubling the filter functions of the camera aperture. The events of these nights altogether suggest the digital recompositing of the characters, their setting, and their things. The next day, Micah records Katie as she sits in midrange of the camera and the television screen, occupying the same space as the Ouija. The film thereby repositions the flesh as one more node or relay, one more machine in an intercommunicating network of them.

The demon ruffles the sheets covering the couple as they sleep on "Night #19." It switches the upstairs lights on and off, as Katie awakens, claiming that she can feel it "breathing." She then says that she "can feel it watching me," the film's most unmistakable expression of the demon's retracing of the off-screen work of the digicam, which also watches Katie, for example, at this moment in a medium shot. Searching for answers, Micah surfs the Internet and finds a webpage about another woman's dealings with visitations of the demonic. Katie cursorily examines the woman's "bio," and then says, "I'm gonna go lie down." She thus "image-hosts" this woman, who also "lies down" in the thumbnail on the webpage, assuming the role of a "version" or "replay" of a "reality" that only comes into narrative significance online. The secret of the demon's motives and actions thus comes to seem a matter of downloading Internet content, which in this scene, in the manner of ipsocentric reason, calculates the catastrophic ending of the film. However, since reason offloads the unreasonableness of its own sovereignty on to that which exceeds it and which it thus works on, the demon remains unpredictable, still invisible to the camera that nevertheless re-orchestrates its trace into a narrative sequence of separate dramatic intensities. As Katie shouts at Micah, "You and your stupid camera are the problem," she declaims the camera's sovereign upconverting of "reality" and also its excessive digitization of everything in it.

The demon's shadow slides across the room on "Night #20," much like the camera's shadow earlier in the film, and it drags Katie through the doorway. The next day, Micah says that "it looks like something bit [her]," as she stares in a trancelike state, almost speechless. He then wrestles a crucifix from Katie's fingers and throws it in the fireplace. He takes the camera off the couch after a jump cut, tracking the crucifix as the fire consumes it. He implores them to get in the car and drive away, resignedly muttering, when Katie refuses, "I don't know what the hell is going on, but this is insane." These scenes almost totalize the AIllusion of the film, or rather its first two constituent terms. As the meta-image of the camera, the demon extends its manipulation of the visual register into the *mise-en-scene* and ultimately these characters' flesh. The camera, in short, clicks on Katie and drags this "icon" from one side of the screen to the other, so that the Ouija "cursor" converges with "point and shoot" digital technologies. When Micah says "something bit" Katie, then, we might see this simple declarative statement as a word-play on "byte," on the eight data-bits that make up the octet. In effect, this "something" that traces out the couple's technological internment also reengineers Katie's flesh into a sort of malware, a (non)modern "demonic possession" in which external media and internal cortical-muscular networks indivisibly form an intelligent machine.

The film's final scene, "Night #21," which an intertitle says occurs on October 8, 2006, shows Katie completely under the demon's influence. She awakens at 1:27 A.M. and, then, in another fast motion compression of time, enacts the role of the digicam, watching Micah sleep until 3:15 A.M., when she descends the stairs and screams. He follows Katie, also screams, and in one minute crashes into the camera, toppling it from its mount and decentering the film. The camera, as it falls to the floor, cants to the right, as in the opening scene when Micah tells Katie to "Kiss the camera." The timer disappears from the right side of the screen as Katie reappears, standing in the middle of the door frame. The camera shuts down, the film cuts out, and an epilogue graphic tells us that "Katie's whereabouts remain unknown." On "Night #21," the chronological order of the narrative shuts down with the timer's countdown on the screen, suggesting that the film's characters, *mise-en-scene*, and viewer experience cross over into the instantaneity of digital arbitration and signal-processing that replaces the categorical-historical succession of events. This scene thus marks a redefinition of the secret as not so much an interior space the responsible self can monitor so that it can die with a clear conscience. The secret that the film refers to concerns the subject's "whereabouts," especially as the anchors of its material nature, its analogical self-experience, and the illusion-allusion tradeoff of its myth-making exercises seem inadequate to explain its technological reduction to manageable information. The secret *Paranormal Activity* reveals is that, at the center of its drama, at the center of the camera's optical sensitivities, and even at the center of its characters', filmmakers', and audience's sovereign reason, the demonic returns, fathoming without directly clarifying the "unspoken" of the flesh, the "unthought" of the machine, and the "unforeseeable" misfires that might occur when they meet. If the demon is the camera, then the characters are the wires that connect it up with the minds of its viewers, the film's very own digitizable flat-screens.

NOTES

1. Pierre Bourdieu argues that the vertical integration and increasing concentration of market share characteristic of transnational media corporations subordinate cultural production to the commercially widest distribution channels (224). The "emergence" of creatively "autonomous universes" free of the rule of financial interest now faces the threat of an "involution," meaning "a regression from work to product, from author to engineers or technicians deploying technical resources they have not invented themselves (such as the vaunted 'special effects')." He thus concludes, in a manner fairly descriptive of the trailers for *Paranormal Activity*, that the "quasicynical" organization of our cultural resources work to "seduce the largest possible number of viewers by playing to their basic drives which other technicians, the marketing specialists, attempt to predict," or more aptly in the case of this film, program (227).

2. Umberto Eco, after quoting Carducci's *Hymn to Satan*—notably "Hail, O Satan, O Rebellion, O avenging force of reason!"—usefully distinguishes science, as that which "proceeds slowly," from technology, which offers us "everything instantly" (105–6). He moreover argues that technology, which makes us "lose sight of the chain of cause and effect," especially through the mass media, resembles magic, which also assumes that "it is possible to go from cause to effect without taking intermediate steps" (105–7).

3. Paul Ricœur, in *The Symbolism of Evil*, discusses the "exile" of the soul in dualistic myth-systems, which contrast "the soul as the Same" to "the body as the Other" (283, 298). This "Other" undergoes "symbolic transmutation" into a "counterpole of thought," into "the border between the inner and the outer," and thus into the sign of death and defilement (336, 338). Its evil consists not so much in its essence as in the "direction" of its mortality, in its unlikeness to the consistency of the idea (339). It therefore comes to function as the site of the "soul's captivity," not of the "origin of evil," which rather obtains in the confusion of interior with exterior, in the disruption of the "community of the soul with truth," and in the "consecration of multiplicity in ourselves" (341, 343–44).

4. Technological modernity converges upon the nonmodern in *Paranormal Activity*, with the film's viewers occupationally similar to what Bruno Latour theorizes as "quasi-objects," social in their determination, although not mere "receptacles of society," and also real, objective, and somewhat nonhuman, although not mere elements of nature either (53). In the film, especially with its use of a counter to segment its narrative set-pieces and to underscore its characters' increasing connectivity with their technological environment, time comes to mark the replacement and recombination of things rather than a succession of world-historical events (72, 74).

5. Renata Salecl argues, "Life is like a computer game in which the subject can play with his or her identity, can randomly follow fashion rituals," and so on (159). She attributes certain forms of self-mutilation, such as cutting, tattooing, and elective

surgery, to "the fact that life appears as a screen on which everything is changeable has resulted in a desperate search for the real behind the fiction" (160). However, the "cut in the body" might equally suggest the subject's somewhat crude attempts to "wear" the code-artifices of the technological environment, to show off the flesh's receptivity to implants, information channels, and other types of instrumentation, and thus to experience its compatibility with them *in vivo*.

6. In *Escape from Evil*, Ernest Becker discusses the anthropological tendency "to split things into contrasts and complementarities" and those who use it argue that we thus function "naturally just like the computer [...] the logical fulfillment of basic human nature," meaning that "the mystery of mind and symbolism might well be traceable down to simple neural circuits" (10). The upshot of this argument, then, is that we come to take the machine, not the soul, as our true "eternity symbol," as that "which transcends both life and death" (141).

The Indigestibility of the World: Birthing the Posthuman in Spielberg's *A.I.*

Todd A. Comer

Recent scholarship on the "posthuman" emphasizes embodiment, finitude, the humanizing work of representation, and ontological relation; it also tends toward a critique of dualism, transcendence, and the centering of the Human. These motifs are all emphasized to some extent because of an increasing awareness of the ethical limitations of Humanism, which seems in most formulations dualistic and, hence, violent: N. Katherine Hayles refers to the "liberal humanist subject," a notion of identity which indicates a subject's "freedom" from society (3). Neil Badmington discusses how a Cartesian humanism posits a notion of identity in which every human shares an "essence," the human essence, to rationally differentiate "the true from the false" (Descartes' phrase), displacing God and centering Humanity (*Posthumanism* 3–4). And Derrida writes of "man and humanism, the name of man being the name of that being who, throughout the history of metaphysics or of ontotheology — in other words, throughout his entire history — has dreamed of full presence, the reassuring foundation, the origin and end of play" (292).

There have been numerous recent texts on posthumanism, including fine texts by Elaine L. Graham and Badmington. With her emphasis on an ethics of birth, Graham's argument in *Representations of the Post/Human* provides a particularly good counterpoint for what follows. Graham opposes "necrophilia" to "natality," desiring to replace the West's focus on death with birth, and thereby emphasize our "shared origin in birth which necessarily embeds us in common experiences, both biological and social, and commits all living beings to sociability, interdependence and embodiment" (81). Graham, following Bruno Latour, posits that there are two "epistemological strategies" in modernity that ensure its "ontological stability" (33–34): The first strategy is "purification," the categorizing of "species, classes and states of being." The second strategy is "translation," a process by which hybrids are made of nature and culture. It is purification, of hybridity and of modernity's others, that naturalizes modernity's "privileged categories" (i.e., the Human). The "post/human," which is not a "condition" but an "intervention" that allows us to recognize the constructed nature of humanism (37), occurs at the moment that this purification process falters due to a "greater profligacy" of hybrids (35). She writes:

> At the boundaries of humanity, machines and nature, the impossibility of fixed definitions is shown forth in the proliferation of contemporary signs and wonders. In their capacity to show up the "leakiness" of bodily boundaries ... this emergent array of hybrid creatures are arguably "monstrous" not so much in the horror they evoke but in their exposure of the redundancy and instability of the ontological hygiene of the humanist subject [12].

Graham's book lacks a close focus on space and ontology, making it difficult to see how this "instability" precisely operates. Against what I see as her basic argument that the confrontation with hybrids causes a post/human "intervention," I will argue for a sublime confrontation with birth.

Badmington's *Alien Chic: Posthumanism and the Other Within*, by contrast, describes in much greater detail the ontological nature of the "posthuman." His Derrida-inflected argument does not attempt to show that we are now in a period of "posthumanity" (145), so much as show how the binary of human/alien deconstructs itself as it oscillates between presence and absence, and in this "wandering" is the "possibility of posthumanism." He writes of *Roswell*, a television series:

> The human is never quite at home with itself, and never without the alien ... Within its stories, the signifiers "human" and "alien" are rearticulated until the relationship between them is no longer one of absolute difference. Neither the human nor the alien is ever entirely revealed in the plenitude of opposition; there is a repeated deferral, an endless retreat from humanism [134].

The problem, often, is love, he argues in relation to 1956's *Invasion of the Body Snatchers* (141–143), for "desire escapes its vows," leading humans to desire aliens in a decidedly non-human fashion, undermining the binary, and giving rise to the posthuman (138). Desire, he continues, "never falls under the control of the subject of humanism" (140). (In what follows, desire will play, in large part, the opposite role: Desire *sustains* the human until a certain absolute representation is engineered.)

While the human subject generally conforms to what others, including Graham and Badmington, have said about its foundation in "absolute difference" or its strategy of "purification," I argue that the embodied activities that create humanism are localized within the family. Specifically, families teach us how to eat in the literal embodied sense and, more importantly, in the following ontological sense: Family is the space within which we learn how to digest (or, in a Latourian sense, purify) the world — the *essential* mark of humanism. Subjectivity is created by *ingesting* a world of difference. Such poor (i.e., violent) table manners are fueled by an incessant, if illusory, traumatic lack which creates the desire that orients and, concomitantly, creates hungry subjects. This digestive (and representational) cycle is the essence of humanism, fueling the engineering of the world into more and more human dimensions. But what happens at the apex of this trajectory when humans engineer their ultimate mirror, that is, an artificial entity which perfectly mirrors back to them their humanity?

This essay uses Steven Spielberg's *Artificial Intelligence (A.I.)* to argue that something has changed: "Posthumanity" has appeared because this digestion has paused. To be Human is to lack, to always drive forward while repressing the past, the artifice of our *birth,* as we mold the world in our image. However, in a strange way, with cloning and other technologies, this digestion is interrupted; "we" humans have succeeded too well in our masterful creation of an absolute representation of humanity, and have lost our impetus. This mastery, secondly, leads us to experience birth in a new way. No longer can we easily digest birth (and its others) and move on. No, birth now surrounds us like an immense, sublime ocean, undermining us as desiring subjects.[1]

Family Identity, Narrative, and the Limits of Digestion

A.I. begins in mourning. Martin, the son of Monica and Henry, is cryogenically frozen due to a medical condition for which science has yet to find a cure. He exists as both present and absent, alive and dead, and this is a reality that is excruciating for Monica. Their doctor says to Henry,

"She is in the most difficult position of feeling she should mourn the death of your son. After five years your instincts tell you to mourn him, too. But medicine assures us that mourning is inappropriate, that Martin is merely pending, so all her grief goes undigested." Death, an ontological wound in presence, is difficult to *digest*, but what we have here — through the advancement of medicine — is a cryogenic state with which humans have no previous coping experience (indeed, in a much more material sense than in the case of death, Martin *is* still present and absent). Even so, Monica reads to her son. She reads *The Adventures of Robin Hood*, specifically the pages dealing with the birth of Maid Marian's son, also named Martin. *Robin Hood*, as a birth narrative in this case, operates as a therapeutic narrative, assimilating the experience of "mourning" (or cryogenic freezing). The issues that I wish to elaborate on are nicely introduced here. Either subjectivity is gathered together into a well-bordered absolute with the assistance of narrative, or it is torn, "exposed" (Jean-Luc Nancy, *Inoperative* 39) to a world of relation (both of presence *and* absence) that it cannot fully digest.

We only begin to see how some of these issues are coupled in a different manner after David enters the frame. In a situation which approximately duplicates that of Monica and Martin, Professor Hobby designs David after the likeness of his deceased son, also named David. David, as an artificial creation of Humanity, here operates similarly to narrative in that he also assuages mourning. David is intended as a child substitute for couples, like Monica and Henry, who cannot have children or whose children are terminally ill and resigned to a cryogenic state. As an artificial creation he serves to heal the familial world and preserve its sense.

David is the result of an attempt to create a "mecha" that will precisely model human emotional responses. As Sheila, a mecha, informs us, "love is first widening my eyes a little bit and quickening my breathing a little" and so on. Like a human, David will also love and not just artificially *simulate* its physiological manifestations. Hobby's implicit assumption, of course, is that human, or *real*, identity is not in any way a matter of simulation. On the side of the real is immanent identity, a subjectival being which does not ostentatiously rehearse how to act (based on an exterior movement, or imitation), but (seemingly) reacts immediately, wholly out of itself, and with ease to the call for emotion. This is what it means to be Human; anything else is artificial and the lesser half of the binary.

Trauma has exposed the family to the outside, to a non-recognition (Nancy, *Inoperative* 43). This family unit, or representation, is dispersed in the aftermath of Martin's illness. Directly following a scene in which David is glancing over a series of family pictures which include Martin (but not David), Henry is shown explaining the rules according to which David can be imprinted. As he explains, a bathroom mirror reflects them not once, but in perhaps a dozen perspectives, as if they have their existence, somehow, outside of themselves. Both of these scenes underline the fragility of the family representation; the former in particular, in light of the absence of David from the pictures, foregrounds the painful disjunction of the idea and reality of the family — such representations can simply not keep up with a reality full of sickness and death.

Before imprinting, David appears detached, with the family yet not recognizing Monica as mother (he is both *in* and *outside* of the family representation). When David is finally imprinted by Monica, he is her only child and, hence, "special," insofar as he is *immediately* with Monica. Imprinting becomes an act of mythmaking in which it is less the words than their enunciation that is essential to drawing David into the presence of the family. After David listens to the series of random words that constitutes imprinting, he responds immediately by referring to Monica as "Mommy." The work of narrative is precisely to give back identity and heal the family representation by making it once again immanent, erasing that deferral to the outside. In this case, Monica's narrative gathers the family and gives them back a sense of themselves as a family. This state lasts until Martin's recovery forces David to *mediate* around him before he can reach Monica. Such prolonged "mediation" foregrounds the work, the construction and artifice, that goes into that supposedly intimate relationship which we term real or natural. What had stabilized into a traditional family unit, is strained, though not broken. Neither David nor Martin feel fully in the presence of their mother, prompting Martin to emphasize the real/artificial binary as a way of excluding David from the family proper and assimilating him to the outside. The ultimate object of this violence is the return of a world of immanence without the mediating presence of an other (boy). Ultimately, David is digested through his exclusion to the outside, "fully" within the mecha side of the binary.

Of course, such an immanent position is never anything but an illusion. In light of the film's many photographs, it becomes a question, we could say, of who will be included in the family portrait — the mythic representation of the family. In this struggle between David and Martin the problem is that the family does not yet constitute a clear picture for itself now that the former has returned. The struggle is completely over the question of how this family representation will be delineated and bordered and, ultimately, who will be included, and who will be excluded to the "outside." The very work of identity then amounts to the creation of a ("real") monad, a subject or essence, which perpetually elides (or digests) its ("artificial") birth outside itself.

Embodied, and Performing Humans

Thus far I have shown how representation operates as a means of creating that which is really human and, consequently, the violent digestion of that which suggests our existence outside of ourselves. In what follows I will undermine this opposition between "real" and "artificial" and show how identity is created through a hermeneutic movement that places us inextricably with others. Much of *A.I.*'s muted horror can be traced to this displacement of the above binary. For instance, the horror of the early scenes is bound up in David's strange manner prior to his imprinting. Consider his first appearance at the dinner table. He silently stares at Monica and Henry as they eat until he finally picks up an empty glass and "drinks." Then he stares squarely at Monica and, having no stomach, mimics her eating, once again with no food. When some pasta fails to make it into Monica's mouth, a few threads hanging, undigested, out the right corner, he laughs loudly, and hysterically. Why is the viewer spooked by this scene? We are horrified because the scene confronts us with identity's groundlessness. Identity's essence *is* existence if we understand existence as the constant self-interpretation that occurs prior to rational consciousness and inserts us in the world in a profound referential manner (Dreyfus 12–17). Each of us "embodies an understanding of what it means to be" in our reliance on shared social practices. Heidegger writes that the "closest kind of association is not mere perceptual cognition, but, rather, a handling, using, and taking care of things which has its own kind of 'knowledge'" (German page numbers 67). In this case, it is both Monica's failure to digest, and David's im*proper* laughter that foregrounds this groundless identity construction.

The *knowledge* that David is not "real" does not balance out the fact that he appears human. The Flesh Fair provides a telling instance of how David is interpreted as real because he conforms to social practice. This "celebration of life" is defined by its opposition to all that is artificial. An announcer shouts, "What about us? We are alive and this is a celebration of life. And this is a commitment to a truly human future!" About to have David killed, Johnson-Johnson argues that while David is a product of "artistry" and craftsmanship, he only "perform[s]," or simulates, and is only the most recent of "insults to human dignity." The crowd saves David, but less because he looks human than because he acts like one. When David pleads for his life a member of the crowd shouts that he "looks like a boy" but only after commenting that mecha "do not plead for their lives." In conforming to normative social practices, David finds empathy.

I am reminded of Heidegger's example of the "handy" tool which is taken for granted until it is broken (73–74). Once broken its relation ("reference") to its wielder and the world around it is made *conspicuous*. The state of being broken forces us to recognize our relation and dependence on the world around us, which is to say, that we are *in the world* and not monadic subjects. David's eventual ill-advised and literal ingestion does land him in a mecha[nic] shop, but I want to emphasize conspicuousness on the level of social etiquette: David and Monica's faulty "eating" can be read in at least two ways. To return to the motif of digestion, it can be understood as a metaphor for the impossibility of immanence. While our ingestion scoops up the exterior world and tidily assimilates it to our insides, it always misses something, the pasta lolls out of the corner of the mouth, we fumble the fork and it clatters across a plate. The digestion of difference (or artifice, in terms of the Flesh Fair) is doomed to failure.

Secondly, David's "eating" foregrounds the socialization process which might be better described as a *hermeneutic* process. It highlights the fact that we are not essence but existence, creating, interpreting, and practicing our being, constantly searching for a resolution of reality with the idea we have of that reality, whether our idea is of the family, or the Humanist subject which are, indeed, the same in this context. Jean-Luc Nancy makes a distinction between the architecture of "meaning" and the metaphysical *signification* that results from the open architecture of the hermeneutic circle. Meaning is essentially "open" in that the "subject" constantly anticipates meaning; meaning therefore cannot be a prior origin or telos, but is rather formed because of this lack and through anticipation: "understanding is possible only by an anticipation of meaning which is or constitutes meaning itself" (Raffoul xii). Essentially, David's mimicking of "eating" then is a hermeneutic attempt to inscribe himself in such a way that he closes the gap between his inept social skills (reality) and a particular idea of table etiquette. Whether this is read as the actual act of ingestion or, more generally, as an issue of the assimilation of difference in which success would amount to being part of the family and/or fully human, the end result would be metaphysical. His actions should be thought of as a matter of signification, an attempt to resolve the distance between the sensible and the intelligible which would then amount to the *presentation* of "meaning" in, for instance, a family portrait (Nancy, *Gravity* 22–23).

David's letters are perhaps the best way to see how the hermeneutic and representational work together. While one of these letters might indicate the presence of a fully present myth, the entire series with differing configurations — "DEAR MOMMY/I'M REALLY OUR SON/AND I HATE TEDDY/HE IS NOT REAL," or "DEAR MOMMY/I'M YOUR LITTLE/BOY AND SO IS/MARTIN BUT NOT/TEDDY" — demonstrates David's anguished hermeneutic attempt to resolve this tension between reality and the human family. He writes several letters because he is attempting to correctly signify an idea of family that remains distant. The stakes of this resolution are high: "Before the terrifying or maddening abyss that is opened between the possibility that thought is empty and the correlative possibility that reality is chaos ... signification is the assurance that closes the gaping void by rendering its two sides homogeneous. Reality has an order to it, and reason orders the real" (Nancy, *Gravity* 23). And it is upon the human subject that all of this hinges. This closing of the hermeneutic circle is simultaneously the work of the subject and what makes the subject *be* in the first place.

All of this also dramatizes how the subject and narrative are not immediate and immanent, but the product of a prior hermeneutic exteriority, or mediation, which is continually erased as the subject becomes present: Shortly after the mecha woman (mentioned above) describes love, she begins applying cosmetics to her face. There is an immediate cut to Monica who is engaged in the same act. The act of putting cosmetics on is associated with the simulation of love and then, crucially, identified with the human Monica. The ostentatious binary between humans and mecha would place *immediate* action on the side of humanity. Here that binary is strained, or founders, perhaps, from the viewers' standpoint: Both "organic" and "mechanical" life forms require a resolution of the sensible and intelligible before a "real" emotion (identity) can be presented. Both mecha and orga have to engage in an unconscious hermeneutic work before they can be seen as real. Immanence and identity, once again, only exist as such when this prior practice or *birthing is repressed*. Such a moment of signification is what creates "commonsense" metaphysical distinctions such as that between "real" and "artificial." Badmington's work is deeply interested in such moments in which the "absolute difference" between alien and human is undermined, as alien features are found in the human, or human features are found in the alien. With Badmington, I agree that at such moments "the boundaries marked out with such confidence and clarity by anthropocentrism have been breached" (*Alien Chic* 131), at least for the viewer. To a large extent, Spielberg's film does, in fact, operate formally in such a way, though all such breaches need, additionally, to be framed by what Darko Suvin describes as the essential work of science fiction: "cognitive estrangement" (4). *A.I.* estranges us from humanity, and from our world, making the viewer see both in a new, denaturalized light. However, with my ultimate emphasis on a diegetic sublime, I am after something more radical than estrangement.

Interrupting Humanism: Birth and the Posthuman

In Rouge City, David asks Dr. Know how a mecha can be made real. He is told to travel to the "end of the world where the lions weep" and seek out Hobby. In this future world, global warming has melted the ice caps. The oceans have become bloated and overrun countless cities. Most of Manhattan's buildings are covered by water. Lady Liberty, perhaps *the* Humanist icon, barely lifts her enlightened torch above the waves. This is *Man*hattan, "a mecha restricted zone," where Man (fails to) resist(s) that which would undermine his identity and reveal his artificial nature. In the first few moments of the film, a voiceover explains that millions have starved in this future world and that first world nations have "licensed pregnancy" and turned to mecha as a means of ensuring a stable way of life. The narrator refers to mecha as an "essential ... economic link in the chain mail of society," nicely summing up both the economic nature of identity as well as its obsessive construction of an inside and an outside.

As the voiceover commences, we see the ocean followed by a fade into a statue of a man with outstretched hands and a peacock base which conveys a sense of flight, power, and immortality. It is the business logo of Cybertronics, David's manufacturer. As the camera draws back, we realize that we are behind a rain-swept window looking out at the statue. Perhaps the oldest trope for birth, water is also a metaphor for that which erodes immanence. It is that which all representations, statues, and mecha are created to shield humans from, like chain mail, or the pane of glass shutting out the rain in this scene. It is fitting then that while the Cybertronics statue, window, and rain are still in view, Hobby begins his speech about how inventing a mecha "has been the dream of man since the birth of science," advocating the design of a mecha who will not simulate: David. Opposed to the rain of difference outside, Hobby is concerned with a mythic birth of immanent subjects that will fend off the horror of death — his son's — and the indefatigable rain (of difference) on the outside.

This is, as another series of statues suggests, an impossibility. On the flight into Manhattan, several identical stone lions, iconic symbols of power, are found weeping, gushing water out of both eyes and mouths. If subjectival identity is a matter of bringing the outside in, digesting difference, here is an inversion of that movement. The leonine, immanent interior has been exposed to the outside. Just as the melting icecaps suggest humanity's inability to manage or assimilate nature, this vomited water points to the failure of the Humanist subject, and to the indigestibility of the world, and to the posthuman. David meets Hobby only after he has murdered another david, confirming his humanity through his efficacious elimination of difference. Hobby affirms that David is the only David, implying his individuality and his humanity, only to add that his son was "one-of-a-kind" and that David was at least "first-of-a-kind." This tension between simultaneously recognizing humanity and undermining it continues when Hobby tells David that he is "a real boy, at least as real as I've ever made one." For him, David is a "success" story, the first mecha to desire and dream. Shattered, David tells Hobby that his "brain is falling out." When Hobby leaves to collect David's "real mothers and fathers," David wanders around a manufacturing center, his womb. A dozen boxed davids stand in a line while others hang from the ceiling on what resemble meat hooks. Two lines of life-size boxes are each marked "David" and "Marlene." Ad copy on the outside says, "At Last — A Love of Your Own." At a particularly crucial moment, David looks through the eyes of another david. This face, without a cranium, is exposed to the world around it, specifically to the rain and window discussed earlier. David's murder and meeting with Hobby occurs in the room adjacent to the aforementioned window. It is through this window that David walks only to deliberately drop to the water below. If the window and the building amount to humanist enclosures, the digestive spatiality of the Humanist subject is reversed as David leaves the building. A suggestive shot at the surface of the ocean follows. The camera begins filming while still placed within what we can only suppose to be the building that David fell from only to move forward through shattered glass to the outside and to the rain. The camera recapitulates David's indigestion.

Subjectivity, co-originary with representation, arises as we have seen through the digestion of difference. David's tortuous and repetitive attempts to write the family/Humanist narrative are all concerned with exactly such a digestion of difference in which the subject recognizes his self in that which is other, becoming in this way human. However, in the experience of the *birth* of these other davids, David's digestion is stalled, and spatially reversed. Such a confrontation with birth — by contrast to the myriad examples of digestion in the film — exceeds the rational, assimilative abilities of David, who, until this moment, was able to quite easily scoop up the exterior world of difference and interiorize it. David's idea of the family (Human) founders before this sublime experience of birth which undermines representational closure. We do not need Lyotard or Nancy to tell us, though they do, of the sublime nature of birth (Nancy, *Birth* 2; Lyotard, "Unbeknownst" 47). The digestive logic (spatial, rational, representational, ontological) developed thus far in the essay has been turned inside-out in the face of this, the raw experience of birth. A Latourian reading of this moment would emphasize the row of davids as examples of the proliferation of nature-culture hybrids, undermining modernity. Such a reading is possible, but not quite as telling as what I have developed above. David, after all, has already murdered one other david, and the very fact that David could be digested by a human family indicates the incredible purifying power present in the film. Birth is the logical trigger for this posthuman exposure, ultimately, because of the spatial logic. If Humanism is defined by a rationalizing ingestion, the logical opposite, birth, is defined, literally, by an expulsion — the brain of the rational subject somewhere outside of itself, in the other.

This spatial exposure entails David's "recognition"—one cannot in light of the experience described above neglect the scare quotes — that he will not become immanent, or real. While in the lab, David sees how all these other davids are not only constructed but also boxed; if boxes operate as a metaphor for subjectivity, he also sees how very insubstantial the lines we draw between the "inside" and "outside" are. He "recognizes" that he cannot be rid of the artificiality that plagues him and all humans for that matter. In this moment of representational indigestion, David confronts the impossibility of immediate presence, the fact that identity is born through an exteriority that cannot be erased. For the Humanist subject to be interrupted, digestion must stop, opening up the borders of the self so that the interior movement is reversed: The "self" opens to the outside, and to others; a posthuman ethics would begin with this spacing. With Badmington (*Alien Chic* 153) and Graham (228), I would also locate the posthuman in the spacing of Derridean *différance*. Against the rigid *difference* of, say, a binary between human and alien, what happens at this moment is that David's representational faculties — which are on the side of difference — break down, confronting him with his existence in an endlessly *deferred* series of relations.

Humanist Completion, Cloning, Hospitality

Just as David gets his dream in *A.I.*'s final scene — immanence — and (apparently) dies, so, too, does humanity. Hobby informs us that it has been the dream of "man since the birth of science" to create a real being. David, as a tool of narrative, represents the completion of signification for both Hobby and the family. Monica has lost a son, prompting the desire for and creation of David to heal the family representation. Hobby, of course, is confronted with much the same circumstances as his own son's death predates his Davidic simulacrum. This parallel justifies telescoping the obsession with a familial representation onto the much larger stage of humanism.

Contemporary critics of postmodernism argue that philosophy, the world, is ill (in the absence of its "Martin") and has lost its hold on absolutes like God, morality, and Man (Nancy, *Gravity* 21–35). Paradoxically, it is the very charge that meaning has been lost that provides meaning with its vitality — to return to the dynamic of anticipation and the hermeneutic circle. This illness stands in for a lack that is less absent than present "at a distance." Such an illusory absence is crucial as it is what creates the desire which fuels the modern project whose ultimate object is the presentation of an absolute Subject. Meaning (David/Martin), once returned, then has to move away again to ensure that this crude dialectic of lack and desire continues.

As we have seen, Hobby's speech inscribes a teleological history whose fulfillment, whose "dream" and desire, is embodied in David. His objective is the resolution of the sensible (David *as* representation) and the intelligible (the idea of Man) in which "each presents the other" (22–23). Assuming the chasm between the sensible and intelligible, signification is the absolute "resolution" of the two which, at the furthest end, amounts to *"the very model of a structure or system that is closed upon itself,"* a definition of the seamless monad (original's emphasis). It is also — to point out what may be obvious by now — the utter opposite of the sublimity, which is defined by the impossibility of representing an otherwise intelligible idea (Lyotard, *Postmodern Condition* 78). In the same way that David's letters were an attempt to align the sensible (words) with the intelligible (an idea of the family), David himself operates for the Humanist project. As a feat of engineering David amounts to an absolute representation of the Humanist subject. There can be no greater Humanist feat than to make an entity that mirrors the self, desiring, dreaming, and lacking. By making David (really) human, the world has been fully represented and science can be at ease because this representation signals the end of that distant lack and the desire that it creates (49).

Yet it is a profoundly disturbing success in that it is only the dialectic of lack and desire that creates the orientation or project that gives identity to the subject. The closure of the hermeneutic circle is therefore also a non-subjectival opening. First, a bit more on this limit from Nancy's *The Gravity of Thought*:

> In its completed form, this circle is as follows: the subject of signification recognizes itself as the ultimate signified. This amounts to saying that the process or structure of signification recognizes and signifies itself as its own subject. Thus, the *meaning* of the *subject* ... is situated at once in a constant and infinite presence-at-a-distance *and* in a perfect ontological identity with the subject whose meaning it constitutes; the uniformly evasive presence of meaning constitutes its substantiality [original's emphasis; 43–44].

At the point of total representation, lack and its corollary, desire, are gone and with them the subject. What remains as a "subject" "recognizes" that identity is less immanent than a play between absence ("presence-at-a-distance") and presence ("perfect ontological identity"). The subject "recognizes" that its substance is grounded not in signification, but in the perpetual movement or architecture of meaning by which signification comes into being. Subjectivity requires an inexhaustible lack, so that, in a way, the subject is confronted with a structural paradox: to complete the Humanist project is to die. When Hobby tells David that he is "real" because he is the first mecha to desire and dream, he explains in the simplest terms that subjectivity is grounded in lack. We are who we are because we are constantly projecting ourselves toward that illusory lack. Subjectivity is revealed, in other words, as *in-sign-ificant*, as lacking a ground as it moves perpetually from *here* to *there* (51). Having become a real boy, his subjectivity is endangered along with the essential inertia that is the project of subjectivity (and having completed its project in David, the same is true for humanism).

As I have demonstrated, there is no essential difference between orga and mecha. Both simulate and operate hermeneutically in the world, trying to resolve the tension between the sensible and intelligible in a representation. Whereas humans had been able to elide this exposition in seamless representations, at the end of humanism this cannot be ignored: The recognition of "insignificance" is the signature trait of our time. This is again, to say the least, considerably different than Graham's argument: Rather than an overabundance of hybrids that may no longer be "purified," what we see here is a mechanical boy who *is* really human (at least in terms of Hobby's definition)—at which point the Humanist edifice collapses.

A.I. focuses and furthers this discussion by foregrounding the fact of bioengineering. With the film's emphasis on androids this will seem strange until it is recalled that David is an identical twin of Hobby's son—as are all the davids on the manufacturing line—and that the A.I. at the end of the film clone Monica for a brief rendezvous with David. While David is an android, my analysis takes Hobby (for whom David exhibits the essential qualities of humanity) at his word, and uses this android's human experience to discuss the biotechnological world that we humans now inhabit. The dialectic of lack and desire stalls because reproductive science interrupts the rational subject in two ways, both as a completion, and as a confrontation with our birth. Biological science has been perfected to such an extent that it not only confronts us with our birth, but does so *incessantly* due to its increasingly expansive place in society. We may be able, as David does, to digest one copy, but when we are confronted with the artificial manner in which we are born, our digestion fails and "we" are brought, finally, face to face with the indigestibility of the world. The subjectival mastery over birth has made it possible to move beyond a subjectival birth: Posthumanity experiences a state of constant birth.

Cloning is not a simple extension of subjectival power. It is also an interruption of subjectivity and thereby a confrontation with our insubstantiality, our existence outside of ourselves with others. This is an endless birth because cloning is endless; innumerable davids can be made of one David and, more importantly, it is endless because the "subject," in the face of this birth, is incapable of creating the mental representations that would reduce this reality to the well-bordered stability of a Human, Family, National being.

When, for instance, Hobby informs David that he will return momentarily with David's real mothers and fathers, the immanent notion of the family self is replaced with a notion of the self constructed via an impersonal web of communal activity. David cannot interiorize this "family" or "birth" in a representation when his presence is endlessly deferred. The rational mind cannot truly digest its relation to all humans, let alone its construction in a womb that looks more like a factory floor than an intimate domicile. Humanism is a sentimental myth which is exposed at the moment we are forced — as we are more and more — to confront our birth in the world.

Ethically, this entails an understanding of identity as less immanent than deferred, a spacing in which what once was a subject — absolute, monadic, solipsistic — is now exposed to others. "Posthumanity" would be defined by spacing, a non-subjectival awareness of each singularity's existence outside of his or her self. Opposed to the digestion of presence and absence seen in David's personal path toward total signification, this exposure would interrupt simple immanent representations. Instead of seamless borders of self, the subject's "interior" would be radically exposed. (While in the mecha shop for ingesting real food, David attempts to touch his chest cavity. The mechanic slaps his hand away. In this new space, hands will not be swatted.) While *Artificial Intelligence* signals the interruption of the subject, it concomitantly signals the birth of a singularity whose existence is defined by "artificiality," once this word has been drained of all metaphysical vestiges. Nor, lest I be misunderstood, is this a new individual, shorn of the past, and now somewhere *simply* beyond humanism, as if that were possible.

Spielberg's film ends with a representation of such a singularity. The A.I. at the film's end, descendants of David and others of his time, while curious, do not recapitulate the obsession with subjectivity that is seen in humans and David. Our first telling image of this other order is glimpsed in their choice of transportation. Their transport, for lack of another name, is not a seamless representation of tin and rivets, but a rough-cut rectangle in which the seams are ostentatious. Nothing appears to hold the sides of this vehicle together but transparent spacing. Its interior is totally exposed to the outside. Having served its purpose, the ship explodes in dozens of pieces to be, assumedly, stacked to the side. It is a (strategically essential) representation to be used for a short time and abandoned. The A.I. who leave the transport discover David, frozen, immobile and trapped in a seamless helicopter-like bubble by contrast. He is foreign to them. He is an intruder, demanding and increasingly rude. Yet they remain hospitable. David's alterity is not digested and put to work in the manner so well modeled by Martin, David, or Hobby's humanism. When the statue of the Blue Fairy collapses at David's touch, the A.I. recreate and animate her. Monica is even brought back for 24 hours of illusory communion with David. This is not the world of abandonment and exposure of the A.I., yet they acquiesce to the fantasies of this young boy. Exposed to the end of humanism, it is such a hospitality that beckons to us.

NOTE

1. This essay began as a chapter in my 2005 dissertation (*At the Limit of Subjectivity: Ethics, Community, Birth, and the Posthuman in the Narratives of Thomas Pynchon, Samuel R. Delany, Steven Spielberg, and Joel and Ethan Coen*). In light of space considerations, I have eliminated much of the theoretical armature. The film sustains the above argument, though I willingly acknowledge my theoretical debt to the work of Jean-Luc Nancy whose language I emulate. Numerous people have read this essay along the way, including David Sheridan, Dawn Comer, Scott Michaelsen, Eyal Amiran, Patrick O'Donnell, and A.C. Goodson. Thank you all for your assistance.

Afterword: Afterwards

Patrick Fuery

Every age has its own sense of terror. To paraphrase Tolstoy, all happy ages are alike; every age of terror is terrified in its own way. So it must seem to each age that their sense of terror is beyond comparison, beyond all that has gone before. And because of this there is almost inevitably a sense of uniqueness about the terror—a terror like no other. The shadow of terror that pervades "us" (Western culture at the beginning of the 21st century) stretches back to colonial Europe and through to 9/11. The weight of those seemingly impossible events and acts have given our times a difficult and complex history. In many ways it was 9/11 that marked the moment when the West (or at the very least the U.S.) shifted from a terror defined by the events of the 20th century to a new configuration that has in many ways determined the sensibilities of the 21st century. Part of this sensibility is embedded in the fact that we inhabit an age that is mediated and remediated like no other. Cinema, the exemplar here, has devised a discursive practice that means it does not simply represent a sense of terror, it has the capacity to create it, replay it, archive, and serve as a cultural memory as well. The cultural terror of our age is bound up with the eternal recurrence. Our terror is played out in ways that have come to define it; we have a performativity of terror that exceeds what even Baudrillard imagined.

One of the key shifts that took place with the events of 9/11, and its aftermath, is that terror for the West became entwined with terrorism; but this was a particular type of terrorism that is invested in the complex relations of the internal and external. It is not difficult to trace this back to other terrors—one only has to think of the cultural paranoia cinema of the 1950s to see that the threat becomes more forceful when it is seen as

Afterword

an external force manifested internally. The threat from within (from all our literal and metaphoric ideas about the viral through to the idea of sleeper cells lying in wait to be activated) is also about the deconstruction of the social order in itself. It is a meditation on how strong cultural identity is and can be held. The social discursive practices — and cinema has been one of the most significant since its inception — contribute, critique, and expose this. We see this in many guises as the shift in the paradigms of terror almost inevitably marks self reflection. Within that paraphrased Tolstoy line, the post–9/11 is defined by a number of unique attributes as it has become a terror unlike any other. A key to this is the (digital — and I would include the cinematic in that) mediation in which we live and experience events (and their knowledges) with more speed, more information, more repetition, and more access than ever before. The post–9/11 terror is bound up to these returns, and this has shaped, and is shaped by, the cultural order of things.

If it is the case that all ages have their sense of terror, we might be a little more circumspect in regard to the sublime. There are three "ages" of theorizing the sublime — Longinus (1st or 3rd century A.D.); Burke and Kant (mid 1700s); and Lyotard (the latter part of the 20th century). It is a curious twist of history, expression, and co-incidence that we witness two "ages" (our current one is still in formation) that are defined by terror. If we put Longinus to one side (there is so little known about him that this is a reasonable thing to do), we note that 1793–94 was known as the Reign of Terror due to the French Revolution; and our (theoretical) age of post-modernity and post-structuralism marks the beginning of a new version of terrorism, with a revisitation of the sublime. The challenge that this sets any theory of the sublime is that it cannot simply argue that the theoretical mechanisms and processes can be universally applied to different versions of terror. If the terror is unique (even if the manifested signifiers appear as universals), then it needs a well defined theoretical apparatus to be able understand it. If we want to understand the nature of a terror at a point in time and/or culture, then we need a system of thought that is capable of examining both universals and particulars. In many ways this is precisely the task that Lyotard sets himself to when he investigates the sublime from that dominant Kantian model.

Added to this idea that each age sees its terror as no other is the version of terror found within the sublime itself. No matter which trajectory that terror has taken that we adopt in the history and practice of the sublime, one thing remains constant. This is the idea that "terror" in the sublime must be seen as a different typological order; or, put another way, it must be part of a different categorical aspect, to all other versions of terror. We cannot think of the terror that inhabits the sublime as the same as any other terror because to do so renders it redundant in the determination of the sublime, and brings in to question the hermeneutic value of the sublime as a category itself. We cannot think of the terror that the sublime produces as the same as other versions of terror, for this is why the idea of the sublime has philosophical and aesthetic value (it is the basis, at least within this context of the aesthetic, of the Kantian notion of judgment). Finally, we must think of the terror in the sublime as different from all other terrors because this is fundamentally what it is — different and unique. It is precisely this sense of terror and the sublime as being sutured together that drives the need to understand "terror" as something altogether different whenever we encounter the sublime. Defining this order (the precisions and nuances) of terror is a complex and extensive enterprise, but some notes toward how terror is unique within the sublime (and vice versa) will serve here to locate this sublime-specific terror within the cinematic. More than this, so specific is this typological order of terror that to understand it we need to think of it as something beyond terror. At its most extreme it is a kind of meta-terror — an excess that leads us to reflect on what the *noumena* of terror might be. Here we witness the relationship of the internal and external foregrounded once more.

It might be argued that cinema fits into this discussion in a curious fashion. It is certainly seductive to think of this interpretation of sublime and terror in terms of cinematic exemplars — that is, cinema becomes the textual examples to demonstrate this version of terror — but this is a seduction that should make us ill at ease. What I would like to suggest here is that cinema (or at least a certain type and part of cinema) should not be employed to illustrate the philosophical and aesthetic ideas of the sublime, but rather be seen as part of the very process. In other words, cinema is not the textual variation or illustration, it is actually part of the formation and iteration of the sublime itself. I want suggest that cinema has provided a certain function within its lifetime that has made a dynamic contribution to the cultural formation of the sublime, and this in turn has played a part in shaping various aspects of Western cultural life. This is the idea that the sublime, as a cultural process, interplays with the cinematic, which has gone on to produce a unique version of the sublime.

Here, then, is our first proposition of sublime terror and cinema: that our engagement with "reality" (be it objective, textually construed, cinematic, psychical, and so on) is mediated, but in this mediation is the underlying terror of losing the capacity to be the active agent in the processes of perception and interpretation. The Surrealists knew this; as did Leni Riefenstahl and Sergei Eisenstein, operating as they were at different ends of the political propaganda spectrum; Hitchcock certainly did and constructed an entire philosophy of suspense around it; and, as a final example here, John Ford, in his Westerns, demonstrated this. In a way all "pure" cinema does this, although it is not always with a sublime result. I would also argue that once it passes into cinematic convention (that is, becomes a recognizable, representable, and repeatable, device) then the sublime possibilities are lost.

The fear/terror (recalling that the German term [*furcht*] may mean dread, fear, terror, as well as angst) that is at play in this negotiation of reality emerges through the sublime. It is worth reminding ourselves at this point that Kant's notion of the subjective is highly reflexive, demanding that the spectator (and the examples are predominately visual in Kant) reflect on his/her relationship to what is being beheld. As Gasché points out in *The Idea of Form*: "The 'subjective' principle is thus a principle for mere [*bloss*] reflection, that is, for an isolated use by the power of reflection — though, as Kant repeatedly reminds us, it is not without relation to the understanding as the faculty of concepts in general" (Gasché 32).[1] The fear of the loss of such a reflexive site/sight can be interpreted as sublime in part because of the sensation of being overcome and of having to give up the power of "judgement" (both teleological and aesthetic). What is significant here is that this fear is not a straightforward negative one, which is why it can be seen as part of the sublime; it is heavily imbued with a sense of pleasure and even desire. As cinema spectators we desire this status of the vision machine, this investment of the spectator in the gaze of cinema itself. The greatest pleasure — perhaps *jouissance* is not too strong a term here — emerges from this giving up the site of subjectivity to allow a new, hybridized subjectivity that has become part of the cinematic text itself. In Kant's terms, this is the awe and excess that sweeps over us when we experience the sublime.

Terror in the sublime can be seen as a specific type of transformative process. If we were to argue that all terror transforms (from states of non-terror to the terrified) then it is important to understand what makes the transformative attributes of terror in the sublime somehow different. This is precisely what we find in Kant's "judgement" contribution, but in some ways we also see this in Edmund Burke's ideas on terror as the specificity of the sublime. In *A Philosophical Enquiry into the Origin of our Ideas of the Sublime and Beautiful,* Burke is adamant on this qualification: "Whatever is fitted in any sort to excite the ideas of pain, and danger, that is to say, whatever is in any sort terrible, or is conversant about terrible objects, or operates in a manner analogous to terror, it is a source of the sublime; that is, it is productive of the strongest emotion which the mind is capable of feeling" (Burke 39). We can go even further back to the historical origins and note that in Longinus' discussion of Sappho, this quality of being overcome (swooning) is essential to understanding the process. From Longinus to Burke to Kant and on to the recent works of Lyotard we see this recurrence of the transformative processes of the sublime. It is this transformative power of the terror in the sublime that defines the unique attributes of this process. The cultural determination of the sublime is entwined with the terror of the age. This collection of essays is part of that self-reflexive examination of cultural sensibilities as they articulate a version of terror unique to its time.

NOTE

1. Gasché offers an excellent and persuasive discussion regarding Kant's use of the term "merely" (*bloss*), demonstrating how the English translation is far from adequate. The German word also carries with it the sense of pure, as well as open and manifest. Here we need to see that this is a pure reflection and not, as implied in the word "mere," an inferior or lesser reflection.

Patrick Fuery is a professor and chair of English at Chapman University in Orange, California. He was previously professor of film studies at the University of London, a professor of film at Sussex University, and director of research and professor of film studies at Newcastle University (Australia). He is the author of eight books, most recently *Madness and Cinema* (Palgrave) and *Cultural Studies and Critical Theory* (Oxford University Press).

Selected Bibliography

Adorno, Theodor W. *The Culture Industry.* Ed. J.M. Bernstein. New York: Routledge, 1991. Print.
Adorno, Theodor Wilhelm, and Max Horkheimer. *The Dialectic of Enlightenment.* Trans. John Cumming. New York: Verso, 1997. Print.
Agamben, Giorgio. *Homo Sacer.* Trans. Daniel Heller-Roazen. Stanford: Stanford University Press, 1998. Print.
———. *Remnants of Auschwitz: The Witness and the Archive.* Trans. Daniel Heller-Roazen. New York: Zone Books, 1999. Print.
———. *The Signature of All Things: On Method.* Trans. Luca D'Isanto and Kevin Attell. New York: Zone Books, 2009. Print.
———. *State of Exception.* Trans. Kevin Attell. Chicago: Chicago University Press, 2005. Print.
A.I.: Artificial Intelligence. Dir. Steven Spielberg. Perf. Haley Joel Osment and Jude Law. DreamWorks Pictures, 2002. DVD.
The American Nightmare. Dir. Adam Simon. IFC, 2000. DVD.
Arthur, Paul. "The Four Last Things." *The End of Cinema as We Know It: American Film in the Nineties.* Ed. Jon Lewis. New York: New York University Press, 2001. 342–55. Print.
Ashfield, Andrew, and Peter de Bolla, eds. *The Sublime: A Reader in British Eighteenth-Century Aesthetic Theory.* Cambridge: Cambridge University Press, 1996. Print.
Badmington, Neil, *Alien Chic: Posthumanism and the Other Within.* New York: Routledge, 2004. Print.
———, ed. *Posthumanism.* New York: Palgrave, 2000. Print.
Bataille, Georges. "The 'Old Mole' and the Prefix Sur in the Words *Surhomme* [Superman] and *Surrealist.*" *Visions of Excess: Selected Writings, 1927–1939.* Ed. Allan Stoekl. Minneapolis: University of Minnesota Press, 1985. 32–44. Print.
———. "The Use Value of D.A.F. de Sade (An Open Letter to My Current Comrades)." *Visions of Excess: Selected Writings, 1927–1939.* Ed. Allan Stoekl. Minneapolis: University of Minnesota Press, 1985. 91–102. Print.
Baudrillard, Jean. *The Spirit of Terrorism and Requiem for the Twin Towers.* Trans. Chris Turner. London: Verso, 2002. Print.
Becker, Ernest. *Escape from Evil.* New York: Free Press, 1975. Print.
Benjamin, Walter. *Illuminations.* Trans. Harry Zohn. New York: Schocken, 1969. Print.
———. *Illuminations: Essays and Reflections.* Ed. Hannah Arendt. New York: Schocken, 2007. Print.
Bilal, Wafaa. "... and Counting." *Wafaa Bilal.* March 2010. Web. 11 July 2011.

Selected Bibliography

Black Swan. Dir. Darren Aronofsky. Perf. Natalie Portman, Mila Kunis, Vincent Cassel and Barbara Hershey. Fox Searchlight Pictures, 2011. DVD.
Bonitzer, Pascal. "Lignes et voies (*Macadam à deux voies*)." *Cahiers du Cinéma* 266–267 (May 1976): 68–70. Print.
Bordwell, David. *The Poetics of Cinema*. New York: Routledge, 2007. Print.
_____. *The Way Hollywood Tells It: Story and Style in Modern Movies*. Berkeley: University of California Press, 2006. Print.
_____, and Kristen Thompson. *The Classical Hollywood Cinema: Film Style and Mode of Production to 1960*. New York: Columbia University Press, 1985. Print.
Boundas, Constantine, ed. *The Deleuze Reader*. New York: Columbia University Press, 1993. Print.
Bourdieu, Pierre. "Culture Is in Danger." *Sociology Is a Martial Art: Political Writings by Pierre Bourdieu*. Ed. Gisèle Sapiro. New York: The New Press, 2010. 222–33. Print.
Brison, Susan. *Aftermath: Violence and the Remaking of a Self*. Princeton: Princeton University Press, 2002. Print.
Brockman, John. *The Third Culture*. New York: Simon & Schuster, 1995. Print.
Brown, Michelle. "'Setting the Conditions' for Abu Ghraib: The Prison Nation Abroad." *American Quarterly* 57.3 (2005): 973–997. Print.
Bryant, Martin. "The Guardian's 9/11 mistake shows we're still learning the boundaries of Twitter." *The Next Web*. 13 September 2011. Web. 13 September 2001.
Bukatman, Scott. "The Artificial Infinite: On Special Effects and the Sublime." *Alien Zone II: The Spaces of Science Fiction Cinema*. Ed. Annette Kuhn. London: Verso, 1999. 249–75. Print.
Burke, Edmund. *A Philosophical Enquiry Into the Origin of Our Ideas of the Sublime and Beautiful*. Ed. James T. Boulton. London: Routledge, 1958. Print.
_____. *A Philosophical Enquiry Into the Origin of Our Ideas of the Sublime and Beautiful*. Oxford: Oxford University Press, 1998. Print.
Butler, Judith. *Precarious Life: The Powers of Mourning and Violence*. London: Verso, 2006. Print.
Campbell, Jim, artist. *Accumulating Psycho*. 2004. Media installation.
_____. *Illuminated Average #1, Hitchcock's Psycho*. 2000. Media installation.
_____. *Night Light*. 1995/1998. Media installation.
Carroll, Noël. "Film, Emotion, and Genre." *Passionate Views*. Eds. Carl Plantinga and Greg M. Smith. Baltimore: Johns Hopkins University Press, 1999. 21–47. Print.
Caryl, Christian. "Predators and Robots at War." *The New York Review of Books* 29 September 2011. Web. 16 October 2011.
Chalmers, David. "Facing Up to the Problem of Consciousness." *Journal of Consciousness Studies* 2.3 (1995): 200–219. Print.
Clark, Andy. *Natural Born Cyborgs: Minds, Technologies, and the Future of Human Intelligence*. New York: Oxford University Press, 2003. Print.
Cloverfield. Dir. Matt Reeves. Perf. T.J. Miller and Jessica Lucas. Paramount Pictures, 2008. Film.
CNN. "Details of Army's abuse investigation surface." *CNN*. 21 January 2004. Web. 13 October 2006.
Coleridge, Samuel Taylor. *Lectures 1808–1819 on Literature. The Collected Works of Samuel Taylor Coleridge* Vol. 5:2. Eds. Reginald Anthony Folks and Kathleen Coburn. London: Routledge and Kegan Paul, 1987. Print.
Comer, Todd A. "At the Limit of Subjectivity: Ethics, Community, Birth, and the

Selected Bibliography

Posthuman in the Narratives of Thomas Pynchon, Samuel R. Delany, Steven Spielberg, and Joel and Ethan Coen." Diss., Michigan State University, 2005. Print.
Comolli, Jean-Louis. "Le fantome de Personne." *Cahiers du Cinéma* 188 (March 1967): 20. Print.
Creed, Barbara. *The Monstrous Feminine: Film, Feminism, Psychoanalysis*. New York: Routledge, 1993. Print.
Csicsery-Ronay, Jr., Istvan. "On the Grotesque in Science Fiction." *Science Fiction Studies* 29 (2002): 71–99. Print.
Cubitt, Sean. *The Cinema Effect*. Cambridge: MIT Press, 2004. Print.
Cvek, Sven. *Towering Figures: Reading the 9/11 Archive*. Amsterdam: Rodopi, 2011. Print.
Daney, Serge. *Postcards from the Cinema*. Trans. Paul Douglas Grant. Oxford: Berg, 2007. Print.
"Dark Places." Santa Monica Museum of Art. 2005. Media installation.
Dasgupta, Partha. "Digitalization." ASU Ira A. Fulton School of Engineering. 24 December 2001. Web. 18 April 2011.
Davis, Mike. *Buda's Wagon: A Brief History of the Car Bomb*. New York: Verso, 2007. Print.
de Certeau, Michel. *The Practice of Everyday Life*. Berkeley: University of California Press, 1988. Print.
Déjà Vu. Dir. Tony Scott. Perf. Denzel Washington. Touchstone Pictures, 2007. DVD.
Deleuze, Gilles. *Cinema 2: The Time-Image*. Trans. Hugh Tomlinson and Robert Galeta. Minneapolis: University of Minnesota Press, 1989. Print.
_____. *Difference and Repetition*. Trans. Paul Patton. New York: Columbia University Press, 1994. Print.
de Rougemont, Denis. *The Devil's Share: An Essay on the Diabolic in Modern Society*. Trans. Haakon Chevalier. New York: Meridian, 1956. Print.
Derrida, Jacques. *The Gift of Death and Literature in Secret*. Trans. David Wills. Chicago: University of Chicago Press, 1995. Print.
_____. *Memoires: For Paul de Man*. New York: Columbia University Press, 1989. Print.
_____. *Politics of Friendship*. Trans. George Collins. New York: Verso, 1997. Print.
_____. *Rogues: Two Essays on Reason*. Trans. Pascale-Anne Brault and Michael Naas. Stanford: Stanford University Press, 2005. Print.
_____. *Writing and Difference*. Trans. Alan Bass. Chicago: University of Chicago Press, 1978. Print.
Doane, Mary Ann. *The Emergence of Cinematic Time: Modernity, Contingency, the Archive*. Cambridge: Harvard University Press, 2002. Print.
Dog Day Afternoon. Dir. Sidney Lumet. Perf. Al Pacino. Warner Home Video, 1997. DVD.
Dogville. Dir. Lars Von Trier. Perf. Nicole Kidman, Lauren Bacall and James Caan. Lions Gate, 2004. DVD.
Donnie Darko. Dir. Richard Kelly. Perf. Jake Gyllenhaal. 20th–Century–Fox, 2003. DVD.
Dopaso, Andrea. "*Spider-Man* Commentary." *Spider-Man* Trilogy Box-set, Sony Pictures, 2007. DVD.
Douthat, Ross. "Less than Monstrous." *National Review* 11 February 2002: 55. Print.
Dreyfus, Hubert. *Being-in-the-World*. Cambridge: MIT Press, 1997. Print.
Dykstra, John. "*Spider-Man* Commentary." *Spider-Man* Trilogy Box-set, Sony Pictures, 2007. DVD.

Selected Bibliography

Eco, Umberto. "Science, Technology, and Magic." *Turning Back the Clock: Hot Wars and Media Populism.* Trans. Alastair McEwen. Orlando: Harvest, 2006. 103–11. Print.

Editorial. "Rushing Off a Cliff." *The New York Times* 28 September 2006. Web. 13 October 2006.

Eisenman, Stephen F. *The Abu Ghraib Effect.* London: Reaktion, 2007. Print.

Elsaesser, Thomas. "The Blockbuster: Everything Connects, But Not Everything Goes." *The End of Cinema as We Know It: American Film in the Nineties.* Ed. Jon Lewis. New York: New York University Press, 2001. 11–22. Print.

———. "The Mind-Game Film." *Puzzle Films: Complex Storytelling in Contemporary Cinema.* Ed. Warren Buckland. Chichester, UK: Wiley-Blackwell, 2009. 13–41. Print.

Enstad, Robert. "Public Safety's Concerns Force Great America to Scrap Ride." *Chicago Tribune.* 12 March 1986. Web. 14 May 2012.

The Fountain. Dir. Darren Aronofsky. Perf. Hugh Jackman and Rachel Weisz. Warner Bros. Pictures, 2006. DVD.

1408. Dir. Mikael Hafstrom. Perf. John Cusack and Samuel L. Jackson. Weinstein Co., 2007. DVD.

Freud, Sigmund. *Beyond the Pleasure Principle.* In *The Standard Edition of the Complete Psychological Works of Sigmund Freud.* Trans. James Strachey. Vol. 18. London: Hogarth Press, 1955. Print.

———. "Mourning and Melancholia." *On Metapsychology.* London: Penguin, 1991. Print.

———. "The Psychotherapy of Hysteria." *The Pelican Freud Library.* Vol. 3. Harmondsworth: Penguin, 1974.

Friedman, Roger. "*Cloverfield*: Horror Film Not Sensitive about 9/11." *Foxnews.com.* 16 January 2008. Web. 13 September 2011.

Frohne, Ursula. "That's the Only Now I Get: Immersion und Participation in Video-Installations by Dan Graham, Steve McQueen, Douglas Gordon, Doug Aitken, Eija-Liisa Ahtila, Sam Taylor-Wood." *Media Art Net.* Goethe-Institut. n.d. Web. 19 July 2012.

Frost, Laura. "Black Screens, Lost Bodies: The Cinematic Apparatus of 9/11 Horror." *Horror After 9/11: World of Fear, Cinema of Terror.* Eds. Aviva Briefel and Sam Miller. Austin: University of Texas Press, 2011. 13–39. Print.

Gabler, Neil. "This Time, The Scene Was Real." *The New York Times* 13 September 2001. Web. 13 September 2001.

Gasché, Rodolphe. *The Idea of Form: Rethinking Kant's Aesthetics.* Stanford: Stanford University Press, 2003. Print.

Ghosts of Abu Ghraib. Dir. Rory Kennedy. HBO Documentary Films, 2007. Film.

Gilligan, Carol. *In A Different Voice: Psychological Theory and Women's Development.* Cambridge: Harvard University Press, 1993. Print.

Girard, René. *I See Satan Fall Like Lightning.* Trans. James G. Williams. Maryknoll: Orbis, 2009. Print.

Gladstone, Jim. "Beyond the Hoods: The Abu Ghraib Images of Daniel Heyman," *Six Magazine.* 6 June 2007. Web. 16 October 2011.

Gordon, Douglas, artist. *24 Hour Psycho.* 1993. Media installation.

———. *24 Hour Psycho Back and Forth and To and Fro.* 2010. Media installation.

Graham, Elaine L. *Representations of the Post/Human: Monsters, Aliens and Others in Popular Culture.* New Brunswick, NJ: Rutgers University Press, 2002. Print.

Grant, Barry Keith. "'Sensuous Elaboration': Reason and the Visible in the Science

Selected Bibliography

Fiction Film." *Liquid Metal: The Science Fiction Film Reader*. London: Wallflower Press, 2004. 17–23. Print.
Grusin, Richard A. *Premediation: Affect and Mediality After 9/11*. New York: Palgrave-Macmillan, 2010. Print.
Guthrie, Marisa. "Spike Lee: Why I Haven't Made a Feature Film in Three Years," *The Hollywood Reporter* 30 June 2001. Web. 5 July 2011.
Harrison-Kahan, Lori. "Inside *Inside Man*: Spike Lee and Post-9/11 Entertainment." *Cinema Journal* 50.1 (Fall 2010): 39–58. Print.
Hartley, David. *Observations on Man, His Frame, His Duty, and His Expectations*. 6th ed. London: Thomas Tegg & Son, 1834. Print.
Harvey, David. *New Imperialism*. Oxford: Oxford University Press, 2005. Print.
Hayles, N. Katherine. *How We Became Posthuman: Virtual Bodies in Cybernetics, Literature, and Informatics*. Chicago: University of Chicago Press, 1999. Print.
Hegel, G.W.F. *Phenomenology of Spirit*. Trans. A.V. Miller. London: Oxford University Press, 1977. Print.
Heidegger, Martin. *Being and Time*. Trans. Joan Stambaugh. Albany: State University of New York Press, 1996. Print.
Hepburn, Ian. "Why @911tenyearsago was a bad taste blunder by the Guardian." *False Doorway*. 11 September 2011. Web. 13 September 2011.
Hoberman, Jim. "Meet the Depressed." *Village Voice* 24 October 2007. Web. 9 August 2011.
Hoefer, Carl. "Causal Determinism." *Stanford Encyclopedia of Philosophy*. The Metaphysics Research Lab, 2010. Web. 26 May 2012.
Hutcheon, Linda. *A Theory of Parody. The Teachings of Twentieth-Century Art Forms*. New York: Methuen, 1985. Print.
Inception. Dir. Christopher Nolan. Perf. Leonardo DiCaprio, Ellen Paige and Ken Watanabe. Warner Home Video, 2010. DVD.
Inglourious Basterds. Dir. Quentin Tarantino. Perf. Brad Pitt, Christoph Waltz, Mélanie Laurent and Michael Fassbender. Universal, 2009. DVD.
Inside Man. Dir. Spike Lee. Perf. Denzel Washington, Clive Owen and Jodie Foster. Universal, 2006. DVD.
Isaacs, Bruce. *Toward a New Film Aesthetic*. London: Continuum, 2008. Print.
Jackie Brown. Dir. Quentin Tarantino. Perf. Pam Grier, Samuel L. Jackson and Robert Forster. Miramax, 1997. DVD.
Jameson, Fredric. "Class and Allegory in Contemporary Mass Culture: *Dog Day Afternoon* as a Political Film." *Signatures of the Visible*. New York: Routledge, 1992. 35–54.
———. "Postmodernism, or the Cultural Logic of Late Capitalism." *New Left Review* I/146 (1984): 53–92. Print.
———. *Postmodernism: Or, the Cultural Logic of Late Capitalism*. Durham: Duke University Press, 1991. Print.
———. *Signatures of the Visible*. New York: Routledge, 1992. Print.
Junod, Tom, "Falling (Mad) Man." *Esquire*. 30 January 2011. Web. 7 May 2012.
———, and Andrew Chaikivsky. "The Falling Man." *Esquire*. September 2003. Web. 7 May 2012.
Kant, Immanuel. *The Critique of Judgement*. Oxford: Oxford University Press, 1952. Print.
———. *The Critique of Judgement*. Rev. ed. Oxford: Oxford University Press, 2007. Print.
———. *Critique of Judgment*. Trans. J.H. Bernard. *eBooks@adelaide*. University of Adelaide, 2010. Web. 19 July 2012.

Selected Bibliography

———. *Critique of Judgement*. Trans. J.H. Bernard. New York: Hafner, 1951. Print.
———. *Critique of the Power of Judgment*. Trans. Paul Guyer and Eric Matthews. Cambridge: Cambridge University Press, 2001. Print.
———. *Critique of Pure Reason*. Trans. Paul Guyer and Allen Wood. Cambridge: Cambridge University Press, 1999. Print.
———. *Observations on the Feeling of the Beautiful and Sublime*. London: University of California Press, 1960. Print.
Keane, Stephen. *Disaster Movies: The Cinema of Catastrophe*. 2nd ed. London: Wallflower, 2006. Print.
Kearney, Richard. "Terror, Philosophy and the Sublime: Some Philosophical Reflections on 11 September." *Philosophy Social Criticism* 29 (2003): 23–51. Print.
Keenan, Thomas. "Publicity and Indifference." *Human Rights Project at Bard College*. 12 November 2003. Web. 16 October 2011.
Kinder, Marsha. "Hot Spots, Avatars, and Narrative Fields Forever: Bunuel's Legacy for New Digital Media and Interactive Database Narrative." *Film Quarterly* 55.4 (2002): 2–15. Print.
King, Geoff. *Donnie Darko*. London: Wallflower Press, 2007. Print.
———. *Spectacular Narratives: Hollywood in the Age of the Blockbuster*. London: I.B. Taurus, 2000. Print.
King Kong. Dir. Merian C. Cooper and Ernest B. Schoedsack. Perf. Fay Wray, Robert Armstrong and Bruce Cabot. Turner Home Entertainment, 2006. DVD.
Klein, Naomi "'Never Before!' Our Amnesiac Torture Debate." *The Nation*. 26 December 2005. 11–12. Print.
Koolhaas, Rem. *Delirious New York*. New York: Monacelli Press, 1994. Print.
Kracauer, Siegfried. *Theory of Film: The Redemption of Physical Reality*. Oxford: Oxford University Press, 1960. Print.
Kristeva, Julia. *Black Sun: Depression and Melancholia*. Trans. Leon S. Roudiez. New York: Columbia University Press, 1989. Print.
———. *Powers of Horror: An Essay on Abjection*. New York: Columbia University Press, 1982. Print.
———, and Katharine A. Jensen. "The Pain of Sorrow in the Modern World: The Works of Marguerite Duras." *PMLA* 102.2 (1987): 138–152. Print.
LaCapra, Dominick. *Writing History, Writing Trauma*. Baltimore: Johns Hopkins University Press, 2001. Print.
Lanzmann, Claude. "Why Spielberg Has Distorted the Truth." *Guardian Weekly* April 1994: 14. Print.
Latour, Bruno. *We Have Never Been Modern*. Trans. Catherine Porter. Cambridge: Harvard University Press, 1993. Print.
Le Corbusier. *La Ville Radieuse*. Paris: Vincent Freal, 1964. Print.
Levinas, Emmanuel. *God, Death and Time*. Trans. Bettina Bergo. Palo Alto: Stanford University Press, 2000. Print.
———. *Otherwise Than Being: Or Beyond Essence*. Pittsburgh: Duquesne University Press, 1998. Print.
Lukács, Georg. *The Theory of the Novel*. Trans. Anna Bostock. Cambridge: MIT Press, 1971. Print.
Lurie, Susan. "Falling Persons and National Embodiment: The Reconstruction of Safe Spectatorship in the Photographic Record of 9/11." *Terror, Culture, Politics: Rethinking 9/11*. Eds. Daniel J. Sherman and Terry Nardin. Bloomington: Indiana University Press, 2006. 44–68. Print.

Selected Bibliography

Lyotard, Jean-François. "Acinema." *The Lyotard Reader.* Ed. Andrew Benjamin. Oxford: Blackwell, 1989. 169–180. Print.
———. "Adorno as the Devil." *Telos* 19 (1974): 127–138. Print.
———. "An Answer to the Question: What Is the Postmodern?" *The Postmodern Explained: Correspondence 1982–1985.* Sydney: Power, 1992. 1–16. Print.
———. *The Differend. Phrases in Dispute.* Trans. Georges van den Abbeele. Manchester: Manchester University Press, 1988. Print.
———. "Discussions, or Phrasing 'after Auschwitz.'" *The Lyotard Reader.* Ed. Andrew Benjamin. Oxford: Blackwell, 1989. 360–391. Print.
———. *Heidegger and the Jews.* Trans. Andreas Michel. Minneapolis: University of Minnesota Press, 1990. Print.
———. *The Inhuman: Reflections on Time.* Trans. Geoffrey Bennington and Rachel Bowlby. Cambridge: Polity Press, 1991. Print.
———. *Lessons on the Analytic of the Sublime.* Trans. Elizabeth Rottenberg. Stanford: Stanford University Press, 1991. Print.
———. *Lessons on the Analytic of the Sublime.* Trans. Elizabeth Rottenberg. Stanford: Stanford University Press, 1994. Print.
———. *The Postmodern Condition: A Report on Knowledge.* Trans. Geoffrey Bennington and Brian Massumi. Minneapolis: University of Minnesota Press, 1984. Print.
———. "The Sublime and the Avant-Garde." *Artforum* 22.8 (1984): 36–43. Print.
———. "Unbeknownst." *Community at Loose Ends.* Ed. Miami Theory Collective. Minneapolis: University of Minnesota Press, 1991. 42–48. Print.
Manovich, Lev. "Data Visualization as New Abstraction and Anti-Sublime." 2002. 17 July 2012. Web. MS Word Doc.
———. "Database as Symbolic Form." 1998. 17 July 2012. Web. MS Word Doc.
Massumi, Brian. *Parables for the Virtual: Movement, Affect, Sensation.* Durham: Duke University Press, 2002. Print.
Mathews, Peter. "Spinoza's Stone: The Logic of *Donnie Darko.*" *Post Script* 25.1 (2005): 38–48. Print.
McCormack, Jon, and Alan Dorin. "Art, Emergence, and the Computational Sublime," *networked_performance.* 2006. Web. 19 July 2012.
McCoy, Kevin, and Jennifer McCoy, artists. *Horror Chase.* 2003. Media installation.
McGowan, Todd. *The End of Dissatisfaction? Jacques Lacan and the Emerging Society of Enjoyment.* Albany: State University of New York Press, 2004. Print.
McNeill, Eddy. "State Urged to Inspect Thrill Rides." *Chicago Tribune* 24 May 1984. Web. 14 May 2012.
McQuire, Scott. "Impact Aesthetics: Back to the Future in Digital Cinema?" *Convergence* 6 (2000): 41–61. Print.
Melnick, Jeffrey P. *9/11 Culture: America Under Construction.* Chichester, UK: Wiley-Blackwell, 2009. Print.
Mey, Kerstin. *Art and Obscenity.* New York: I.B Tauris, 2007. Print.
Minority Report. Dir. Steven Spielberg. Perf. Tom Cruise. 20th Century-Fox, 2002. Film.
Mirzoeff, Nicholas. *Watching Babylon: The War in Iraq and Global Visual Culture.* New York: Routledge, 2005. Print.
Mitchell, W.J.T. *Cloning Terror: The War of Images, 9/11 to the Present.* Chicago: Chicago University Press, 2011. Print.
———. "The Unspeakable and the Unimaginable: Word and Image in a Time of Terror." *ELH* 72.2 (2005): 291–308. Print.

Selected Bibliography

Mystic River. Dir. Clint Eastwood. Perf. Sean Penn, Kevin Bacon and Tim Robbins. Warner Home Video, 2004. DVD.
Nancy, Jean-Luc. *The Birth to Presence.* Trans. Brian Holmes, et al. Stanford: Stanford University Press, 1993. Print.
──. *The Gravity of Thought.* Trans. François Raffoul and Gregory Recco. Atlantic Highland, NJ: Humanities Press, 1987. Print.
──. *The Inoperative Community.* Trans. Peter Connor. Minnesota: University of Minnesota Press, 1991. Print.
Ndalianis, Angela. "Special Effects, Morphing Magic, and the Nineties' Cinema of Attractions." *Meta-Morphing: Visual Transformations of the Culture of Quick-Change.* Ed. Vivian Sobchack. Minneapolis: University of Minnesota Press, 2000. 251–71. Print.
Nicholson, Mervyn. "Boring *Psycho.*" *Bright Lights Film Journal* 71 (February 2011). Web. 19 July 2012.
Nietzsche, Friedrich. *The Birth of Tragedy.* Trans. Shaun Whiteside. London: Penguin, 1993. Print.
──. *The Gay Science: With a Prelude in Rhymes and an Appendix of Songs.* Trans. Walter Kaufmann. New York: Vintage, 1974. Print.
──. *On the Genealogy of Morals and Ecce Homo.* Trans. Walter Kaufmann. New York: Vintage, 1969. Print.
──. *Thus Spoke Zarathustra: A Book for None and All.* Trans. Walter Kaufmann. London: Penguin, 1978.
──. *The Will to Power.* Trans. Walter Kaufmann. New York: Random House, 1967. Print.
Orr, John. *The Art and Politics of Film.* Edinburgh: Edinburgh University Press, 2000. Print.
Outer Space. Dir. Peter Tscherkassky. Poet Picture Productions, 1999. Film.
Paranormal Activity. Dir. Oren Peli. Perf. Katie Featherston, Micah Sloat and Mark Fredrichs. Paramount, 2007. DVD.
Pascal, Blaise. *Pensées.* Trans. A. J. Krailsheimer. London: Penguin Classics, 1995. Print.
Persona. Dir. Ingmar Bergman. Perf. Liv Ullman and Bibi Andersson. Svensk Filmindustri, 1966. Film.
Peyser, Andrea. "Heart of Stone." *The New York Post* 18 Sept. 2002. Print.
Pi. Dir. Darren Aronofsky. Perf. Jean Gullette and Mark Margolis. Lions Gate, 1999. DVD.
Pierson, Michele. *Special Effects: Still in Search of Wonder.* New York: Columbia University Press, 2002. Print.
Poe, Edgar Allan. "The Imp of the Perverse." *Edgar Allan Poe: Poetry and Tales.* New York: The Library of America, 1984. 826–833. Print.
──. "The Philosophy of Composition." *Essays of American Essayists.* New York: The Colonial Press, 1900. 255–267. Print.
──. "The Pit and the Pendulum." *Edgar Allan Poe: Poetry and Tales.* New York: The Library of America, 1984. 491–506. Print.
Pollin, Robert, and Heidi Garrett-Peltier. "The US Employment Effects of Military and Domestic Spending Priorities." *Institute for Policy Studies.* October 2007. Web. 11 July 2011.
The Poseidon Adventure. Dir. Ronald Neame. Perf. Gene Hackman and Ernest Borgnine. 20th Century-Fox, 1999. DVD.
Psycho. Dir. Alfred Hitchcock. Perf. Anthony Perkins. Universal Studios, 1998. DVD.

Selected Bibliography

Raffoul. François. "Preface." *The Gravity of Thought*. Atlantic Highlands, NJ: Humanities Press, 1987. vii–xxxii. Print.

Rajiva, Lila. *The Language of Empire: Abu Ghraib in the American Media*. New York: Monthly Review Press, 2005. Print.

Rancière, Jacques. "The Ethical Turn of Aesthetics and Politics." *Critical Horizons* 7.1 (2006): 1–20. Print.

———. "The Ethical Turn of Aesthetics and Politics." *Aesthetics and Its Discontents*. Cambridge: Polity Press, 2004. 109–32. Print.

———. *The Future of the Image*. New York: Verso, 2007. Print.

The Raven. Dir. James McTeigue. Perf. John Cusack and Alice Eve. Intrepid Pictures, 2012. Theatrical Release.

Ray, Gene. *Terror and the Sublime in Art and Critical Theory: From Auschwitz to Hiroshima to September 11*. New York: Palgrave Macmillan, 2005. Print.

Redfield, Marc. "Virtual Trauma: The Idiom of 9/11." *diacritics* 37.1 (Spring 2007): 55–80. Print.

Reich, Robert. "Our Only Existing Jobs Program Is the Military—An Insane Way to Keep Americans Employed." *AlterNet*. 12 August 2010. Web. 11 July 2011.

Requiem for a Dream. Dir. Darren Aronofsky. Perf. Ellen Burstyn, Jared Leto and Jennifer Connelly. Artisan, 2001. DVD.

Reservoir Dogs. Dir. Quentin Tarantino. Perf. Tim Roth, Harvey Keitel, Michael Madsen and Steve Buscemi. Artisan, 1997. DVD.

Ricœur, Paul. *The Symbolism of Evil*. Trans. Emerson Buchanan. Boston: Beacon Press, 1967. Print.

Rodowick, David. *Reading the Figural, or, Philosophy After the New Media*. Durham: Duke University Press, 2001. Print.

———. *The Virtual Life of Film*. Cambridge: Harvard University Press, 2007. Print.

Sack, Warren. "Aesthetics of Information Visualization." *Context Providers: Conditions of Meaning in Media Arts*. Eds. Margot Lovejoy, Christiane Paul and Victoria Vesna. Toronto: Intellect, 2011. Print.

Salecl, Renata. *(Per)versions of Love and Hate*. New York: Verso, 1998. Print.

Sanjek, David. "Same as It Ever Was: Innovation and Exhaustion in the Horror and Science Fiction Films of the 1990s." *Film Genre 2000*. Ed. Wheeler Winston Dixon. Albany: SUNY Press, 2000. Print.

Santilli, Paul. "Culture, Evil, and Horror." *American Journal of Economics and Sociology* 66.1 (January 2007): 173–193. Print.

Sartre, Jean-Paul. *Existentialism and Human Emotions*. New York: Citadel Press, 1985. Print.

Schopenhauer, Arthur. *The World as Will and Representation*. Vol. 1. Eds. Judith Norman, Alistair Welchman and Christopher Janaway. Cambridge: Cambridge University Press, 2010. Print.

Schrader, Paul. *Trancendental Style in Film*. Berkeley: University of California Press, 1972. Print.

Shaviro, Steven. *Post Cinematic Affect*. The Bothy: John Hunt, 2010. Print.

Shaw, Philip. *The Sublime*. London: Routledge, 2006. Print.

Slocum, David J., ed. *Terrorism, Media, Liberation*. New Brunswick, NJ: Rutgers University Press, 2005. Print.

Snibbe, Scott, artist. *Visceral Cinema: Chien*. 2005. Media installation.

Sobchack, Vivian. *Screening Space: The American Science Fiction Film*. New Brunswick, NJ: Rutgers University Press, 1987. Print.

Selected Bibliography

Sontag, Susan. "The Imagination of Disaster." *Against Interpretation and Other Essays*. New York: Octagon, 1978. 209–225. Print.

———. "The Imagination of Disaster. *Liquid Metal*. Ed. Sean Redmond. London: Wallflower Press, 2004. 40–47. Print.

———. "Regarding the Torture of Others," *The New York Times Magazine* 23 May 2004. Web. 13 October 2006.

Source Code. Dir. Duncan Jones. Perf. Jake Gyllenhaal and Michelle Monaghan. Summit Entertainment, 2011. DVD.

Spence, Louise. "Teaching 9/11 and Why I'm Not Doing It Anymore." *Cinema Journal* 43.2 (2004): 100–104. Print.

Spisak, Neil. "*Spider-Man* Commentary." *Spider-Man* Trilogy Box-set, Sony Pictures, 2007. DVD.

Standard Operating Procedure. Dir. Errol Morris. Sony Pictures Home Entertainment, 2008. DVD.

Steyn, Mark. "Inflicting Real Pain." *The Spectator* 22 September 2001: 56–58. Print.

Stoljar, Daniel. "Physicalism." *Stanford Encyclopedia of Philosophy*. The Metaphysics Research Lab, 2009. Web. 26 May 2012.

Strange, Carolyn. "The 'Shock' of Torture: a Historiographical Challenge." *History Workshop Journal* 61 (2006): 135–152. Print.

Stuart, Jan. "The Brooding Mind of 'Donnie Darko.'" *Los Angeles Times* 26 October 2001. Web. 9 August 2011.

Superman. Dir. Richard Donner. Perf. Christopher Reeve. Warner Bros., 1978. Film.

Suspicion. Dir. Alfred Hitchcock. Perf. Cary Grant, Joan Fontaine and Cedric Hardwicke. RKO Radio Pictures, 1941. Film.

Suvin, Darko. *Metamorphoses of Science Fiction*. New Haven: Yale University Press, 1980. Print.

Telotte, J. P. *Replications: A Robotic History of the Science Fiction Film*. Urbana: University of Illinois Press, 1995. Print.

Terminator 2. Dir. James Cameron. Perf. Arnold Schwarzenegger. TriStar Pictures, 1991. Film.

Thompson, Kristin. "Cinematic Excess." *Ciné-Tracts* 1.2 (Summer 1977): 54–63. Web. 16 October 2011.

Travers, Peter. "Scare Tactics." *Rolling Stone* 7 September 2008: 88. Print.

Tuck, Greg. "When More Is Less: CGI, Spectacle, and the Capitalist Sublime." *Science Fiction Film and Television* 1.2 (2008): 249–273. Print.

Turse, Nick. "Bringing the War Home: The New Military-Industrial-Entertainment Complex at War and Play." *TomDispatch*. 16 October 2003. Web. 11 July 2011.

———. *The Complex: How the Military Invades Our Everyday Lives*. New York: Metropolitan Books, 2008. Print.

Two-Lane Blacktop. Dir. Monte Hellman. Perf. James Taylor, Dennis Wilson, Warren Oates and Laurie Bird. Universal, 1971. Film.

2012. Dir. Roland Emmerich. Perf. John Cusack and Amanda Peet. Columbia Pictures, 2009. Sony Pictures Home Entertainment, 2010. DVD.

Virilio, Paul. *Open Sky*. Trans. Julie Rose. New York: Verso, 1997. Print.

———. "The Primal Accident." *The Politics of Everyday Fear*. Ed. Brian Masumi. Minneapolis: University of Minnesota Press, 1993. 211–220. Print.

Wakeman, Jessica. "On *Cloverfield* and 9/11." *The Huffington Post*. 21 January 2008. Web. 14 May 2012.

Selected Bibliography

Walters, James. "Potential Worlds." *Alternative Worlds in Hollywood Cinema: Resonance Between Realms*. Bristol, UK: Intellect, 2008. 107–14. Print.
War of the Worlds. Dir. Steven Spielberg. Perf. Tom Cruise. Paramount Pictures, 2005. Film.
Wigoder, Meir. "The 'Solar Eye' of Vision: Emergence of the Skyscraper-Viewer in the Discourse on Heights in New York City, 1890–1920." *The Journal of the Society of Architectural Historians* 61.2 (June 2002): 152–169. Print.
Williams, Bernard. *Shame and Necessity*. Berkeley: University of California Press, 2008. Print.
Wood, Robin. *Hollywood from Vietnam to Reagan*. New York: Columbia University Press, 1986. Print.
The Wrestler. Dir. Darren Aronofsky. Perf. Mickey Rourke, Marisa Tomei and Evan Rachel Wood. Fox Searchlight Pictures, 2009. DVD.
Wright, Evan. *Generation Kill: Devil Dogs, Iceman, Captain America and the New Face of American War*. New York: Berkley Caliber, 2005. Print.
Yeo, Rob. "Cutting Through History." *Cut: Film as Found Object in Contemporary Video*. Ed. Stefano Basilico. Exhibition catalog for *Cut: Film as Found Object*, organized and presented by the Milwaukee Art Museum. Milwaukee: Milwaukee Art Museum, 2004. 13–28. Print.
Ziskin, Laura. "*Spider-Man* Commentary." *Spider-Man* Trilogy Box-set, Sony Pictures, 2007. DVD.
Žižek, Slavoj. "The Clash of Civilizations at the End of History." www.childrenof men.net. 2006. Print.
_____. *The Parallax View*. Cambridge: MIT Press, 2006. Print.
_____. *The Sublime Object of Ideology*. London: Verso, 1989. Print.
_____. *Welcome to the Desert of the Real! Five Essays on September 11 and Related Dates*. London: Verso, 2002. Print.
Zorn, Eric. "Behind the Screams." *Chicago Tribune* 19 May 1991. Web. 17 May 2012.

About the Contributors

Michael J. **Blouin** is an assistant professor of English and the humanities at Milligan College. His work has appeared in *The Journal of American Studies* and *Extrapolation*, and his book *Japan and the Cosmopolitan Gothic* is expected in 2013. His research interests include transnationalism, U.S.-Japan cultural relations, and the American Gothic.

Donald **Callen** teaches philosophy at Bowling Green State University. His recent work focuses on topics conjoining existentialism, scientific materialism, aesthetics, narrative theory and cinema. His "Image and Action in the Time of the Dismal Tide," in *Rhizomes* (Summer 2008), explores ethical concepts in David Cronenberg's *Eastern Promises*.

Todd A. **Comer** teaches film, literature, and comics at Defiance College. He has published on Joel and Ethan Coen, Samuel R. Delany, Flann O'Brien and Doctor Who. He co-edited, with Joseph Michael Sommers, *Sexual Ideology in the Works of Alan Moore: Critical Essays on the Graphic Novels* (McFarland, 2012) and is editing a collection on Occupy Wall Street.

Sven **Cvek** works in the American Studies program, Faculty of Humanities and Social Sciences at the University of Zagreb. His book *Towering Figures: Reading the 9/11 Archive* is forthcoming (Rodopi). His interests include contemporary US literary and popular cultural production, problems of globalization, visuality, and the new media.

Larrie **Dudenhoeffer** is an assistant professor of English and film studies at Kennesaw State University and the author of "Hitchcock-eyed: Ocular Dys/function in Alfred Hitchcock's *Rear Window*" in *Cinephile* and "Monster Mishmash: Iconicity and Intertextuality in Tobe Hooper's *The Texas Chain Saw Massacre*" in *The Journal of the Fantastic in the Arts*.

Marco **Grosoli,** completed his Ph.D. in film studies with a dissertation on the corpus of writings (2600 articles) by André Bazin. His other research interests are French New Wave, film theory and media studies. His essays have appeared in *Fata Morgana*, zizekstudies.org, *Film Comment*, and several edited collections and he regularly contributes to *Cinergie*, *La Furia Umana*, and *Sentieri Selvaggi*.

About the Contributors

Seung-hoon **Jeong** is an assistant professor of cinema studies at New York University, Abu Dhabi. He specializes in film theory in relation to diverse modes, areas and periods of cinema. He received Korea's Cine21 Film Criticism Award in 2003, and a Domitor essay award in 2007. He has published on many topics and filmmakers such as Werner Herzog, Michael Haneke, Peter Greenaway and Apichatpong Weerasethakul.

Kartik **Nair** is in the cinema studies Ph.D. program at New York University. His M.Phil. dissertation focused on the low-budget horror films of the Ramsay Brothers. He has previously freelanced as a copy editor with Sage, written movie reviews for Campus 18, and served as an editor on the 9th Osian's-Cinefan *Film Festival Bulletin*.

Lloyd Isaac **Vayo** is an instructor of arts and humanities at Concordia University–St. Paul. He is working on sound studies and 9/11, including the use of voice recordings of the hijackers in popular media. His publications have appeared in the journals *Popular Music and Society* and *Rhizomes: Cultural Studies in Emerging Knowledge*, and in edited volumes on 9/11.

John P. **Warton** is an assistant professor in film and media at the University of Edinburgh. He has been an instructor of film and video production in Los Angeles, Portland, Oregon, and Nairobi, Kenya.

Holly **Willis** is the author of *New Digital Cinema: Reinventing the Moving Image* and editor of *The New Ecology of Things*, essays on pervasive computing. She is also an assistant research professor in the School of Cinematic Arts at the University of Southern California and director of academic programs for USC's Institute for Multimedia Literacy.

Scott **Wilson** is the associate head and senior lecturer in the Department of Performing and Screen Arts at Unitec, Institute of Technology in Auckland, New Zealand, having previously taught at the University of Auckland and at Victoria, University of Wellington. His interests lie in popular culture, cinema theory, monster movies and critical and cultural studies.

Index

Abrams, J.J. 33; *Cloverfield* (film) 9–10, 16, 29, 32–36, 39–41, 76, 145
Abu Ghraib 46, 48–53, 55–56
The Abu Ghraib Effect (print) 50; *see also* Eisenman, Stephen F.
Accumulating Psycho (media installation) 126
Adorno Theodor W. 11, 91–92, 95, 104, 117; "... as the Devil" 92
The Adventures of Robin Hood (film) 168
aesthetic 6–7, 10, 23, 33, 38, 45, 50, 57, 59–62, 64–67, 69, 71–74, 86, 91–93, 102, 106, 112, 116, 121, 124, 133, 136–138, 141, 143–145, 148–149, 152, 183, 184
Agamben, Giorgio 97, 99–101; *Homo Sacer* (print) 99, 101; *Remnants of Auschwitz* (print) 100; *The Signature of All things* (print) 97; *State of Exception* (print) 99
Airport (film) 75
Aitken, Doug 124–125
alien 15–16, 26, 124, 144, 166, 173, 176
Alien (film) 130; *see also* Scott, Ridley
AMC 27
American 19, 21, 33, 36, 42–43, 50–51, 54, 56, 73, 83–84, 96, 101–102, 104, 114; American cinema 126; American decline 28; American flag 46; American Romanticism 118
The American Nightmare (film) 132; *see also* Simon, Adam
amor fati 66, 67, 71
anti-Semitism 92; Nazi 11, 53–54, 89, 90, 91–96, 101–102
apocalypse 16, 75–76, 78–80, 84, 86–87, 146
Apollonian 59–61
Armageddon (film) 59–61
Aronofsky, Darren 57, 59–61, 69; *Black Swan* (film) 10, 57, 60, 65, 68; *Pi* (film) 67; *Requiem for a Dream* (film) 60, 68; *The Wrestler* (film) 59
Art and Obscenity (print) 38
"The Artificial Infinite: On Special Effects and the Sublime" 136; *see also* Bukatman, Scott
Artificial Intelligence (film) 12, 167, 170, 173, 176, 178–180; David (character) 168–180; Dr. Know (character) 173; Henry (character) 167–170; Martin (character) 167–169, 172, 176, 180; Monica (character) 167, 168–172, 176, 178, 180; Professor Hobby (character) 168, 173–174, 176–180; Sheila (character) 168; *see also* Spielberg, Steven
Ashfield, Andrew 140
askēsis 152
Auschwitz 91, 95–97, 100–101
autopoeisis 82, 87
avant-garde 11, 90, 123
Avatar (film) 145

Badmington, Neil 165–167, 172, 173, 176; *Alien Chick: Posthumanism and the Other Within* (print) 166; *Posthumanism* (print) 165
Basilico, Stefano 125
Bataille, Georges 111–112
Baudrillard, Jean 15–16, 26, 181
Berg, Nick 56
Bergman, Ingmar 90; *Persona* (film) 90
Benjamin, Walter 35, 39, 104
Beyond the Pleasure Principle (print) 35; *see also* Freud, Sigmund
Bilal, Wafaa 43; "...and Counting" (performance) 43
biopolitical 90, 99–101
The Birth of Tragedy (print) 57, 59–60; *see also* Nietzsche, Friedrich
Black Sun: Depression and Melancholia (print) 32, 37
Black Swan 58, 60, 68; *Black Swan* (film) 10, 57, 60, 65, 68; Leroy, Thomas (character) 57–58, 65; Lily (character) 57, 66; Nina (character) 57–58, 60, 68–69; *see also* Aronofsky, Darren
Blade Runner (film) 26; *see also* Scott, Ridley

201

Index

Bordwell, David 119–120, 144
Boundas, Constantine 65, 67
Brison, Susan J. 31
Brockman, John 87
Brown, Michelle 56
Bryant, Martin 41
Bukatman, Scott 134, 136–137, 148; "The Artificial Infinite: On Special Effects and the Sublime" 136
Buñuel, Luis 128–129; *Un Chien Andalou* (film) 129
Burke, Edmund 7, 45, 134–135, 139, 184; Burkean 7, 12, 141, 143, 148; *A Philosophical Enquiry into the Origin of Our Ideas of the Sublime and Beautiful* (print) 141, 185
Burstyn, Ellen 68
Bush, George H.W. 80, 84–85
Bush, George W. 49, 80
Butler, Judith 30, 43; *Precarious Life: The Powers of Mourning and Violence* (print) 30
The Butterfly Effect (film) 85

Campbell, Jim (artist) 126; *Accumulating Psycho* (media instillation) 126; *Illuminated Average #1, Hitchcock's Psycho* (media instillation) 126; *Night Light* (media instillation) 126
Cartesian 116, 165
catastrophe 11, 15–16, 24, 72–76, 80, 86–87, 100, 142, 145
Chalmers, David 64
Chicago, Illinois 19, 21, 103, 138; Millennium Park 110
Un Chien Andalou (film) 129
Children of Men (film) 145
Chrysler Building 21, 36
Clark, Andy 155
"The Clash of Civilizations at the End of History" 84; *see also* Žižek, Slavoj
The Classic Hollywood Cinema: Film Style and Mode of Production to 1960 (print) 119; *see also* Thompson, Kristin
Cleveland, Ohio 21
Cloning Terror: The War of Images, 9/11 to the Present (print) 56; *see also* Mitchell, W.J.T.
Close Encounters of the Third Kind (film) 136; *see also* Spielberg, Steven
Cloverfield (film) 9–10, 16, 29, 32–36, 39–41, 76, 145; *see also* Reeves, Matt
Coleridge, Samuel Taylor 140–141; *1818 Lectures on European Literature* (print) 141
"Common Ground: Melodramas of 9/11" 55; *see also* Cvek, Sven
Comolli, Jean-Louis 90
The Complex: How the Military Invades our Everyday Lives (print) 56; *see also* Turse, Nick
"The Concept of Cinematic Excess" 56; *see also* Thompson, Kristin
Crandall, Jordan (artist) 130
Creed, Barbara 121; *The Monstrous Feminine: Film, Feminism, Psychoanalysis* (print) 121
Cruise, Tom 77
Csicsery-Ronay, Istvan, Jr. 23
Cubitt, Sean 31
Cusack, John 145
Cvek, Sven 10, 42, 55; "Common Ground: Melodramas of 9/11" 55

Daney, Serge 86
Dark City (film) 75
The Dark Knight (film) 26; *see also* Nolan, Christopher
"Dark Places" (media installation) 130–131
Dasgupta, Partha 159
"Data Visualization as New Abstraction and Anti-Sublime" 129; *see also* Manovich, Lev
De Rerum Natura (print) 143
de Bolla, Peter 140
Debord, Guy 144
de Certeau, Michel 20
Decter, Joshua 130
Déjà vu (film) 76, 78; *see also* Scott, Tony
Deleuze, Gilles 65, 67, 83, 114–115, 117; Deleuzian 83, 106
Delirious New York (print) 19; *see also* Koolhaas, Rem
demon 12, 68–70, 119, 150–163
De Rougemont, Denis 150–151; *The Devil's Share: An Essay on the Diabolic in Modern Society* (print) 150
Derrida, Jacques 67, 83, 150–153, 165–166; *The Gift of Death and Literature in Secret* (print) 152; *Rogues: Two Essays on Reason* (print) 153
determinism 61, 63, 64, 77
deus ex machina 76, 87
The Devil's Share: An Essay on the Diabolic in Modern Society (print) 150; *see also* de Rougemont, Denis
Dialectic of Enlightenment (print) 91; *see also* Adorno, Theodor W.
DiCaprio, Leonardo 107
The Differend (print) 95–96, 141; *see also* Lyotard, Jean-François
Dionysian 10, 59–60
Disney 138–139
Doane, Mary Ann 35
Dog Day Afternoon (film) 53; *see also* Lumet, Sidney

Index

Dogville (film) 99; see also von Trier, Lars
Donner, Richard 78; *Superman* (film) 78
Donnie Darko (film) 10–11, 72, 74, 77–78, 85; Cunningham, Jim (character) 80; Donnie Darko (character) 78–87; Frank (character) 78, 81, 83–84, 86–87; Grandma Death (character) 78, 86; Gretchen (character) 81, 86; see also Kelly, Richard
Dopaso, Andrea 22
Dorin, Alan 129
Douthat, Ross 33, 36
Drew, Richard 17–18, 25
Dukakis, Michael 84
Dunst, Kirsten 22
Dykstra, John 21

Eastwood, Clint 99; *Mystic River* (film) 99
1818 Lectures on European Literature (print) 141; see also Coleridge, Samuel Taylor
Eisenman, Stephen F. 50, 65; *The Abu Ghraib Effect* (print) 50
Emmerich, Roland 12, 15–16, 135, 145, 147; *The Day After Tomorrow* (film) 16, 76, 145; *Godzilla* (film) 15, 145; *Independence Day* (film) 15, 37, 75, 145; *2012* (film) 12, 76, 135, 144–148
The End of Dissatisfaction? (print) 115; see also McGowan, Todd
The Entity (film) 119, 122; see also Furie, Sidney J.
Escher, M.C. 79
Evil Dead 2: Dead by Dawn (film) 128; see also Raimi, Sam
The Exorcist (film) 157

Fahrenheit 9/11 (film) 28; see also Moore, Michael
"The Falling Man" 17, 27; see also Junod, Tom
Featherston, Katie 150
Fight Club (film) 87
Forkscrew 51
Foster, Jodie 46
1408 (film) 106, 117; Enslin, Mike (character) 106–107, 111
Fredrichs, Mark 156
Freud, Sigmund 30–31, 35, 97; *Beyond the Pleasure Principle* (print) 35; Freudian 31, 74, 97; Freudian immemorial 97; Freudian Thing 72; "The Psychotherapy of Hysteria" 30
Friedman, Roger 36–37
Frohne, Ursula 124–125; "That's the Only Now I Get: Immersion and Participation in Video-Installations by Dan Graham, Steve McQueen, Douglas Gordon, Doug Aitken, Eija-Liisa Ahtila, Sam Taylor-Wood" 124
Frost, Laura 28
Furie, Sidney J. 122; *The Entity* (film) 119, 122

Gabler, Neil 37
Garrett-Peltier, Heidi 47
The Gay Science: With a Prelude in Rhymes and an Appendix of Songs (print) 68; see also Nietzsche, Friedrich
Geneva Convention 49
genocide 86, 139
German 72, 90–92, 94–96, 98, 102, 145, 170, 184–185; Nazi 11, 53–54, 89, 90, 91–96, 101–102
Ghostbusters (film) 75
Ghosts of Abu Ghraib (film) 56; see also Kennedy, Rory
The Gift of Death and Literature in Secret (print) 152; see also Derrida, Jacques
Gilligan, Carol 71; *In a Different Voice: Psychological Theory and Woman's Development* (print) 71
Girard, René 153
Gladstone, Jim 56
G[g]od 1, 20, 63, 72, 74–75, 78, 81, 86–87, 146, 150, 165, 176; godlike 79
God, Death, and Time (print) 70
Godzilla (film) 15, 34, 40, 145; see also Emmerich, Roland; Honda, Ishirô
Gordon, Douglas 11, 124; *24 Hour Psycho* (media installation) 11, 124–125
Graham, Elaine L. 165–167, 176, 178; *Representations of the Post/Human: Monsters, Aliens and Others in Popular Culture* (print) 165
Grant, Barry Keith 137, 142, 144, 149
The Gravity of Thought (print) 177; see also Nancy, Jean-Luc
Greengrass, Paul 28; *United 93* (film) 28, 76
Gremlins (film) 75
ground zero 18, 26, 40, 54; see also September 11
Groundhog Day (film) 120
Grusin, Richard A. 9, 16, 24, 76, 87
Guthrie, Marisa 42
Gyllenhaal, Jake 103

Harrelson, Woody 145
Harrison-Kahan, Lori 42–43
Hartley, David 141; *Observations on Man, His Frame, His Duty, and His Expectations* (print) 141, 159
Hayles, N. Katherine 151, 155, 165
Hegel, G.W.F. 87, 117; Hegelian 95, 105, 112

Index

Hellenistic 91
Hellman, Monte 90; *Two Lane Blacktop* (film) 90
Hepburn, Ian 41
hermeneutic 2, 38, 70, 170–172, 176–178, 183
Hershey, Barbara 122
Heyman, Daniel 50, 56
Hitchcock, Alfred 26, 123–126, 184; *Psycho* (film) 123, 126–128; *Vertigo* (film) 26–27
Hoberman, Jim 87
Hollywood 10, 15–16, 27, 37, 40, 48, 55–56, 72–75, 77–78, 85–87, 91, 107, 111–112, 115, 119–120, 127, 145
Homo Sacer (print) 99, 101; *see also* Agamben, Giorgio
Honda, Ishirô 34; *Godzilla* (film) 34
Horkheimer, Max 91–92; *The Dialectic of Enlightenment* (print) 91
Horror Chase (media installation) 128–129; *see also* McCoy, Jennifer; McCoy, Kevin
Howard, Bryce Dallas 24
humanity 8, 15, 56, 59, 71, 145, 165–168, 172–174, 176, 178; humanism 12, 165–167, 173, 175–176, 178–180; posthumanism 12, 165–166; posthumanity 166–167, 178–179
Hurricane Katrina 76, 137
Hutcheon, Linda 51

I Am Legend (film) 16; *see also* Lawrence, Francis
Illuminated Average #1, Hitchcock's Psycho (media instillation) 126; *see also* Campbell, Jim
"The Imagination of Disaster" 34; *see also* Sontag, Susan
immemorial 95, 97, 134; immemorial trauma 86
"Imp of the Perverse" 103, 105; *see also* Poe, Edgar Allan
In a Different Voice: Psychological Theory of Women's Development (print) 71; *see also* Gilligan, Carol
In the Shadow of No Towers (print) 43; *see also* Spiegelman, Art
Inception (film) 106–107, 111, 117; Cobb, Dom (character) 107, 111; *see also* Nolan, Christopher
Inconvenient Evidence (media installation) 50
Independence Day (film) 15, 37, 75, 145; *see also* Emmerich, Roland
Inglourious Basterds (film) 11, 88–90, 92–93, 95–97, 101; Donowitz, Donny (character) 94; Dreyfuss, Shoshanna (character) 89–90, 92–93, 96, 102; Goebbels (character) 91, 96; Goldfarb, Harry (character) 60; Hitler, Adolf (character) 90, 96; Raine, Lieutenant Aldo (character) 94, 100; Selznick, David O. (character) 91; Stiglitz, Hugo (character) 98; Von Hammersmark, Birgit (character) 98; Zoller, Fredrick (character) 92; *see also* Tarantino, Quentin
The Inhuman: Reflections on Time (print) 117; *see also* Lyotard, Jean-François
The Inoperative Community (print) 1, 95, 168; *see also* Nancy, Jean-Luc
Inside Man (film) 10, 42–49, 52–55; *see also* Lee, Spike
Invasion of the Body Snatchers (film) 166
iPod 51–52
Iraq 10, 43, 46–47, 49–50, 54; the iRaq 51; Iraqis 43, 49, 56

Jackie Brown (film) 89; *see also* Tarantino, Quentin
Jackson, Peter 147; *King Kong* (film) 147
Jacob's Ladder (film) 85
Jameson, Fredric 56, 106, 109, 111, 113, 117–118, 134–136, 144; "Postmodernism: Or, the Cultural Logic of Late Capitalism" 118, 134; *Signatures of the Visible* 117
Jesus 75, 79, 81, 87
John Carter (film) 145
USS *John F. Kennedy* 146
Jones, Duncan 11, 103; *Source Code* (film) 11, 103–105, 107–118
jouissance 73, 89, 92, 115, 184
jumping 18; *see also* leap
Junod, Tom 17, 23, 25, 27–28; "The Falling Man" 17, 27
Jurassic Park (film) 75, 86; *see also* Spielberg, Steven

Kant, Immanuel 31–32, 58–63, 71, 73–74, 77, 123, 128–129, 131, 133, 139–141, 182, 184–185; *The Critique of Judgment* (print) 31, 123; *Critique of Pure Reason* (print) 62; *Critique of the Power of Judgment* (print) 59, 73; Kantian 59–62, 73–75, 88–91, 93, 140, 182–183; *Observations on the Feeling of the Beautiful and the Sublime* (print)141
Kapó (film) 86
Keane, Stephen 87
Kearney, Richard 31
Keenan, Thomas 56; "Publicity and Indifference" 56
Kelly, Richard 74, 78; *Donnie Darko* (film) 10–11, 72, 74, 77–78, 85
Kennedy, Rory 56; *Ghosts of Abu Ghraib* (film) 56
Kill Bill (movie) 89; Bill (character) 89; Bride (character) 89

204

Index

Kinder, Marsha 127
King, Geoff 87, 144
King, Stephen 106; *1408* (print) 106
King Kong (film) 147; King Kong (character) 96; original *King Kong* (film) 87; *see also* Honda, Ishirô; Jackson, Peter
Koolhaas, Rem 19–20, 25; *Delirious New York* (print) 19
Kracauer, Siegfried 134; *Theory of Film: The Redemption of Physical Reality* (print) 134
Kristeva, Julia 32, 37, 121–123, 132; *Black Sun: Depression and Melancholia* (print) 32, 37; "The Pain of Sorrow in the Modern World: The Works of Marguerite Duras" 32; *Powers of Horror: An Essay on Abjection* (print) 121
Kubrick, Stanley 109, 136; *The Shining* (film) 109; *2001: A Space Odyssey* (film) 136

Lacanian 83, 118
LaCapra, Dominick 44–45
Lanzmann, Claude 72–74, 86
Las Vegas, Nevada 147
The Last Temptation of Christ (film) 81
Latour, Bruno 163, 166
Lawrence, Francis 16; *I Am Legend* (film) 16
leap 17, 19, 60, 97; leaping 97; *see also* jumping
Lee, Spike 10, 42, 45; *Inside Man* (film) 10, 42–49, 52–55
Lessons on the Analytic of the Sublime (print) 88; *see also* Lyotard, Jean-François
Levinas, Emmanuel 70; *God, Death and Time* (print) 70
Los Angeles, California 146–148
Lucas, George 136; *Star Wars* (film) 136
Lukaćs, Georg 105; *The Theory of the Novel* (print) 105
Lumet, Sidney 53; *Dog Day Afternoon* (film) 53
Lurie, Susan 43, 55
Lyotard, Jean-François 1, 5, 7, 8, 74, 88–92, 94–97, 99–100, 102, 111–112, 116–117, 140–141, 143, 149, 175, 177, 182, 185; "Acinema" 89, 94; "Adorno as the Devil" 92; "An Answer to the Question: What Is the Postmodern?" 92; *The Differend* (print) 95–96, 141; "Discussions, or phrasing 'after Auschwitz'" 95, 100; *Heidegger and the Jews* (print) 96–97; *Lessons on the Analytic of the Sublime* (print) 88; Lyotardian 7, 11–12, 88, 90, 97, 112; *The Postmodern Condition: A Report on Knowledge* (print) 5, 74; "The Sublime and the Avant-Garde" 93; "Unbeknownst" 175

Mad Men (television series) 27–28
Maguire, Toby 22
Malevich 93; *Black Square* (media instillation) 93
Manhattan 16, 19–22, 25–26, 37, 87, 173–174
Manovich, Lev 120, 127, 129
Massumi, Brian 135–136
Mathews, Peter 81; "Spinoza's Stone: The Logic of *Donnie Darko*" 81–82
The Matrix Revolutions (film) 147
May, Karl 102
McCormack, Jon 129
McCoy, Jennifer 128; McCoy, Kevin 128; *Horror Chase* (media installation) 128–129
McGowan, Todd 115–116, 118; *The End of Dissatisfaction?* (print) 115
McQuire, Scott 144
McTeigue, James 114; *The Raven* (film) 113–114
Melnick, Jeffrey P. 29
Memento (film) 127
memorialization 10, 29, 36
Messiah 81, 85
Mey, Kerstin 38; *Art and Obscenity* (print) 38
Minority Report (film) 76–77; *see also* Spielberg, Steven
Misery (film) 106
Mitchell, W.J.T. 50, 56; *Cloning Terror: The War of Images, 9/11 to the Present* (print) 56
modernity 20, 35, 153, 155, 166; postmodernity 8, 182; technological modernity 152, 163
Molina, Alfred 22
Monaghan, Michelle 103
The Monstrous Feminine: Film, Feminism, Psychoanalysis (print) 121
Moore, Michael 28; *Fahrenheit 9/11* (film) 28
Morris, Errol 56; *Standard Operating Procedure* (DVD) 56
Moses 72, 75
mourning 26, 29–33, 40, 74, 167, 168; *see also* trauma
My Own Private Idaho (film) 85; *see also* Van Sant, Gus

Nancy, Jean-Luc 1, 95, 168, 171–172, 175–177, 180; *The Gravity of Thought* (print) 177; *The Inoperative Community* (print) 1, 95, 168
NASA 20–21
New Orleans, Louisiana 76, 137
New York, New York 10, 15–21, 24, 26–27, 33–34, 36–41, 45–46, 49–50, 137
Nicholson, Mervyn 126

205

Index

Nietzsche, Friedrich 57, 59–61, 65, 67–71, 82, 84; *The Gay Science: With a Prelude in Rhymes and an Appendix of Songs* (print) 68; Nietzschean 60, 75, 85; *Thus Spoke Zarathustra: A Book for None at All* (print) 61, 69
Night Light (media installation) 126
9/11 12, 5, 9–10, 12–13, 15–19, 21, 23, 25–49, 52–55, 76, 80, 83, 87, 99–100, 117, 137, 143, 145, 148, 181–182; *see also* September 11
Nolan, Christopher 26–27, 106–107, 111; *The Dark Knight* (film) 26; *Inception* (film) 27, 106–107, 111, 117; *Memento* (film) 127

Oklahoma City bombing 76, 137
Orr, John 144
The Others (film) 85
Otis, Elisha 20
Owen, Clive 46

The Parallax View (print) 74, 77, 82; *see also* Žižek, Slavoj
paranoia 57–58, 65–66, 181
Paranormal Activity (film) 150–155, 177–178, 162–163; Dr. Fredrichs (character) 156–157; *see also* Peli, Oren
Pascal, Blaise 70; *Pensées* (print) 70
Peet, Amanda 147
Peli, Oren 12, 150; *Paranormal Activity* (film) 150–155, 177–178, 162–163
Persona (film) 90
Peyser, Andrea 17
"Philosophical Horror" 132; *see also* Santilli, Paul
"The Philosophy of Composition" 105; *see also* Poe, Edgar Allan
Pi (film) 67; Max (character) 63; Robeson, Sol (character) 63; *see also* Aronofsky, Darren
"The Pit and the Pendulum" 113; *see also* Poe, Edgar Allan
Playstation 47–48
Poe, Edgar Allan 103–104, 114; "The Imp of the Perverse" 103, 105; "The Philosophy of Composition" 105; "The Pit and the Pendulum" 113
The Poetics of Cinema (print) 120; *see also* Bordwell, David
Pollin, Robert 47
Pontecorvo, Gillo 86
The Poseidon Adventure (film) 75
Posthumanism and the Other Within (print) 166; *see also* Badmington, Neil
"Postmodernism: Or, the Cultural Logic of Late Capitalism" 118; *see also* Jameson, Fredric

Powers of Horror: An Essay on Abjection (print) 121; *see also* Kristeva, Julia
Precarious Life: The Powers of Mourning and Violence (print) 30; *see also* Butler, Judith
Predator (film) 130
premediation 9, 16–19, 24, 76, 87
Psycho (film) 123, 126–128; *see also* Hitchcock, Alfred
"The Psychotherapy of Hysteria" 30; *see also* Freud, Sigmund
"Publicity and Indifference" 56; *see also* Keenan, Thomas

racial profiling 42, 46, 54
Raimi, Sam 18, 21–22, 25–26, 128; *Evil Dead 2: Dead by Dawn* (film) 128; *Spider-Man* (film) 9, 15, 18–19, 21–23, 25–28; *Spider-Man 2* (film) 21–22, 25–26; *Spider-Man 3* (film) 21, 24–26
Rajiva, Lila 56
Rancière, Jacques 72, 99, 120; "The Ethical Turn of Aesthetics and Politics" 72, 150–151
The Raven (film) 113–114; *see also* McTeigue, James
Ray, Gene 2, 31, 40, 54; *Terror and the Sublime in Art and Critical Theory: From Auschwitz to Hiroshima to September 11* (print) 2, 31
redemption 18, 23, 58, 74–75, 78, 80, 84
Redfield, Marc 143
Reeves, Matt 16, 32, 145; *Cloverfield* (film) 9–10, 16, 29, 32–36, 39–41, 76, 145
Reich, Robert 48
Reiner, Rob 106; *Misery* (film) 106
Remnants of Auschwitz (print) 100; *see also* Agamben, Giorgio
Requiem for a Dream (film) 60, 68; *see also* Aronofsky, Darren
Reservoir Dogs (film) 88; Mr. Brown (character) 88; *see also* Tarantino, Quentin
Rodowick, David 97, 120
Rogues: Two Essays on Reason (print) 153; *see also* Derrida, Jacques
Roswell (television series) 166
Run Lola Run (film) 127

Sack, Warren 129
Sanjek, David 144
Santilli, Paul 132
Sartre, Jean-Paul 58
Schindler's List (film) 72, 86; *see also* Spielberg, Steven
Schopenhauer, Arthur 141; *The World as Will and Representation* (print) 141
Schrader, Paul 117; *Transcendental Style in Film* (print) 117
Schwarzenegger, Arnold 76

Index

science fiction 21, 75, 134–144, 149, 173
Scorsese, Martin 81, 87; *The Last Temptation of Christ* (film) 81
Scott, Ridley 26; *Blade Runner* (film) 26
Scott, Tony 76; *Déjà Vu* (film) 76, 78
Selby, Hubert, Jr. 68–69
September 11 2, 6, 10, 15 17–18, 23, 29, 31–32, 41–43, 55; see also 9/11
Shame and Necessity (print) 69; see also Williams, Bernard
Shaviro, Steven 120; *Post Cinematic Affect* (print) 120
Sherman, Cindy 125
The Shining (film) 109; see also Kubrick, Stanley
Shoten, Kadokawa 40; *Cloverfield/Kishin* (print) 40; see also Togawa, Yoshiki
The Signature of All Things (print) 97; see also Agamben, Giorgio
Signatures of the Visible (print) 117; see also Jameson, Fredric
Silent Running (film) 136
Simon, Adam 132; *The American Nightmare* (film) 132
Singer, Bryan 20; *Superman Returns* (film) 20–21
The Sixth Sense (film) 85
Sky Captain and the World of Tomorrow (film) 145
Sloat, Micah 150
Snibbe, Scott 128–129; *Visceral Cinema: Chien* (media installment) 128–129
Sobchack, Vivian 142
Sontag, Susan 15, 34, 56; "The Imagination of Disaster" 34
Source Code (film) 103–105, 107–118; Christina (character) 103, 110; Rutledge (character) 108–110, 112–113; Stevens, Captain Colter (character) 103–104, 107–118
Spence, Louise 40; "Teaching 9/11 and Why I'm Not Doing It Anymore" 40
Spider-Man (film) 9, 15, 18–19, 21–23, 25–28; Doctor Octopus (character) 22; Green Goblin (character) 22; Parker, Peter (character) 22; Spider-Man (character) 20–25, 87; *Spider-Man 2* (film) 21–22, 25–26; *Spider-Man 3* (film) 21, 24–26; Stacy, Gwen (character) 24; Watson, Mary Jane (character) 22; see also Raimi, Sam
Spiegelman, Art 43; *In the Shadow of No Towers* (print) 43
Spielberg, Steven 72, 76, 136, 165, 167, 173, 179–180; *Artificial Intelligence* (film) 12, 167, 170, 173, 176, 178–180; *Close Encounters of the Third Kind* (film) 136; *Minority Report* (film) 76–77; *Schindler's List* (film) 72, 86; *War of the Worlds* (film) 16, 34, 39
Spisak, Neil 22
Standard Operating Procedure (film) 56; see also Morris, Errol
Star Wars (film) 136; see also Lucas, George
Stargate (film) 145; see also Emmerich, Roland
Statue of Liberty 16, 46
Steyn, Mark 37
Stoljar, Daniel 71
Stuart, Jan 80
sublime 1–3, 5–13, 18–19, 22–23, 29, 31–32, 36, 38, 43–45, 48, 50–55, 57–59, 62–67, 70–79, 82–93, 97, 103–105, 110–115, 117, 121–123, 125–144, 146–149, 151, 166–167, 173, 175, 182–185
"The Sublime and the Avant-Garde" 93; see also Lyotard, Jean-François
Superman (film) 78; Superman (character) 21, 78–79; *Superman Returns* (film) 20–21; see also Donner, Richard; Singer, Bryan
Suvin, Darko 173
Swan Lake 57–58

Tarantino, Quentin 11, 88; *Death Proof* (film) 1; *Inglourious Basterds* (film) 11, 88–90, 92–93, 95–97, 101; *Jackie Brown* (film) 89; *Reservoir Dogs* (film) 88
"Teaching 9/11 and Why I'm Not Doing it Anymore" 40; see also Spence, Louise
technophobia 86
Telotte, J.P. 21
Terminator 2 (film) 75–76
terror 1–2, 5–7, 9–10, 13, 16–17, 19, 23, 32, 42–48, 50–56, 59, 64, 73, 80, 82, 86–87, 99, 101, 121, 128, 130, 134, 136, 138–139, 141–143, 147–148, 151, 181–185; terrorism 10–11, 16, 34, 48, 54, 85, 99, 101, 181–182; terrorist 11, 15, 18, 32, 34, 46, 53, 76, 80, 83–84, 90, 99, 101, 103; war on terror 97, 101
Terror and the Sublime in Art and Critical Theory (print) 2, 31
Thater, Diana 125
"That's the Only Now I Get: Immersion and Participation in Video-Installations by Dan Graham, Steve McQueen, Douglas Gordon, Doug Aitken, Eija-Liisa Ahtila, Sam Taylor-Wood" 124; see also Frohne, Ursula
Theory of Film: The Redemption of Physical Reality (print) 134; see also Kracauer, Siegfried
The Theory of the Novel (print) 105; see also Lukács, Georg

Index

Thompson, Kristin 56, 119; "Cinematic Excess" 48, 56, 94
Thus Spoke Zarathustra: A Book for None at All (print) 61, 69; *see also* Nietzsche, Friedrich
Times Square 21–22
Titanic (film) 75, 86
RMS Titanic 141
Togawa, Yoshiki 40; *Cloverfield/Kishin* (comic) 40; *see also* Shoten, Kadokawa
torture 46, 49–52, 55–56, 98, 113
totalitarian 11, 91, 94
trauma 6, 9–12, 16, 18, 29, 31–40, 44–45, 76, 83–84, 86, 126, 130, 135, 148, 168;
traumatic 9–10, 16, 27–32, 34–35, 37, 39, 44–46, 54–55, 72, 87, 167
Travers, Peter 33
Trumball, Douglas 136
Tscherkassky, Peter 11, 119, 122, 133; *Outer Space* (film) 11, 119, 121–122, 133
Tuck, Greg 147
Tumbling Woman 17
Turse, Nick 47, 56
Twelve Monkeys (film) 75, 78
24 Hour Psycho (media installation) 11, 124–125; *see also* Gordon, Douglas
Twilight Zone (television series) 28, 138
Twin Towers 10, 15, 17–18, 20, 23, 26, 36, 46, 148; *see also* World Trade Center
Two Lane Blacktop (film) 90; *see also* Hellman, Monte
2001: A Space Odyssey (film) 136; *see also* Kubrick, Stanley
2012 (film) 145; Frost, Charlie (character) 145–146; Gordon (character) 145–148; Jackson (character) 146–147; Kate (character) 145, 147

United 93 (film) 28, 76; *see also* Greengrass, Paul
United States 17, 46, 49, 54–55, 80
urbanization 24
utopia 86, 105–106, 109, 111–112, 118

Vanilla Sky (film) 85
Van Sant, Gus 85; *My Own Private Idaho* 85
Varela, Francisco 87
Vatican City 146
Vertigo (film) 26,-27; *see also* Hitchcock, Alfred
Virilio, Paul 24–26; "The Primal Accident" 26
Visceral Cinema: Chien (media installation) 128–129
von Trier, Lars 99; *Dogville* (film) 99

Wakeman, Jessica 41
Wall, Jeff 125
Walters, James 87
War of the Worlds (film) 16, 34, 39; *see also* Spielberg, Steven
Washington, Denzel 46
Washington, D.C. 137, 146
Welcome to the Desert of the Real! Five Essays on September 11 and Related Dates (print) 38, 83
Wigoder, Meir 20
The Will to Power (print) 61; *see also* Nietzsche, Friedrich
Williams, Bernard 69; *Shame and Necessity* (print) 69
The World as Will and Representation (print) 141; *see also* Schopenhauer, Arthur
World Trade Center 15, 17–18, 20, 37, 41, 80, 87; *see also* Twin Towers
World War II 45, 54–55, 101
The Wrestler (film) 59, 60; Randy (character) 59, 60, 69; *see also* Aronofsky, Darren
Wright, Evan 50–51

Yellowstone National Park, Wyoming 146

Ziskin, Laura 22, 25
Žižek, Slavoj 15, 77, 82, 84, 140–141; "The Clash of Civilizations at the End of History" 84; *The Parallax View* (print) 74, 77, 82

www.ingramcontent.com/pod-product-compliance
Ingram Content Group UK Ltd.
Pitfield, Milton Keynes, MK11 3LW, UK
UKHW042003140426
5217IPUK00015B/949